# CARMELITE WISDOM
### and
# PROPHETIC HOPE

## Treasures Both New and Old

Carmelite Studies
Volume 11

# CARMELITE WISDOM
## and
# PROPHETIC HOPE

## Treasures Both New and Old

Carmelite Studies
Volume 11

EDITED BY MARY FROHLICH, R.S.C.J.

ICS Publications
Institute of Carmelite Studies
Washington, D.C.

ICS Publications
2131 Lincoln Road NE
Washington, D.C. 20002-1199

www.icspublications.org

© Washington Province of Discalced Carmelites, Inc., 2018

*Published with Ecclesiastical Approval*

Book and cover design by Rose Design

Cover photo: "Glory Window" in stained glass by Gabriel Loire, Chapel of Thanksgiving, Dallas, Texas.

Printed in the United States of America

**Library of Congress Cataloging-in-Publication Data**
Names: Frohlich, Mary, editor.
Title: Carmelite wisdom and prophetic hope : treasures both new and old / edited
  by Mary Frohlich, R.S.C.J.
Description: First [edition]. | Washington, D.C. : ICS Publications, 2018. |
  Series: Carmelite studies ; Volume 11
Identifiers: LCCN 2018001057 | ISBN 9781939272638 (alk. paper)
Subjects: LCSH: Carmelites--Theology. | Wisdom--Religious
aspects--Catholic
  Church. | Teresa, of Avila, Saint, 1515-1582. | John of the Cross, Saint,
  1542-1591.
Classification: LCC BX3202.3 .C365 2018 | DDC 248.088/25573--dc23
LC record available at https://lccn.loc.gov/2018001057

ISBN 978-1-939272-63-8

10 9 8 7 6 5 4 3 2 1

# Contents

## PART III:

### *Prophetic Intimations from Teresa of Ávila*

# Acknowledgments

We gratefully acknowledge permission from the following publishers and/or publications to include these essays or revised versions of these original essays in this volume:

### Constance FitzGerald, O.C.D.

"From Impasse to Prophetic Hope: Crisis of Memory"

The Catholic Theological Society of America for "From Impasse to Prophetic Hope: Crisis of Memory," by Constance FitzGerald, O.C.D., originally published in *Proceedings of the Catholic Theological Society of America* 64 (2009): 21–42. Licensed under Creative Commons: https://ejournals.bc.edu/ojs/index.php/ctsa/article/view/4923/0/by/3.0/

### Sandra M. Schneiders, I.H.M.

"The Jesus Mysticism of Teresa of Avila: Its Importance for Theology and Contemporary Spirituality"

*The Berkeley Journal of Religion and Theology*, Berkeley, Calif., for "The Jesus Mysticism of Teresa of Avila," by Sandra M. Schneiders, I.H.M., originally published in special issue, Berkeley Journal of Religion and Theology 2, no. 2 (2016): 43–74.

# Foreword

The Carmelite tradition has had a remarkable renewal in the years following the Second Vatican Council. A resurgence in Carmelite studies in the English-speaking world has been greatly assisted by new translations of critical sources, with updated annotations. Scholars have produced new studies of Carmel, its history, and its spirituality. Through its publishing ministry, ICS Publications, the Institute of Carmelite Studies (ICS) has shared, and to great effect, the results of this scholarly activity. A strength of Carmel is its extensive literary tradition, providing rich material for study, reflection, prayer, and meditation.

In 1983, a group of Carmelite and Discalced Carmelite men and women gathered to study their shared tradition. This Carmelite Forum sponsored summer seminars in the Carmelite tradition at Saint Mary's College, Notre Dame, Indiana. The initial focus was the spirituality of St. Teresa of Ávila and St. John of the Cross. Talks and workshops made use of past and present scholarship. Eventually the Rule of Carmel and other saints of Carmel, ancient and contemporary, were summer themes. These summer sessions began to delve more deeply into the tradition, making connections with contemporary issues.

Some authors in this present volume were among those pioneers who brought Carmelite scholarship forward and made it available to an ever wider audience. The work of the Carmelite Forum, after twenty-eight years, has been continued in the Carmelite Institute of North America. The latter Institute, begun in 1993, is a joint project of the Carmelite Orders to make the tradition available for contemporary pilgrims in faith.

The Carmelite tradition has continually explored humanity's experience of God. Carmelite analysis, language, and symbolism endeavor to articulate an experience which is basically ineffable. The language of Carmel and the lives of its saints provide a vocabulary for transcendent experience. Along with objective statements of speculative theology, Carmel has contributed to the church a language of imagination, a rich symbolic expression of divine experience. Among the images are: an interior castle, a dark night, a little way, and a contemplative landscape called *the Land of Carmel*, a biblically inspired metaphorical place of encounter with God. It is a language and land of yearning, desiring, seeking, which ultimately ends in silence, surrender, and love.

The popular image, *dark night,* is identified with the spirituality of Carmel. The careful presentation in these pages of the original meaning of *dark night,* as described by John of the Cross, conveys an experience of God's love which is a healing of the soul and its deepest attachments. The image has become a widely used expression for a variety of difficulties. St. John Paul II expanded its meaning to include many of the serious problems facing the world.

The articles in this volume particularly focus on wisdom, hope, and prophecy, especially as understood and practiced in Carmel. The study of Wisdom, identified by Christians with the Son of God, confirms Carmel's commitment to the following of Christ. Carmel's focus on Wisdom demonstrates the centrality of the humanity of Jesus in Carmel's spirituality. Rooted in the Old Testament, Lady Wisdom has been interpreted as an expression of the mystery of God in feminine imagery.

Carmel has also become more aware of its prophetic inheritance. The figure of the prophet Elijah has emerged as a balance to the interiority of Carmel and to an individualized spirituality. Convinced that justice is integral to the Gospel, the church has better defined its principles of social justice. In turn, Carmel has become more available and responsive to our contemporary world and its need for community, justice, and depth of meaning. Contemplation should be the deepest source of compassion for our world. The contemplative waits in hope with all who live in hope and wait on God's mercy. Lived in a variety of lifestyles, contemplative prayer in Carmel nourishes active service of the church and the world.

Carmelites, as well as other scholars, continue to mine the rich heritage of this ancient tradition. The articles in this volume are an example of the scholarly work being done today. The quality of the articles is a tribute to the expertise of these authors. *Carmelite Wisdom and Prophetic Hope*, published by ICS Publications, is an act of stewardship offering essays which maintain the tradition, explore its depths, and suggest promising paths for future studies.

JOHN WELCH, O.CARM.
St. Elias Priory
Joliet, Illinois

# Introduction

MARY FROHLICH, R.S.C.J.

The human community is facing unprecedented challenges in our time. The extreme violence of technologically enhanced war; massive population movements, often leaving millions as essentially homeless refugees; the psychological stress of ever-escalating cultural change; and rising global levels of addiction, suicide, and despair: these are only a few of the markers of a pivotal era in which life itself appears to be at risk. Looming behind all of these is the threat of ecological catastrophe due to out-of-control climate change, toxic chemical pollution, and resource depletion. What does the Carmelite tradition have to offer in such a time?

From the tradition's origins in the late twelfth century until now, Carmelites have been known chiefly for their dedication to the practice of silent and solitary contemplation. Today there is renewed interest in the contemplative and mystical traditions, as well as growing realization that these traditions are not meant to be the preserve only of celibate religious who have the privilege of ample time and space for their practice.[1] Nonetheless, a tendency to draw a sharp line between contemplation and action often remains strong. The notion that the depth of contemplation and the power of action on behalf of a just and harmonious world might grow in tandem, rather than reciprocally, has not yet been well integrated into mainstream Christian thinking.

This book takes up the question of what gift the deeply contemplative Carmelite tradition brings to a time so desperately in need of intelligent, morally responsible, globally coordinated action in response to its profound material challenges. From that question a second emerges: could it be that the Carmelite tradition and other contemplative traditions are also at a turning point, from which they will emerge significantly changed? If we truly live at a "turning of the ages," the scope and scale of change will reconfigure all parties. These essays explore various facets of that momentous shift.

"Wisdom in the Carmelite Tradition" was the theme of the Carmelite Summer Seminar at St. Mary's College in South Bend, Indiana, in 2009. The essays by Keith Egan, Daniel Chowning, Vilma Seelaus, and Kevin Culligan were first given as lectures or workshops at that gathering. As the seminar amply demonstrated, intimacy with divine wisdom is at the very core of the Carmelite contemplative tradition. Wisdom has also come to the fore more and more frequently in both theological and scientific discussions of the changed paradigms that are needed for the radical newness of many aspects of the challenges the human community faces today.[2] A renewed understanding of wisdom may offer a way to name the common root of justice and holiness—the human and divine wholeness that has the potential to set both soul and world aright.

As for "prophetic hope," this is a theme that has been gaining increasing prominence in Carmelite self-understanding in recent years. The root tradition of Elijah as the archetypal founder of the Order and the model of the intensely lived Carmelite life is being revivified for a new time. The Carmelite Institute's Fifth National Conference in 2007, for example, explored the theme of "The Prophetic Dimension of our Carmelite Rule." In several groundbreaking essays—one of which is included in this anthology— Constance FitzGerald has articulated the crucial role of contemplation in giving birth to the prophetic consciousness for which our times call. FitzGerald is among those who are reinvigorating a tradition of prophetic Carmelite women—and men—that can be traced all the way back to Teresa of Ávila, foundress of the Discalced Carmelite branch of the Order.

Part I, "Orientations to Wisdom and Prophetic Hope, Ancient and New," offers four very distinct entry points to the questions being explored in this volume. My first essay, "Contemplative Wisdom in an Axial Age: The Carmelite Tradition," explores the pivotal character of the present era as one uniquely in need of a fresh appropriation of both wisdom and prophecy. Karl Jaspers proposed the term "axial age," a concept that was updated by Thomas Berry and Brian Swimme when they identified the upheaval of our time as the birth pangs of an "Ecozoic Era" in which humans must fully accept the responsibilities of our membership in the community of life.[3] In this time of global crisis, not only biblical scholars and theologians but also scientists and psychologists search for a renewed concept of "wisdom." Slowly, a more integrated view of the relation between contemplation and action is replacing attitudes that have tended to place a gulf between them. Within the Carmelite tradition itself, such mid-twentieth-century figures as Edith

Stein and Titus Brandsma model a call to public prophetic witness that is a significant shift from Carmelite norms of earlier generations. This essay aims to sketch a broad evolutionary framework for these developments, in order to lay the groundwork for other essays that focus on more specific aspects of the volume's themes.

Keith Egan's "Wisdom: A Many-Splendored Tradition" provides a sweeping overview of how "wisdom" has been understood by Christians through the ages. He traces the development of the figure of "Lady Wisdom" from probable roots in ancient goddess figures through its appropriation in the Hebrew Bible, where she is a primary figure of God's personal engagement in his creation. In the New Testament, the themes associated with this image were taken up as central for understanding Jesus. Indeed, in the Christian tradition the core meaning of Wisdom is Jesus himself. Egan traces the main lines of development of the Christian theology of wisdom as a gift of the Holy Spirit that is closely linked to contemplation. He connects this with the Carmelite charism as he notes, "Human wisdom is a great endowment, but the wisdom that comes from the Holy Spirit is as far beyond it as the difference Teresa described between *contentos* and *gustos*—the difference between what humans can do (*contentos*) and what only God can do (*gustos*)."

Constance FitzGerald's essay, "From Impasse to Prophetic Hope: The Crisis of Memory," was originally given as a keynote address at the annual meeting of the Catholic Theological Society of America in 2009. The very fact that FitzGerald, a contemplative Carmelite nun who does not work in a formal academic setting, was invited to give such an address was a stirring confirmation of the recognition by academic theologians that in the current era, contemplation must be at the center of their enterprise. FitzGerald pinpoints the role of "the prayer of no experience"—felt by many today as a confusing emptiness at the heart of prayer—in transforming human selves toward a root openness to God's action in and through them. She identifies this as a "dark passage to prophecy" that is demanded by the harsh reality of a world that is in the process of being destroyed by human selfishness. Her essay offers both a sobering view of the profound challenge of inner transformation that faces us and a vision of a uniquely Carmelite path through this challenge. It is particularly strong in identifying both the character and the cost of the prophetic vocation.

Kees Waaijman, in his essay entitled "The Wisdom of 'Work' in the Carmelite Rule," rounds out the introductory background with a close analysis of the parts of the Carmelite Rule that deal with the necessity of work in the Carmelite life. Work, Waaijman concludes, is essential on the human level both because it gives focus and because it contributes to fulfilling community needs. Yet it also has a mystical meaning, especially highlighted in the Rule's injunction to work in "silence." "Working silently and peacefully," Waaijman observes, "I entrust myself to God who shall bring my work to completion, as he desires it." It does not matter whether one's work is simple manual labor or a task that seems more exalted; all human work, in the view of the Carmelite Rule, contains within itself the whole rhythm of contemplation and action for which we are created. As such, our work is a creative partnership with God. Like Lady Wisdom who in Proverbs 8:30 is depicted as "beside God, like a master worker," so the Carmelite (or anyone inspired by the Carmelite tradition of contemplation) co-creates with God through his or her daily labor.

The four essays of part II, "Wisdom and Prophetic Hope in John of the Cross," explore in depth how John of the Cross placed wisdom at the center of his spiritual theology. As Daniel Chowning's "John of the Cross: A Spirituality of Wisdom" spells out, John was deeply aware of the biblical identification between Jesus and Wisdom. John saw how the image of Wisdom, the Son of God, is imprinted into the very molecular structure of creation, and he understood that our transformation in wisdom is intended to bring that image to life in all its fullness. Chowning reviews John's insights into this process in each of his major writings, finally concluding that for John, "the ultimate goal of all wisdom is to be transformed into the beauty of the Son of God: God's Beautiful Face of Love that has looked upon this world giving it dignity and beauty."

The essay "Carmelite Mysticism as Theology: John of the Cross's Mystical Theology of the Human Person" is one of the last offered by revered Carmelite nun, teacher, and spiritual director Vilma Seelaus (1925–2012). Seelaus identifies two convergent theological strands in John's writings: a theology of presence and a theology of silence. God, writes Seelaus, is an indwelling presence that unceasingly draws the human person to God's tender heart. John's writings explore how that divine presence interacts with the human person. His teachings on the "dark night," for example, spell out the various ways in which we can only apprehend God's overwhelming light and presence as "dark." Gradually the soul realizes that God is "sketching" God's own image in her, and this awakens intense desire for the completion of that image. This can only occur, however, through being drawn ever deeper into "the thicket of God's wisdom" (C 37.2). Here, in the divine thicket, Seelaus finds John articulating a "theology of silence." The silence of deep, transformative contemplation is not a silence that we can create but one into which only God can invite us. In this silence, "the soul's deepest *within* becomes the root of all human activity. God *within* overflows into life's everydayness."

Kevin Culligan's "The Wisdom of Emptiness" begins with the paradox of a Zen koan: "Marvelous existence is true emptiness." Like the koan, the assertions John of the Cross makes about the marvelous fruitfulness of dryness, emptiness, darkness, and suffering are deeply puzzling to us. The key to understanding this paradox, Culligan asserts, is to realize that John is primarily talking about being emptied of *desire* for things other than God. John understands the human person as a "created infinite capacity for God," but as long as one's inner space is filled with desire for finite things, the infinite capacity cannot be realized. John once wrote to the nuns of Beas, "The waters of inward delight do not spring from the Earth. One must open toward heaven the mouth of desire, empty of all other fullness" (Letter 7, Nov. 18, 1586, *Collected Works*). This is to be interpreted not as a rejection of the things of earth in themselves but rather as a willingness to let God fill the "infinite capacity" of our humanity so that we can live the marvelous lives God intends for us on this earth and in eternity.

Edward Howells also deals with paradox as he revisits a theme FitzGerald addressed in her essay: how is it possible that the radical emptying of memory can be at the root of true Christian hope? In "'O Guiding Night!': Darkness as the Way to God in John of the Cross's Mysticism," Howells shows how John of the Cross both employed and revised an Augustinian theology of the person to answer this question. The ordinary use of memory is to store the traces of created things that we have encountered, and "remembering" in this sense grounds our ordinary sense of selfhood. Yet for John the more profound character of memory is not this storage function but what Howells calls "a pure relationality, the purified image of God in the soul, orientated to God for God to possess." The memory, then, must be dispossessed of everything created in order to discover its true hope in being possessed by relation with God. As we are joined with Christ who allowed himself to be dispossessed in order to be with us, infinite hope blossoms in the darkness of a seeming loss of self.

The four essays of part III, "Prophetic Intimations from Teresa of Ávila," each examine how Teresa was gifted as a woman of prophetic wisdom whose life transformed those she encountered, then and now. Sandra Schneiders leads off with a theological analysis in "The Jesus Mysticism of Teresa of Ávila: Its Importance for Theology and Contemporary Spirituality." She first explores how Teresa's spiritual experiences were a genuine form of revelation, the main content of which was the person of the risen Jesus. As a biblical scholar, Schneiders details how Teresa's inaugural intellectual vision of Christ has close parallels with biblical stories of prophets receiving their call. Teresa was well aware of other possible interpretations of her claims, such as delusion, psychological ill health, or the action of the devil, and she developed careful criteria of discernment to demonstrate that her experience was real. Her way of articulating her prophetic wisdom is best described as "theopoetic," meaning that she employed evocative images and stories rather than rational arguments to convey her insights. This style, notes Schneiders, "mediates truth as lovable."

How does a saint's transformation also make a difference in the world? The thesis of my second essay, "How Love Transforms: Teresa and the Impact of Sanctity," is that to understand the impact of a saint, we must study *both* the dynamics of interior transformation *and* the social networks within which the story of that transformation was born and proclaimed. Teresa's family, cultural, and religious context prepared her well to be a woman whose "story of the self" has a vibrant, powerful, enticing effect on those who encounter her, whether during her life or through her writings. The truly essential ingredient in her effectiveness, however, was the transforming event of Christ's action in her soul that she compared to the change from caterpillar to butterfly. Still, even this had to be received, rearticulated, and given a public role within both the communities of women who were her closest disciples and the networks of male ecclesial authorities who controlled the official recognition of sanctity. Thus, Teresa's story graphically shows how the most inward of transformations is always dynamically situated within an expanding web of social relations that both support it and make it concretely fruitful for the mission of Christ.

Tara K. Soughers turns to a study of Teresa's practices in "Seeking Wisdom in Common Vocal Prayers: Teresa of Ávila's Response to the Banning of Vernacular Books on Prayer." Teresa was convinced that the very heart of her reform of Carmel was the practice of contemplative prayer. She herself had discovered wisdom to guide her growth in interior prayer in vernacular books such as Francisco de Osuna's *Third Spiritual Alphabet*, but by the time she set about making her foundations, these books were banned. To make matters worse, even engaging in mental prayer was regarded as dangerous, especially for women. Instead of letting herself be cornered, Teresa responded by demonstrating how the fullness of contemplative prayer can develop by starting from attentive vocal prayer with the simplest liturgical texts, such as the Our Father and Hail Mary. In this way she drilled deep into classical Christian traditions to bring forth a fresh fount of wisdom and make it available to all, without exception.

Finally, in "The Prophetic Charism of the Mystical Life: The Model of Teresa of Jesus," Gillian T. W. Ahlgren engages in a historical study of Teresa's active and prophetic witness during the pivotal years when her reform of the Carmelite tradition came under intense attack. At the very moment that opponents of the reform were preparing to imprison and torture John of the Cross, Teresa was putting the finishing touches on her masterwork on the unitive life, *The Interior Castle*. Ahlgren shows how Teresa lived out what she wrote about the unitive life by using every resource at her disposal to "lament, denounce, bear witness to, alleviate, and remediate a situation that cried out for divine (and human) intervention." Teresa spent her life practicing courageous public advocacy on behalf of the creation and protection of societal spaces where the delicate inner work of contemplation can come to fruition. Thus, within her own context she prophetically models just the kind of societal "education for contemplation" that FitzGerald has frequently proposed.[4]

As is evident, the title themes of wisdom and prophetic hope in the Carmelite tradition are the warp and woof of the book. Other themes that run like bright threads through the various essays, surfacing here and there in fresh combinations, include the reintegration of contemplation and action; human work as co-creation with God; the transforming power of contemplative silence; the paradox of hope blossoming in the midst of loss; and the call for education for contemplation. These essays are rich fare indeed. Like the intoxicating wine and nourishing bread set forth by Lady Wisdom (Prv 9:1–6), they have the potential to inspire us with new vision and, at the same time, to fortify us for the hard labor that life at the "turn of the ages" demands. And in doing that, they bring fresh life to the best prophetic traditions of Carmel.

## Notes

1. See Virginia Manss and Mary Frohlich, *The Lay Contemplative: Testimonies, Perspectives, Resources* (Cincinnati: St. Anthony Messenger Press, 2000).

2. See, for example, Warren S. Brown, ed., *Understanding Wisdom: Sources, Science, and Society* (Philadelphia: Templeton Foundation,

2000); Edward Foley and Robert Schreiter, eds., *The Wisdom of Creation* (Collegeville, Minn.: Liturgical, 2004); Elisabeth Schussler Fiorenza, *Jesus, Miriam's Child, Sophia's Prophet: Critical Issues in Feminist Christology* (New York: Continuum, 1994); Celia E. Deane-Drummond, *Creation through Wisdom: Theology and the New Biology* (Edinburgh, Scotland: T & T Clark, 2000).

3. Thomas Berry and Brian Swimme, *The Universe Story: From the Primordial Flaring Forth to the Ecozoic Era* (San Francisco: HarperOne, 1994).

4. See, for example, Constance FitzGerald, "Transformation in Wisdom: The Subversive Character and Educative Power of Sophia in Contemplation," in K. Culligan and R. Jordan, eds., *Carmel and Contemplation: Transforming Human Consciousness*, 281–358 (Washington, D.C.: ICS Publications, 2000), 281–358.

# Translations and Abbreviations

Scripture quotations are from the *New Revised Standard Version Bible, Catholic Edition, Anglicized Text*, © 1999, 1995, 1989, Division of Christian Education of the National Council of Churches of Christ of the United States of America. Used with permission. All rights reserved.

## St. John of the Cross

Unless otherwise noted, all quotations are taken from *The Collected Works of St. John of the Cross*, translated by Kieran Kavanaugh, O.C.D., and Otilio Rodriguez, O.C.D. (Washington, D.C.: ICS Publications, 1991).

The abbreviations for John's works are as follows:

A   *The Ascent of Mount Carmel*
C   *The Spiritual Canticle*
F   *The Living Flame of Love*
Lt  *Letters*
N   *The Dark Night*
R   *Romances*
SLL  *The Sayings of Light and Love*

In references to both *The Ascent* and *The Dark Night*, the first number indicates the book, the second number refers to the chapter, and the third number refers to the paragraph. For example, A 2.3.4 refers to book two, chapter 3, paragraph 4 of *The Ascent*. Similarly, for *The Spiritual Canticle* and *The*

*Living Flame of Love*, the first number refers to the stanza, and the second number, to the paragraph. Thus, C 3.4 is a reference to stanza 3, paragraph 4 of *The Spiritual Canticle*.

## St. Teresa of Ávila

Unless otherwise noted, all quotations of St. Teresa of Ávila are taken from the Kieran Kavanaugh, O.C.D., and Otilio Rodriguez, O.C.D., translation of *The Collected Works of St. Teresa of Avila*, 3 vols. (Washington, D.C.: ICS Publications, 1976–1985, 1987, 2012).

The abbreviations for St. Teresa's works are as follows:

   C  *The Constitutions*
   F  *The Book of the Foundations*
  IC  *The Interior Castle*
   L  *The Book of Her Life*
  Ltr  *Letters* (same abbreviation for volumes 1 and 2, designating letter number and paragraph)
  ST  *The Spiritual Testimonies*
  W  *The Way of Perfection*

For the *Life*, *Interior Castle*, *Way of Perfection*, and *Foundations*, the first number refers to the chapter, and the second number refers to the paragraph. Thus, L 3.5 refers to *The Book of Her Life*, chapter 3, paragraph 5. Regarding *The Interior Castle*, the first number refers to the dwelling place, the second number refers to the chapter, and the third number refers to the paragraph. Thus, IC 3.4.2 refers to the third dwelling place, chapter 4, paragraph 2.

# PART I

---

*Orientations to Wisdom
and Prophetic Hope, Ancient
and New*

# Contemplative Wisdom in an Axial Age:
## *The Carmelite Tradition*

MARY FROHLICH, R.S.C.J.

MANY COMMENTATORS ON the current era agree that humanity, and the Earth that is our habitat, are at a turning point. The combination of burgeoning human population with repeated exponential leaps in techno-logical capabilities (and corresponding resource usage) has already significantly altered the functioning of every ecosystem on Earth. Thousands of species have already become extinct, and tens of thousands more will follow the same path in the next few decades. Which life forms are cast aside, which thrive, and which barely hold on against massive odds are all now heavily dependent upon human choices. The last time so much global ecosystemic change took place was sixty-five million years ago, when the collision between a giant meteor and the earth caused the extinction of the dinosaurs. The Cenozoic Era, which began at that time, has been the age of mammals, culmi-nating in the emergence of *Homo sapiens* about 175,000 years ago.

3

Commentators have suggested several possible names for the new era that is emerging today. Some scientists have proposed that it be called the Anthropocene, defined as the epoch in which human activity impacts every aspect of Earth's geology and ecosystem function. More specifically, some assert that it will be the Technozoic Era and that human technology will be the overwhelmingly dominant force of the future. Among these, some go so far as to propose that humans will be able to "download" their consciousness onto computers or robots that will then evolve as the next "life" forms.[1] A contrasting viewpoint, however, is that human survival requires that the next age must be the Ecozoic Era, in which the way forward is human collaboration with the existing web of life.[2] On this view, humans do have a unique leadership role but must exercise it as participants who respect the gifts and roles of every member of the community of life. The premise of this book is that the latter is the way of wisdom and that it will require of us an extraordinarily arduous spiritual transition.

In view of the book's specific focus on what the Carmelite contemplative tradition can contribute to such a spiritual revolution, this essay will develop four key themes: (1) the notion of an "axial age"; (2) recent retrievals of "wisdom" as a guiding concept; (3) the emergent integration of contemplation and action; and (4) an evolutionary perspective on the Carmelite tradition and its prophetic roots. These will, I hope, provide background helpful to reading the remaining essays more fruitfully.

# The Present Era as an Axial Age

The notion of the "Axial Period" was proposed by Karl Jaspers in his *Origin and Goal of History* (1953). Jaspers asserted that between 800 and 200 BCE a new level of human consciousness emerged in China, India, Iran, and Palestine, even though these regions did not have significant contact with each other. He wrote, "What is new about this age, in all three areas of the world, is that man [sic] becomes conscious of Being as a whole, of himself and his own limitations. He experiences the terror of the world and his own powerlessness. He asks radical questions. Face to face with the void he strives for liberation and redemption. By consciously recognizing his limits he sets himself the highest goals. He experiences absoluteness in the depths of selfhood and in the lucidity of transcendence."[3] Jaspers emphasized that he understood this simultaneous shift in human consciousness as caused neither by a mystical impulse "from above" nor simply by a biological evolution "from below." He saw it, rather, as an empirical development of culture whose importance is that it founded everything that has been most significant to the human spirit ever since.[4] The chief fruit of this Axial Period, in Jaspers's view, was the emergence of the capacity for personal, individual thought and commitment.

Not surprisingly, Jaspers's idea has attracted considerable critique. It has been pointed out that the six-hundred-year period he selected is fairly arbitrary, since similar developments can be identified both before and after.[5] Moreover, his attempt to describe the developments in China, India, Iran, and Palestine as intrinsically similar to one another has been called a "Procrustean bed," since it is easy to find major differences among them.[6] In spite of Jaspers's insistence that he was not asserting that some sort of "mystical current" ran around the world at that period, many of his critics have detected a disturbing whiff of esotericism in his proposal. Finally, the fact that he called the native cultures of Africa and the Americas (and early Europe, for that matter) "primitive" until such time as they become seeded by these Axial developments has been seen as enhancing cultural imperialism.

Despite these concerns, Jaspers's concept of the Axial Period has entered our vocabulary and has been taken up in transmuted forms by a variety of other thinkers. It has become a "meme"—that is, a unit of cultural information that takes on a life of its own as it passes rapidly into new cultural settings and hybridizes with them.[7] The core of the idea is that there are certain periods in history when a definitive shift takes place in human awareness of self and world. Analogous to the physical changes in a child entering puberty, such a cultural shift occurs as a sudden, noticeable, and disruptive spurt that is followed by a longer period of assimilation and integration. My purpose in using the term here is not to argue for or against the specifics of Jaspers's claims about an Axial Period occurring in 800–200 BCE. My proposal, rather, is that there is quite persuasive evidence that another, perhaps even more significant, shift in human awareness is occurring in our own time.

This claim, of course, is hardly original. A variety of popular writers have presented such a view. Theologian Ewert Cousins, for example, hybridized Jaspers's idea with Pierre Teilhard de Chardin's concept of planetization.[8]

Teilhard had asserted that the present era is the culmination of a centuries-long process of convergence among human cultures, so that humanity is now ready for the leap to a globalized consciousness. Cousins explicitly identified this as a second Axial Period, one of whose chief characteristics is the coming together of the world religions. He then mined the Christian tradition for resources, old and new, to understand and enter wholeheartedly into the change that is upon us. Thomas Berry and Brian Swimme's *Universe Story* elaborated this further, using the language of the Ecozoic Era.

More recently, Bruno Barnhart has argued that the key to this globalized consciousness is a reclaiming of wisdom, which he defines as "participatory knowing: a knowing that is personal, experiential, and tending toward union with that which is known; ultimately centered in 'identity.'"[9] In his view, the history of the West can be interpreted as a parabolic movement from a "sapiential awakening" with the coming of Christ, through a gradual development of individualized and critical consciousness (a "Western Axial Period") in the later Middle Ages, to the present era in which "sapiential Christianity" is ready to be reborn. He believes that only through such a process, including the long period of modern secularization and unbalanced individualism from which we are only now beginning to emerge, can Christ become truly "the heart of the world" in a global unity.

If we are indeed experiencing a new Axial Period, what are some of the characteristics of the newly emerging consciousness? It is undoubtedly too soon to make a fully definitive analysis, since the movement is still in progress. We can, however, name some of the trends. Integration, balance, and flexibility might be some of the key words, as well as integration of material and spiritual; balance between inner and outer; and flexibility and openness to a plurality of persons and traditions. It is in this context that the notion of "wisdom" is emerging within both science and theology as a potential key to a renewed understanding of human maturity and capability.

## The Emergence of "Wisdom" as a Key Concept

In recent decades the concept of "wisdom" has drawn the interest of secular scientists, at the same time that theologians have also placed a renewed focus on its significance.

### Scientific Interest in Wisdom

Although wisdom has traditionally been a religious concept, some scientists have begun attempting to explain its character and role in human life.[10] Widely accepted evolutionary theory presumes that organisms always evolve toward greater reproductive fitness, that is, physiological adaptations that make it more likely they will successfully raise offspring. One approach to locating wisdom scientifically is evolutionary epistemology, a term coined by Donald Campbell to refer to the theory that evolution always proceeds by adaptations that increase an organism's knowledge.[11] In such a view, "wisdom" may be a uniquely effective type of knowledge that fosters human thriving.

Evolutionary epistemologists study the history of human evolution, looking for evidence of what they call "cognition-gaining" adaptations. Anthropologists have arrived at a general consensus that anatomically modern humans emerged approximately 200,000 years ago in Africa and then emigrated outward to the Middle East, Europe, and beyond. These *Homo sapiens* eventually replaced all preceding populations of hominids. In Europe, the archaic population was the Neanderthals and the modern humans were the Cro-Magnons, who arrived there about 40,000 years ago during the Neo-Paleolithic period. These two hominid species interbred, but eventually the Neanderthals were driven to extinction. During this period in Europe there was a comparatively sudden "creative explosion" of decoration and imagery, most dramatically in the underground cave paintings of southwest France and the Basque country of Spain. These give strong evidence that the humans of that era were developing a new level of symbol-making capacity. While some evidence of human symbolic behavior has been found much earlier in Africa, Indonesia, and elsewhere, at the present stage of knowledge the European cave paintings seem to represent a particularly significant leap to a new level of human representational capacity.

Jean Clottes and David Lewis-Williams, among others, have interpreted the cave paintings as evidence of shamanic religious practice in these early *Homo sapiens*.[12] Shamanic consciousness, which is still a capacity of humans today, involves extremely intense imagistic and emotional experiences that very often include a sense of either flying in the heavens or descending to the underworld. In cultures where this has a cultural role, shamans are regarded as persons of special spiritual power who can guide the community in its most important decisions.

The cave paintings suggest that some of these early European cultures began to desire to enshrine the shamans' inner imagery in the outer world so that it could be accessed by others. Clottes and Lewis-Williams's theory is that the cave paintings were created as part of rituals in which people were taken underground in order to be initiated into shamanic consciousness. This externalization of meaningful imagery, which must have required considerable investment of communal resources on the part of the cultures involved, appears to mark the origin not only of religion but also of art and of a much-enhanced ability to use symbols on a practical level to further communal projects. Sophistication in the design and use of tools, as well as of musical instruments and decorative artifacts, surged in the same periods and locations as the cave paintings. In other words, spiritual consciousness, art, and technical power all advanced together.

Franz Wuketits is an evolutionary epistemologist who traces the human cognition-gaining process to a peak in the capacity for rational knowledge, which in his view is what most increases the evolutionary fitness of its possessors.[13] Like many others, he regards religious practice as expressing a primitive level of consciousness that is now nonadaptive and must be left behind in favor of mature reason. In this view, so-called wisdom is not adaptive, since wisdom traditions in a variety of cultures often propose behaviors and attitudes that appear to decrease, rather than increase, reproductive fitness. Celibacy is the most obvious example, since celibates cannot pass on their genes. Other examples of attitudes that appear to contradict the enhancement of reproductive fitness include the proposal that self-sacrifice is an admirable approach to life, as well as admonitions to prefer wisdom to wealth, success, or status.

Yet much evidence at the present time points to the strong probability that rational and technical power alone (e.g., the Technozoic attitude), when lacking the balance of spiritual and moral development, ultimately is destructive to human life. "Wisdom" names the kind of knowledge that combines balanced rationality with roots in a more deeply rooted and more comprehensive level of awareness. In view of the crisis of our times, other scientists continue to search for a perspective that can give credence to wisdom.

Jeffrey Schloss reviewed various scientific proposals for explaining wisdom and concluded that a model of a nested hierarchy of adaptive strategies is most helpful, with wisdom at the top of the hierarchy. In a nested hierarchy each higher level of the hierarchy emerges out of the lower levels and is dependent on them, yet is not fully reducible to them. Schloss defines wisdom as "living in a way that corresponds to how things are. It is not mere knowledge, nor is it mere moral admonition, but it involves deep insight into the functioning, meaning, and purposes of existence along with the ability to discern how to live accordingly, that is, in accord with the way things are."[14] The foundational level of evolutionary adaptation is biological (e.g., genetic) change, but the problem is that this is patently too slow to deal with immediate problems that an individual organism faces. Adaptation through individual learning is a second level that is much quicker, but it too is often unable to take in a broad enough range of information to be successful. In human beings, culture provides a third level of adaptation, passing on the social adaptations developed over many generations to each new member of the social group. Wisdom, Schloss proposes, may be a fourth level of adaptive potential, able to critique culture and to promote even more sensitivity and flexibility in individual and group responses.

## Wisdom in Contemporary Theology

The theme of wisdom is also being retrieved by an increasing number of thinkers as a key to revisioning Christian theology for the challenges of today. Elisabeth Schüssler Fiorenza observes that "a submerged theology of Wisdom, or sophiology, permeates all of Christian Scriptures,"[15] yet for much of Christian history this theme has been neglected in favor of emphasis on the patriarchal imagery of Father and Son. The discovery that the earliest interpretations of Jesus and his ministry drew heavily upon Jewish Wisdom literature has sent scholars back to these texts to reexamine the worldview they present.

Three aspects of Jewish wisdom have been especially important in this retrieval. First, much of Jewish wisdom has a highly practical, down-to-earth orientation. The wise person is depicted as flexible and pragmatic as he or she navigates through everyday challenges of work, politics, friendship, marriage, and family. This theme has some elements in common with the scientific notions of wisdom that emphasize its contribution to moral, economic, and reproductive success.

Second, the wisdom traditions were daring in integrating cultural elements into theology and spirituality. The most noteworthy example is the enigmatic figure of "Lady Wisdom," who shows strong parallels to the goddess traditions of Israel's neighbors. Some scholars think she is a thinly veiled recycling of the Egyptian goddesses Ma'at or Isis, or of an earlier Hebrew goddess named Asherah. Rosemary Radford Ruether, however, concludes that despite the influence of these and other surrounding cultural stories, Lady Wisdom is an original creation of the Hebrew sages. Ruether warns against the naïveté of those who presume that this female imagery for the divine necessarily represents empowerment for women or other marginalized peoples, since it was clearly created for and by elite males.[16] Nonetheless, the intense significance given to this recontextualized cultural imagery provides a model for the creative inculturation of the Gospel within previously alien networks of symbolism. Moreover, the discovery of how deeply early Christology drew on this female figure opens up new directions for woman-friendly theology.

Third, the wisdom traditions provide a cosmic theology of God as active in every dimension of created time and space. It is Wisdom that sets all things in order and rejoices in their ongoing harmonious development. This creation-centered approach balances out the more pervasive salvation-history perspective of the Bible, which celebrates God's acts of election and redemption as events in human history. From the point of view of modern science, the entirety of human history is only a speck in the vastness of the fourteen-billion-year drama of the cosmos. The cosmic dimensions of Hebrew Bible wisdom theology are thus a breath of fresh air for theologians who seek to enter into a serious dialogue with scientific cosmology.

In the New Testament, Paul adds a crucial dimension when he affirms that the wisdom of God is "Christ crucified, a stumbling block to Jews and foolishness to the Gentiles." One of the major critiques of the optimism of a creation-centered wisdom theology is that it does not take evil seriously enough. The declaration that a tortured and humiliated man is "the power of God and the wisdom of God" shocks us into deep meditation on the reality of evil and on the paradox of a broken, powerless God (1 Cor 1:22–25). Christian wisdom is not a grand vision of triumphant glory but a companioning of all that is with merciful compassion. In the words of Bruno Barnhart, "Christian wisdom reduces itself to Jesus Christ—this bodily human being who is divine—and his cross: the physical death of this human being at the center of humanity, history, and cosmos. The mystery of Christ in its actuality is known as one finds oneself at the central point of the cross. . . . The fullness is known in emptiness, as the forms and ideas give way to participation: 'to know nothing among you except Jesus Christ and him crucified.'"[17] The theological study of wisdom climaxes, then, is a mystery that is "beyond reason, unknowable by the rational mind, yet in its dark density . . . the very core of meaning."[18]

# Contemplation and Action: A Brief History

In examining the Carmelite tradition, a key question will be the relationship between its profound contemplative core and whatever contribution it can make to the needs of the present era. In order to explore this in depth, we must first review the history of Christian understanding of the relationship between contemplation and action. This will be done here in very broad strokes, admittedly neglecting a great deal of important subtlety and detail.

## *The First Millennium*

The theology and spirituality of the first millennium of Christianity were dominated by a fundamentally Platonic model of the relationship between God and world. The chief characteristic of such a model is that it presents all of reality as a unified, ordered hierarchy. All things have their origin in God and have a built-in impetus to return to God. The material world is at the apogee of this arc of descent and return; what is material or fleshly is seen as the least real, the most distant from God, and the most riddled with contradiction and corruption. In such a view, contemplation has to do with gaining knowledge of what is most real, that is, God and the most fundamental divine principles of order that underlie the relative unreality of the world as it presents itself to us in everyday life. The pursuit of this kind of contemplation is normally restricted to an elite group who are able to separate themselves from most of the physical, economic, and social demands of ordinary life in order to devote themselves strenuously to the ascent to God.

Two main models of the contemplative Christian stand out in these early centuries. One is the model of the holy bishop, exemplified by Basil of Caesarea, Gregory of Nyssa, Augustine of Hippo, and Gregory the Great, among others. The ideal bishop was understood to be both supremely active and supremely contemplative. At the center of his charism stood intense personal participation in the mystery of Christ, the font from which all his daily activities of administration, teaching, liturgical leadership, and pastoral care flowed. In this sense the bishop was "mystic," although this term did not have the flavor of esotericism that it typically has today. He was also the theologian par excellence, whose theology was truly an expression of knowledge of God.

The second early model is that of the monk, exemplified most famously by Antony of Egypt. The Greek term *monachos* means alone, solitary, single. At the center of this ideal is the singleheartedness of the quest for union with God. Everything in the monk's life must be focused around this one purpose. For this reason he or she practices celibacy, withdrawal into solitude or into a community of other monks, constant prayer, and manual labor. Monks of the early Christian centuries typically sought to separate themselves as much as possible from family issues, political struggles, and economic concerns. Meanwhile, during this whole period the married laity were for the most part not regarded as capable of contemplation, with the occasional exception of wealthy persons who were able to live semi-monastic lives despite their lay status.

Charles Taylor characterizes the normal experience of life during this period as "the enchanted world." The prevalence of belief in spirits (evil or good) and in the power of sacred objects exemplify this worldview. Taylor attributes such beliefs to a self-structure that does not set up strong boundaries between oneself and the world; this "porous self" is constantly subject to being influenced or even possessed by powers that one encounters everywhere—in people, sacred groves, blessed or cursed objects, and so forth.[19] In such a world, contemplatives were regarded with awe and respect because they were believed to be people who participated in God's ability to master the evil or chaotic powers abroad upon the earth. The holy bishop or monk was in himself or herself a uniquely powerful talisman of the harmonious, ordered world intended by God. The ordinary layperson might not be able to *be* a contemplative, but she or he had access to the fruits of contemplation through contact with those whom God had appointed to these exalted roles.

## The Second Millennium

A major theological shift began to emerge in the eleventh century with such figures as Anselm and Abelard, who sought to bring a more systematic approach to theological questions. A cascading series of developments followed: the Scholastic organization of theology by rational categories; the nominalist separation of linguistic meaning from intrinsic meaning; Descartes's separation of mind from materiality; and finally the emergence of modern science, with its methodological reduction of truth to empirical evidence. Charles Taylor describes the changes in everyday mindset that accompanied these shifts as a process of "disenchantment" leading to a "buffered self" that is able to put a clear boundary between itself and external forces. The buffered self has autonomy, self-control, and the ability to manipulate the world for its own benefit to a far greater degree than the porous self. As noted, Bruno Barnhart referred to this shift as the "Western Axial Period," when individual autonomy and critical thinking begin to emerge as social norms. Accompanying it on the social and economic level was what Max Weber called the increasing rationalization of the structures of daily life.[20] In this context, rationalization refers to emphasis on formal structures, ends-means analysis, and efficiency.

The buffered self as the norm for ordinary people did not fully take hold until late in the process, however. Two major models of the contemplative during the transition period (1000–1600) were the visionary woman and the mendicant. Visionary women, exemplified by such figures as Hildegard of Bingen, Mechthild of Magdeburg, Angela of Foligno, and Teresa of Ávila, exhibited characteristics of both the porous self and the buffered self. They were often possessed and overwhelmed by florid visions and ecstasies; yet at the same time, they were assertive, inner directed, and politically astute to a degree unusual in women of their time.[21] Something similar can be said of the mendicants, with Francis of Assisi as the outstanding example. He too was a man of ecstasies whose resistance to the rationalization of society, as manifested in the emerging merchant economy of his time, required rising to a new level of individuality and inner directedness. Both visionary women and mendicants interacted powerfully with the social world of their surroundings through physical witness, speech, and writing. They contributed considerably to the development of theology, even though some aspects of their contemplative wisdom were not fully appreciated in their own times.

In Taylor's view, it was around the beginning of the seventeenth century that European social elites began a concerted effort to make the buffered self the norm for all people, common folk as well as elites. Within a church context this is the era of the catechisms, missions at home and abroad, and church schools, all aimed at bringing the broad masses of the laity (including the "savages" in mission lands) to a new level of personal discipline and interiorization of the faith. The paradox, from the point of view of church professionals, was that as education liberated people from the anxieties and compulsions of the porous self, they also became able to choose unbelief. Between the eighteenth and twentieth centuries the combination of the ever-increasing rationalization of society with this new inner freedom evolved into the present-day reality of Western secular societies where a pluralism of beliefs (and disbeliefs) is considered normative.

During this period (1600–1950), the primary model of the contemplative was the cloistered nun. The cloistered contemplative nun was seen as living out the new ideal of discipline and interiorization to the ultimate degree, and for this reason she was a highly admired figure among the devout. The strict rules of cloister, however, were designed to keep her separated as much as possible from the actual life of both world and church. Her role was to pray in hiddenness and silence; she could not teach, write, theologize, or offer comment on events outside the cloister. Although within the cloister the nuns obviously had to engage in a variety of activities, from the point of view of the outside world they were not "active" but only "contemplative."

For the surrounding secularized society, such nuns were often little more than a rather bizarre curiosity, not to be taken seriously. In the modern era, in short, contemplation was systematically marginalized. Even within the church it was firmly compartmentalized and assigned a functional role (intercessory prayer) rather than being an organic and integral partner in the evolving life of Christian communities. In the secular world it was seen variously as a waste of time, a relic of bygone ages, or even a manifestation of psychological pathology.

## The Third Millennium

This brings us to our own time, heir to this entire history. Naturally it is the most recent history that weighs most heavily upon us, and it has written firmly upon our psyches the assumption that somehow the relationship between "contemplation and action" is deeply problematic. As we have seen, this has not always been so, or at least the issue has been configured very differently in other eras. For Christians of the first millennium, the separation was not really between contemplation and action but rather between those assigned a place at a higher level of the cosmic hierarchy and those assigned to a lower place. For a good portion of the second millennium, the separation was still not between contemplation and action but rather between the spiritually liberated individual and those more constrained by conformity to societal expectations. It is only in recent centuries that the idea has developed either that contemplation is something so separate from "action" that it is best kept in an entirely distinct compartment (e.g., cloister) or that it is an expendable, possibly pathological activity that should wither away with responsible maturation.

There is something to be learned from each of these eras, and also much to be critiqued. The first millennium offers us models of the fully contemplative and fully active person with a powerful role in society, but the weakness of these models is that their enactment is confined to an elite few, almost always male. Moreover, the optimistic and rather simplistic worldview of cosmic unity and hierarchy does not wear well in today's science-savvy culture. The first half of the second millennium offers us models of the spiritually liberated individual, often female, whose ecstatic creativity opens up new vistas of insight and influence. These models have enjoyed a resurgence of interest in recent years, but their weakness is an overemphasis on individual liberation and on "wild" creativity as almost an end in itself. Finally, the recent era of cloistered contemplation offers us a model of the hidden power of contemplative practice, which does not have to make a public splash in order to have its own integrity. Its weakness, of course, is that the contemplative (at this stage normatively female) becomes not only hidden but also lacking in effective means to witness beyond the four walls of the cloister.

As we enter the third millennium of Christianity, it is evident that none of the previous models of the relationship between contemplation and action matches what is emergent in our time. The desire today is for spiritualities that are, in the words of Beverly Lanzetta, "embodied and engaged."[22] The idea that celibacy is an advantage in the spiritual quest has fallen out of favor; the common assumption is that sexual relationship and family are paths that are at least as spiritually fruitful, if not more so. The spiritual equality of women and men is more and more taken for granted. People long for experiences of inner intimacy and spiritual peace but are insistent that this not be disengaged from the hard work of social, political, and ecological peace. Young people flock to programs on interreligious dialogue, convinced that many different religions and spiritualities have valid access to truth. It is normal for serious spiritual seekers to test out contemplative practices from a variety of spiritual traditions. There is a new openness to the idea that taking account of the insights of science is essential to a well-grounded spirituality. This is especially the case with the sciences of ecology, neurophysiology, and physical cosmology. A major question for this book is the exploration of what Carmelite spirituality brings to this emergent vision.

## Carmelite Spirituality in Evolutionary Perspective

Carmelite spirituality, which made its appearance in the late twelfth century, has developed in the context of the patterns described above for the second Christian millennium. While much is unknown about the earliest Carmelites, it is almost certain that they were originally individuals who made their way to Mount Carmel as pilgrims or as

disillusioned Crusaders, settled there to lead an eremitical life of prayer and penance, and subsequently chose to
band together and request a Formula of Life from the local
patriarch, Albert of Jerusalem. Since Mount Carmel was
revered as the place where the prophet Elijah had defeated
the false prophets (1 Kgs 18:16–45), these men claimed
him as their founding model. The Formula of Life, given
sometime between 1209 and 1214, later became the Carmelite Rule. It establishes Carmelites in a communal way
of life centered in solitary contemplation, meditation on
the Word of God, and the Eucharist.

While some aspects of this spirituality appear similar to
the monastic spirituality of the first Christian millennium, its
actual originating context is the form of eremitical spirituality that flourished between the tenth and thirteenth centuries.
The hermits of this era did not necessarily spend the majority
of their time in solitude but rather sought to imitate as closely
as possible the life of Jesus and the apostles as they understood
it. Part of this ideal was availability to respond spontaneously
to pastoral needs as they arose, yet without getting tied down
to institutionalized commitments.[23] The Carmelite Formula
of Life makes clear that for the first brothers of Carmel, the
highest priority was placed on solitary contemplation, with
other involvements minimized as much as possible. Yet their
location on one of the main routes taken by European pilgrims to Jerusalem must have meant that some ministry to
these travelers—whose alms were also the Carmelites' main
source of funds—was necessary.[24] Within seventy-five years
of their founding, the Carmelites, along with all the other
Latin Christians, had been driven out of the Holy Land. By

then they already had numerous foundations in European cities, where they had taken up the mendicant lifestyle with its combined contemplative and apostolic commitments. This mixed life became the new norm for male Carmelites. Cloister, however, was required of female Carmelites, as it was for other women religious of that era.

Carmelite spirituality, then, came to birth as part of what Bruno Barnhart called the Western Axial Period—the gradual emergence of individualized and critical consciousness among European peoples. Although Carmelites live in community, their roots in the medieval eremitical movement mean that much more emphasis is placed on individual interiority than was typical of most of the earlier monastic movements. Carmelite men studied and taught in the universities from the late thirteenth century onward, participating in the development of Scholastic theology during its peak years. The specific character of Carmelite critical thought came to its climax, however, in the sixteenth century with the writings of John of the Cross. John developed a systematic understanding of the path to mystical union, demonstrating with logical rigor that it requires a thoroughgoing interior critique of every tendency toward attachment—even those to seemingly "spiritual" ideas, images, or feelings.

John's contemporary and mentor, Teresa of Ávila, is one of the medieval women mentioned in the previous section as combining elements of the "porous" and "buffered" self. She experienced visions and ecstasies, sometimes of extreme intensity, and these empowered her bold and creative leadership in the refounding of the Carmelite Order. At a time when mystical women were under great suspicion, she took the risk of teaching on the basis of her own mystical experience. She was acerbic in criticizing and rejecting unjust social conventions whenever she saw them in action. In short, she was a highly independent and creative woman in an era when this was far from the norm of femininity.

Since she did not have the scholastic education that John of the Cross had, Teresa's writings have a very different character. They are vernacular theology, using images, stories, and humor as primary means to teach the spiritual path. Perhaps because of her position at the very end of the medieval period, as well as her intimate acquaintance with John of the Cross and his way of thinking, a semi-systematic approach to the mystical life shines through her decidedly unsystematic and conversational style. This is particularly true in her masterwork, *The Interior Castle*, whose "seven mansions" (*moradas*, more accurately translated as "dwelling places") quickly became normative for the description of Christian spiritual development.

Although there were small numbers of Carmelite nuns before Teresa's time, the female branch of the order expanded exponentially in size and influence after her reform. Before long there were so many women's Carmelite monasteries that many people knew no male Carmelites and simply assumed that all Carmelites were women. In many contexts, the Carmelite nun became the primary exemplar of the cloistered contemplative described in the previous section. She was much revered—although kept at a distance—within church circles, while in secular society she was often regarded with amusement or disdain.

## Carmelites Face the Third Millennium

Three prominent Carmelites of the late nineteenth and twentieth centuries may give hints of a transition period in Carmelite spirituality. Thérèse of Lisieux's lifestyle conformed closely to the model of the cloistered contemplative nun typical of the period between 1600 and 1950, but her *Story of a Soul* broke the mold of female Carmelite silence. The original published edition was heavily edited by Thérèse's Carmelite sisters and others to make her appear to adhere closely to prevailing expectations for a "holy Carmelite," but since Thérèse's own words have become available it has become evident that her real holiness was not so easily tamed. She witnesses unabashedly to a profoundly human and holistic struggle for personal wisdom.[25]

The other two Carmelites, Edith Stein and Titus Brandsma, were both highly educated philosophers who died at the hands of the Nazis in concentration camps during World War II. Each of them combined deep erudition with pastoral approachability and with the strength to surrender their lives in confrontation with public evil. They were seekers of wisdom whose search climaxed in complete identification with Christ crucified, "the power of God and the wisdom of God" (1 Cor 1:24).

While the vocations of Thérèse, Edith, and Titus were certainly extraordinary, they also point to an emerging dimension of Carmelite holiness that has implications for all who draw from the deep springs of this spirituality. The absolute priority of contemplation and the willingness to be radically hidden from the world remain, yet its fruit is a public witness that reverberates far beyond the cloister walls—and even beyond the church. It seems that the original prophetic character of the foundation on Mount Carmel may be, at last, ready to come into its own. The radiance of Carmelite wisdom, we might say, is no longer to be hidden under a bushel basket but rather to be placed on a lampstand for all the world to see.

## Conclusion

This essay has only been able to provide a rough sketch of the vast movements that are shaping our particular moment in time. In fact, these movements are so complex and far-reaching that settled insight into their character may require the passage of decades, or even centuries. Yet for those alive in this moment, there is no time to wait. With the Earth's community of life under threat on every front, we can live with integrity only if we do our best to join all our human energies with the saving project of the God who loves every living being. As the remaining essays of this volume exemplify, the Carmelite contemplative tradition offers deep riches of wisdom that give promise of bearing fruit in the prophetic action that such a moment demands.

### Notes

1. See, for example, David Smith, "2050—and Immortality Is within Our Grasp," *Observer*, May 22, 2005.

2. See Thomas Berry and Brian Swimme, *The Universe Story: From the Primordial Flaring Forth to the Ecozoic Era* (San Francisco: HarperOne, 1994).

3. Karl Jaspers, *The Origin and Goal of History* (New Haven, Conn.: Yale University Press, 1953), 2.

4. Jaspers, *Origin and Goal*, 15–18.

5. Antony Black, "The 'Axial Period': What Was It and What does It Signify?" *Review of Politics* 70, no. 1 (2008): 23–29.

6. James A. Montmarquet, "Jaspers, the Axial Age, and Christianity," *American Catholic Philosophical Quarterly* 83, no. 2 (2009): 239–54.

7. Richard Dawkins, *The Selfish Gene* (Oxford: Oxford University Press, 1989), 186.

8. Ewert Cousins, *Christ in the 21st Century* (New York: Continuum, 1992).

9. Bruno Barnhart, *The Future of Wisdom: Toward a Rebirth of Sapiential Christianity* (New York: Continuum, 2007), 6.

10. See, for example, Robert J. Sternberg, ed., *Wisdom: Its Nature, Origins, and Development* (Cambridge: Cambridge University Press, 1990); Richard P. Honeck, *A Proverb in Mind: The Cognitive Science of Wit and Wisdom* (Mahwah, N.J.: Lawrence Erlbaum, 1997); Warren S. Brown, ed., *Understanding Wisdom: Sources, Science, and Society* (Philadelphia: Templeton Foundation, 2000); and Stephen S. Hall, *Wisdom: From Philosophy to Neuroscience* (New York: Vintage, 2011).

11. Donald T. Campbell, "Evolutionary Epistemology," In *Evolutionary Epistemology, Rationality, and the Sociology of Knowledge*, ed. Gerard Radnitzky and W. W. Bartley (La Salle, Ill.: Open Court, 1974).

12. Jean Clottes and David Lewis-Williams, *The Shamans of Prehistory: Trance and Magic in the Painted Caves* (New York: Abrams, 1996).

13. Franz M. Wuketits, *Evolutionary Epistemology and Its Implications for Humankind* (Albany, N.Y.: SUNY, 1990).

14. Jeffrey P. Schloss, "Wisdom Traditions as Mechanisms for Organismal Integration: Evolutionary Perspectives on Homeostatic 'Laws of Life,'" in Brown, *Understanding Wisdom*, 157. It would be interesting to compare Schloss's notion of wisdom as accord with "the

way things are" with Jon Sobrino's assertion that authentic spirituality is "fidelity to the real." See Sobrino's *Spirituality of Liberation: Toward Political Holiness* (Maryknoll, N.Y.: Orbis, 1988), 14.

15. Elisabeth Schüssler Fiorenza, *Jesus: Miriam's Child, Sophia's Prophet* (New York: Continuum, 1994), 139.

16. Rosemary Radford Ruether, *Goddesses and the Divine Feminine: A Western Religious History* (Berkeley, Calif.: University of California Press, 2005), 90–91.

17. Barnhart, *Future of Wisdom*, 52.

18. Ibid.

19. Charles Taylor, *A Secular Age* (Cambridge, Mass.: Harvard University Press, 2007), 29–41.

20. Max Weber, *The Protestant Ethic and the Spirit of Capitalism*, trans. Talcott Parsons (Mineola, N.Y.: Dover, 2003).

21. Cf. Paul Rorem, "The Company of Medieval Women Theologians," *Theology Today* 60, no. 1 (2003): 82–93.

22. Beverly J. Lanzetta, *Radical Wisdom: A Feminist Mystical Theology* (Minneapolis: Fortress, 2005).

23. Henrietta Leyser, *Hermits and the New Monasticism: A Study of Religious Communities in Western Europe, 1000–1500* (New York: St. Martin's, 1984).

24. Mary Frohlich, "Pilgrimage and the Roots of Carmelite Spirituality," *Studies in Spirituality* 25 (2015): 99–116.

25. See, for example, Mary Frohlich, "Desolation and Doctrine in Thérèse of Lisieux," *Theological Studies* 61, no. 2 (June 1, 2000): 261–79; and Mary Frohlich, "Thérèse of Lisieux and Jeanne d'Arc: History, Memory, and Interiority in the Experience of Vocation," *Spiritus* 6, no. 2 (September 1, 2006): 173–94.

# Wisdom:
## A Many-Splendored Tradition

KEITH J. EGAN, T.O.CARM.

*Among all human pursuits, the pursuit of wisdom is more*
*perfect, more noble, more useful, and more full of joy.*[1]

WHO AMONG US DOES NOT want to be wise? A Ger-
man proverb catches the all too often frustrated desire for
wisdom: "Too soon old, too late smart!" Like other names
for profound realities, the word *wisdom* has countless meanings, from the banal and everyday to the exalted and the
divine. Philosophy as the love of wisdom has since ancient
times sought to answer the numerous questions that the
human mind forever raises. Aristotle claimed that everyone
by nature seeks to know,[2] a conviction that lies at the root of
the search for wisdom. Cultures through the centuries have
had their sages and their ways of learning how to face the
little and big questions of life.

Wisdom is so multifaceted and so many-layered—like
Joseph's many-colored coat—that one must be selective in
what one says about such a rich tradition.[3] I must limit
myself to sampling the Judeo-Christian tradition of wisdom, and specifically to those strands in this tradition that

provide some background to an understanding of what in the wisdom tradition prepared the Carmelites of the sixteenth century to turn to this tradition to explicate their understanding of the contemplative and mystical way of life. My task is to set the table so that others may serve a sumptuous sapiential meal that recalls how Lady Wisdom "set her table" (Prv 9:2), inviting her guests with the words, "Come, eat of my bread and drink the wine I have mixed" (Prv 9:5). Wine has long served as an image for wisdom. May readers find their thirst quenched by the essays that follow this one.

## Biblical Wisdom Literature

The Wisdom literature of the Old Testament generally includes the books of Proverbs, Job, Ecclesiastes (Qoheleth), Ecclesiasticus (Sirach), and the Wisdom of Solomon. The Song of Songs is sometimes considered part of this Wisdom literature. In addition, scholars find snippets of wisdom in a variety of other Old Testament texts. This includes certain Psalms and verses in the Psalms where wisdom is mentioned or there is a wisdom-like saying, for example, "The fear of the Lord is the beginning of wisdom; / all those who practice it have a good understanding" (Ps 111:10).[4]

Two outstanding scholars of Wisdom literature were Gerhard von Rad and Father Roland E. Murphy, O.Carm.[5] Murphy died on the Carmelite feast of Elijah, July 20, 2002. In an interview he explained that he devoted a lifetime of research and writing to the Psalms and to the Wisdom literature because he found that this literature is more "realistic and experiential" than the study of the Pentateuch, which was more of a concern of scholars at the time Murphy began his career.[6] Murphy was a truly memorable teacher. He relished lively texts, and his choice of the texts that he studied immensely enriched English-speaking scholarship on the Wisdom literature of the Bible. Father Raymond Brown, the renowned New Testament scholar, dedicated his *Reading the Gospels with the Church* "To Roland E. Murphy, O.Carm., long-time friend and co-worker in interpreting the Scriptures, in celebration of his eightieth birthday (July 1997). No one has done more to make Old Testament Wisdom living wisdom for believers today."[7] Murphy's *The Tree of Life: An Exploration of Biblical Wisdom Literature* is as fine an introduction to biblical Wisdom literature as can be found anywhere.[8] *Hokmah*, the Hebrew word for wisdom, is more accessible to English speakers because scholars like von Rad and Murphy dedicated their lives and talents to an investigation of the unfathomable riches of wisdom, human and divine. Murphy wrote of this Wisdom literature:

> [Its] most striking characteristic . . . is the absence of what one normally considers as typically Israelite and Jewish. There is no mention of the promises to the patriarchs, the Exodus and Moses, the covenant and Sinai, the promise to David (2 Sm 7). . . . Wisdom does not re-present the actions of God in Israel's history; it deals with daily human experience in the good world created by God. There are hidden connections between Yahwism and wisdom. The Lord of Israel is also the God who gives wisdom to humans (Prv 2:6).[9]

Israel's tradition presents Solomon as the great archetype of Hebrew wisdom. Solomon became wise because in a dream the Lord granted Solomon his desire to have a *leb somea*, a listening heart.[10] Everyone, families and communities, flourish when they give priority to the acquisition of the wisdom that comes with a listening heart. A failure to seek wisdom is a sure ticket to rigid fundamentalism or spineless relativism that saps the vitality of religious cultures. This book offers an opportunity to seek an understanding of wisdom through listening to Carmel's wisdom as articulated by its saints, three of whom are Doctors of the Church and universal Catholic wisdom figures—Teresa of Ávila, John of the Cross, and Thérèse of Lisieux.

Much of the biblical Wisdom literature consists in brief, snappy sayings, as if such wisdom were to say, a word to the wise is sufficient.[11] Here are a few samples of the pithy wisdom sayings: "As a door turns on is hinges, so does a lazy person in bed" (Prv 26:14); "Wisdom is as good as an inheritance, an advantage to those who see the sun" (Eccl 7:11); "A long life baffles the physician; the king of today will die tomorrow" (Sir 10:10); "God loves nothing so much as the person who lives with wisdom" (Wis 7:28); or more religiously, "For I know that my Redeemer lives, and that at the last he will stand upon the earth; and after my skin has been thus destroyed, then in my flesh I shall see God" (Job 19:25–26). If one is tempted to feel wiser than others, there is a wisdom saying to keep one humble: "The first man did not know wisdom fully, nor will the last one fathom her" (Sir 24:28). Biblical wisdom is often cast in what we might think of as secular or daily know-how. However, the biblical context is always articulated with a backdrop that includes a pervasive faith in the God of Abraham, Isaac, and Jacob.

## Lady Wisdom

The attention accorded in recent decades to Lady Wisdom has been warmly welcomed especially by feminist scholars. Roland Murphy begins a chapter on "Lady Wisdom" with this statement: "Lady Wisdom is the most striking personification in the entire Bible."[12] Note that the Hebrew word for wisdom, *Hokmah*, is grammatically feminine, as is the Greek *sophia*, the Latin *sapientia*, the French *sagesse*, the Italian *sagezza*, the Spanish *sabiduría*, and even the German *Weisheit*. Although scholars warn that the move from grammatical gender to sexual gender must be made cautiously, it seems significant that all these words for wisdom are feminine.

Here are a few characterizations of Lady Wisdom:

> On the heights, beside the way, at the crossroads she takes her stand, beside the gates in front of the town, at the entrance of the portals she cries out: "To you, O people, I call, and my cry is to all that live." (Prv 8:2–4)

> Take my instruction instead of silver and knowledge rather than choice gold; for wisdom is better than jewels, and all that you may desire cannot compare with her. I, wisdom, live with prudence, and I attain knowledge and discretion. (Prv 8:10–12)

Perhaps best known are these lines about Lady Wisdom and her relationship to creation and the Creator:

The Lord created me at the beginning of his work, the first of his acts of long ago. Ages ago I was set up, at the first, before the beginning of the earth. When there were no depths I was brought forth, when there were no springs abounding with water. Before the mountains were shaped, before the hills, I was brought forth—when he had not yet made earth and fields, or the world's first bits of soil. When he established the heavens I was there, when he drew a circle on the face of the deep, when he made firm the skies above, when he established the fountains of the deep . . . then I was beside him, like a master worker, and I was daily his delight, rejoicing before him always. . . . For whoever finds me finds life. (Prv 8:22–35)

Roland Murphy's carefully chosen words about Lady Wisdom reveal the divine dimension of Lady Wisdom: "Lady Wisdom is a divine communication: God's communication, extension of self, to human beings."[13] Elizabeth Johnson offers a more detailed feminist characterization of Lady Wisdom: "Given Sophia's activity, which is clearly proper to God alone, this figure is no angel or mere feminine aspect of the divine. Rather Sophia represents Israel's robust God in active, redeeming engagement with the world, and does so [in] a way that uses female images equivalent to the male images used elsewhere in scripture."[14]

Who does not want to be a friend of Lady Wisdom? St. Augustine heard voices in the garden singing, "*Tolle lege*, Take up and read." We shall be much wiser if we take up and read the biblical Wisdom literature. Thérèse of Lisieux,

saint and Doctor of the Church, found warranty for the discovery of her Little Way in the last line of the following quotation from Proverbs: "Wisdom has built her house, she has
hewn her seven pillars. She has slaughtered her animals, she
has mixed her wine, she has also set her table. She has sent
out her servant-girls, she calls from the highest places in the
town, 'You that are simple [little], turn in here'" (Prv 9:1–
4).[15] I suggest that one may legitimately consider Thérèse of
Lisieux to be one of Lady Wisdom's daughters.

## Wisdom in the Christian Scriptures

The patristic scholar Robert Wilken has written that "it was
only after the Resurrection that the followers of Jesus knew
what to make of passages from the Old Testament on Wisdom. Wisdom leaped, as it were, out of the shadows, into
the clear light of day. Now Christians were able to identify
Wisdom with an actual historical person . . . and give
Wisdom a name, Jesus Christ."[16] Wisdom for Christians is
principally and first of all a person, the incarnate God, who
took on our flesh and who as Wisdom is for us the face and
revelation of divine Wisdom.

The Wisdom literature of the Old Testament had a
direct and indirect impact on the authors of the Christian
Scriptures. Jesus proclaimed to his listeners, "The queen of
the South will rise at the judgment with the people of this
generation and condemn them, because she came from the
ends of the earth to listen to the wisdom of Solomon, and
see, something greater than Solomon is here!" (Lk 11:31).
Mark 6:2 reports, "On the Sabbath he [Jesus] began to teach

in the synagogue and many who heard him were astounded. They said, where did this man get all this? What is this wisdom that has been given to him?"

In the Christian Scriptures the name accorded Jesus more than any other is teacher, rabbi, the teacher of God's wisdom. Like sayings of the Old Testament, the wisdom sayings of Jesus appear, for example, in the collection of sayings in Matthew 6:19–7:27, for example, "In everything, do to others as you would have them do to you, for this is the law and prophets" (Mt 7:12). We call that wisdom "the golden rule." Another of Jesus' sayings is, "Not everyone who says to me, 'Lord, Lord,' will enter the kingdom of heaven, but only the one who does the will of my Father in heaven" (Mt 7:21). Jesus says of the wisdom he received from his Father, "All things have been handed over to me by my Father; and no one knows the Son except the Father, and no one knows the Father except the Son and anyone to whom the Son chooses to reveal him" (Mt 11:27; cf. Lk 10:22).

St. Paul and other New Testament writings contain a wisdom Christology:

> Where is the one who is wise? Where is the scribe? Where is the debater of this age? Has God not made foolish the wisdom of the world? For since, in the wisdom of God, the world did not know God through wisdom, God decided, through the foolishness of our proclamation, to save those who believe. For Jews demand signs and Greeks desire wisdom, but we proclaim Christ crucified, a stumbling block to Jews and foolishness to Gentiles, but to those who are the called, both Jews and Greeks, Christ the power of God

and the wisdom of God. For God's foolishness is wiser than human wisdom. . . . He [God] is the source of your life in Christ Jesus, who became for us wisdom from God. (1 Cor 1:20–30)

Colossians 2:3 speaks of Christ "in whom are hidden all the treasures of wisdom and knowledge." Much more could be said about Christ and wisdom in the Synoptic Gospels and in the letters of the New Testament. However, this brief sampling must do for now. It is time to turn to that special sapiential portrayal of Jesus in John's Gospel.

## John's Gospel

Raymond Brown, whose name is synonymous with excellence in Johannine scholarship, has detected many wisdom motifs in John's Gospel. He wrote that "the fourth evangelist saw in Jesus the culmination of a tradition that runs through the Wisdom Literature of the Old Testament."[17] Brown sums up how Jesus is seen as personified Wisdom: "Jesus is the supreme example of divine Wisdom active in history, and indeed divine Wisdom itself."[18] The prologue to John's Gospel uses the metaphor of Word to introduce the story of Jesus, but in fact, this prologue is a retelling of details about Lady Wisdom. Sapiential themes abound in John's Gospel; the Johannine community clearly understood Jesus as personified Wisdom in imagery much like that of Lady Wisdom.

The Gospel of John reveals Jesus, like Lady Wisdom, as one who gives life. "I came that they may have life and have it abundantly" (Jn 10:10). Lady Wisdom had said, "Whoever finds me finds life" (Prv 8:35). In the Last Supper discourses, we see the unique relationship of Jesus to his Father. Jesus prayed, "Father, I desire that those also, whom you have given me, may be with me where I am, to see my glory, which you have given me because you loved me before the foundation of the world" (Jn 17:24). This is just like Lady Wisdom who said, "I was brought forth . . . when he marked out the foundations of the earth" (Prv 8:25 and 29).

Elizabeth Johnson, distinguished professor of theology at Fordham University, has studied carefully the Jewish and Christian traditions of wisdom. Consequently, she and others recognize that another way to deepen our understanding of Jesus Christ, besides those understandings that have been in vogue and from which we have profited immensely, is to know Jesus better within the context of the Sophia/Wisdom tradition. John of the Cross knew and relished this Sophia Christology.[19] We understand John of the Cross better if we have an understanding of this Christology. Here is how Johnson concluded an early study of wisdom Christology:

> Wisdom Christology is an untapped resource of the Christian tradition with the potential to contribute to the redesign of Christology in the face of enormous cultural changes in the position of women. Jesus as the incarnation of Sophia can be thought even in his human maleness to be revelatory of the graciousness of God imaged as female; women as disciples of Jesus-Sophia can fully represent him and share equally in Jesus' saving mission throughout time. All of this is intended not to

the reverse exclusion of men, but toward a community of genuine mutuality and reciprocity.[20]

Johnson sums up the impact of the Sophia tradition on the understanding of Jesus this way: "Far from pointing to a mere feminine dimension of the divine, language about Sophia bespeaks the unfathomable mystery of the living God in female imagery."[21] That statement is no threat to traditional language about Jesus. It is the Spirit of God who has revealed in Scripture the relationship of the imagery of Lady Wisdom to an understanding of who Jesus is as God's Wisdom. What God has revealed may surprise but ought not shock anyone. The incarnate God is a great mystery that cannot be encapsulated in any one image. A wise person is unafraid of truths retrieved from the past. The more wisdom about Jesus that can be plumbed, the stronger will be faith in God's Son whose reality transcends all human understanding.

## Wisdom of the Desert

When Thomas Merton discovered the sayings of the Christians who sought God and holiness in the wilds of the desert, the monk from Gethsemani, Kentucky, called this small collection of sayings *The Wisdom of the Desert*.[22] Merton acknowledged what monasticism knew and practiced for centuries, that these sayings contained valuable lessons about how to live wisely in places where demons could foster illusions. This hard-won wisdom of the desert was passed along from seasoned elders to the young. The worth of the wisdom had its origin in lives of spiritual integrity.[23] What is presumed in these sayings is that the human heart and mind can be easily deceived, but wisdom can be derived from human experience that has been shaped by the Spirit. Wisdom is a necessity to live well, especially when conditions are as precarious as they are in the desert.

A very special repository of the wisdom of the desert is contained in the writings of John Cassian (died c. 435), especially his *Conferences* but also his *Institutes*.[24] These two books by Cassian had an enormous impact on medieval religious life beginning with the Rule of Benedict. In his magisterial study of English monasticism, Dom David Knowles says that the Rule of Benedict cites Cassian "explicitly or implicitly some ninety times, a figure far outnumbering [Benedict's] citations or reminiscences of any other author. As if not content with this, Benedict recommends his favorite author to all his disciples as a pure source of doctrine, and even prescribes that a few pages of [Cassian's] writings should be read in public every day."[25] Cassian's impact on religious life in the West went far beyond the Benedictine Rule. St. Dominic, the founder of the Dominicans, had Cassian's *Conferences* "always at his bedside," and "this book led him to a degree of purity of conscience difficult of attainment, to much light on contemplation and to a high summit of perfection."[26] Another Dominican, St. Thomas Aquinas, kept throughout his life a "habit of regularly reading Cassian's *Collationes*."[27]

John Cassian's writings have shaped Western monastic and religious life like no other text other than the Bible. The Dutch Carmelite scholar Kees Waaijman, in his *The*

*Mystical Space of Carmel: A Commentary on the Carmelite Rule*, studies the Carmelite Formula of Life and the text that it became in 1247, the Carmelite Rule. He finds that John Cassian's *Conferences* and *Institutes* clearly had a major impact on these documents.[28] A study of the principal Carmelite book of spiritual reading until the seventeenth century, *The Institution of the First Monks* by Felip Ribot (d. 1391),[29] contains evidence of Cassian's "profound influence" on Carmelite texts.[30] There is a need for an overall study of Cassian's influence on the Carmelite tradition because, after Scripture, Cassian held sway among the Carmelites until the sixteenth century when Teresa of Jesus and John of the Cross introduced the Carmelite tradition to bridal mysticism.

## Augustine of Hippo

Although I must omit reporting on much of the rich Christian tradition on wisdom, I cannot leave out that great Christian sage of the Western church St. Augustine of Hippo, who has put his stamp on nearly every facet of Christian teachings. Recall that poignant scene (*Confessions* IX, 10, 23–24) when Augustine was ready to sail to Africa from Ostia on the Tiber. Augustine and his mother Monica were leaning against a window looking onto a garden and conversing about things divine. Together, they were lifted up into a kind of ecstasy where they reached "Wisdom through whom all these things are made. . . . Wisdom herself is not made: she is as she always has been and will be forever." Then mother and son "hear him unmediated, whom we love in all things . . . as we now stretch out and in a flash of thought touch that eternal Wisdom who abides above all things."[31] For Monica and Augustine, Wisdom was the Word of God whom they encountered in this unforgettable moment at Ostia when the hearts of mother and son, joined in prayer, leapt beyond the beyond for a glimpse of the divine, the Wisdom of God. What occurred on that memorable day to Monica and Augustine has reminded Christians that all wisdom has it origins in Wisdom, God's only Son.

Augustine wrote a little handbook on faith, hope, and love that begins, "My dearest son, Laurence, it would be impossible to say how much your learning delights me, and how much I desire that you should be wise. . . . This is the kind of person the apostle wants people to be when he says to them 'I want you to be wise in what is good and guileless in what is evil' (Rom 16:19)."[32] Western spirituality has never been the same since Augustine offered it guidance about where to seek wisdom: primarily, of course, in divine wisdom. Augustine's *Confessions* have sent many like Teresa of Ávila into their hearts, into the center of their being, to search for God and God's wisdom. Teresa wrote, "Consider what St. Augustine says, that he sought Him in many places but found Him ultimately within himself."[33]

Augustine speaks eloquently about wisdom in his brilliant masterpiece *On the Trinity*. There he reminds us that "the Father is wisdom, the Son is wisdom, the Holy Spirit is wisdom, and together they are not three wisdoms but one wisdom; and . . . in their case to be is the same as to be wise" (VII, 6). Thus Jesus Christ is God's Wisdom by appropriation. Augustine also says that worship of God is the wisdom of the human community (XIV, 1), and he asks, What could be more beautiful than wisdom? (XV, 7). Always the bishop and pastor, Augustine believed that to live wisely is to follow Jesus (VII, 5). In his *The City of God* (22.4), the Bishop of Hippo mocked the wisdom of the worldly wise when he wrote, citing Psalm 94:11, "The Lord knows our thoughts, that they are but an empty breath."[34] For this wise bishop it is divine wisdom that he seeks, not the wisdom of the "city of this world."

Were the scope of this paper broader, one could also explore where the Holy Spirit is also seen in the tradition as the personification of Wisdom.[35]

## Thomas Aquinas

A Christian voice that one dare not omit in a consideration of Christian wisdom is that of Thomas Aquinas, who is *the* benchmark of wisdom in Western Christian theology. His thought left a lasting imprint on John of the Cross and Teresa of Ávila. While John of the Cross is more Augustinian than Thomist, he studied Thomas carefully at the University of Salamanca, and Teresa was much influenced by her Dominican advisors. We turn to Aquinas especially because he so conscientiously and judiciously gathered up Christian teaching on wisdom. As one of the most perceptive intellects in the Christian tradition, Thomas refined the traditional teaching on wisdom with new insights and, as always, with extraordinary clarity. Know Thomas Aquinas, saint and Doctor of the Church, on Christian wisdom, and there will be little that you do not know about the subject.

Augustine had said, and Thomas agrees, that wisdom is simply the knowledge of divine matters, for wisdom is a participation in divine wisdom. Always logical, Thomas began his *Summa Theologiae* with a discussion about what theology is. He calls what we call theology *sacra doctrina* or sacred teaching. Thomas says that this teaching (based on revelation) is "wisdom above all human wisdom" because this teaching treats of God as the highest of all causes, that is, there is no cause beyond God (*Summa Theologiae*, I, q.1, a.6). Theologians, if docile to the Holy Spirit's gift of wisdom, are, according to Thomas, led by the Spirit to judge rightly about things divine. This statement reminds one of Evagrius of Pontus who saw prayer as theology and theology as prayer. Remember also John of the Cross's conviction that the Holy Spirit is principal guide in the spiritual life.[36]

Thomas knows a wisdom that is a gift of the Holy Spirit. The list of the gifts of the Holy Spirit is taken from Isaiah 11:2: "The spirit of the lord will rest upon him, the spirit of wisdom and understanding, the spirit of counsel and might, the spirit of knowledge and the fear of the Lord." The Vulgate Bible added piety, which makes for seven gifts. Thomas shows how wisdom is more excellent than all the other gifts of the Holy Spirit (*Summa Theologiae*, I-II, q. 68, a.7). These gifts of the Holy Spirit are dispositions that aid in the practice of the virtues; they enable one to be docile to the guidance of the Holy Spirit. This gift of wisdom is closely associated with love/*caritas* (*Summa Theologiae*, II-II, q. 9, a. 2, ad. 1).

Contemplation flows principally from the gift of wisdom, a wisdom that is spurred on by love, *caritas*.

Contemplation is and always has been, of course, a major component of the Carmelite tradition. St. Teresa wrote in *The Interior Castle*, "So I say now that all of us who wear this holy habit of Carmel are called to prayer and contemplation" (5.1.2). Love and wisdom establish a kinship with God and the things of God, known by St. Thomas as connaturality. Contemplation is "the fruit of faith, hope and love under the movement of the gifts of the Holy Spirit. The gifts of wisdom and understanding are like sails that enable a sailboat to be moved through the water by a favorable breeze."[37] If one has had the thrill of sailing, then one has at least a small sense of what it is like to be led by the gifts of the Holy Spirit. When one works at life's issues on one's own, it is exhausting—like pulling one's rowboat by the oars. When the Holy Spirit prompts one, it is like gliding on the waters impelled by a delightful breeze. Human wisdom is a great endowment, but the wisdom that comes from the Holy Spirit is as far beyond it as the difference Teresa described between *contentos* and *gustos*—the difference between what humans can do (*contentos*) and what only God can do (*gustos*).[38]

Thomas Aquinas composed a second *Summa* called the *Summa contra Gentiles*. He begins that work with a discussion of wisdom. There he says that someone is wise who puts things in proper order. A carpenter is wise who knows how to put things where they belong even when creating something new. When one knows how to order things divine, one is simply a wise person led by the Holy Spirit. Thomas says that the pursuit of wisdom makes one more like God, and fosters friendship with God (*Summa contra*

*Gentiles*, 1.1–2). The challenge for Christians is to become as wise as possible in the things of God and together with others to explore courageously and deeply the wonders of the Christian faith.

Aquinas urges his readers to love wisdom and says that we prepare for eternal happiness through wisdom. Thomas contends that one can love only what one knows. Etienne Gilson, an outstanding Thomist scholar, wrote that "a true Thomist" is one who loves.[39] When I love and cherish wisdom, I love Jesus who is Wisdom for us.

Wonder of wonders: the Son of God, birthed in our hearts at baptism, became our brother when the Word of God took on human flesh. Divine Wisdom became a companion, sharing with his followers knowledge of his Father and the secret of how to return to the Creator in whose image and likeness humans were created. The Father and the Son have sent the Holy Spirit to guide humans on their journey, enhancing the life of grace with the gifts of the Holy Spirit, especially with a gift of wisdom that gently fills one's sails so that one may flourish on the ocean of life and eventually enjoy intimacy with God forever. John of the Cross says that it is for this loving intimacy that the human person was created.[40]

## Conclusion

Every human person is called to a loving intimacy with God now and for eternity, to journey as far as the Holy Spirit will take one and as far as the wings of wisdom empower one. What shall it take to journey forward as far as God wills? Is it not better to get halfway up the mountain than to remain at the mountain's bottom? To journey thus is to embrace a holy wisdom that will make it possible, in the words of Luke 5:1–11, to strike out into the deep—*Duc in Altum*, imagery of which Pope John Paul II was fond.[41]

All wisdom, says the book of Sirach (1:1) is from the Lord. Wisdom, divine and human, are God's gifts to humanity. John of the Cross's prayer was, "Transform me into the beauty of divine Wisdom and make me resemble that which is the Word, the Son of God" (Canticle B 36.7). Thomas Aquinas would add that "wisdom as a gift, is not merely speculative but also practical" (*Summa Theologiae* II-II, q. 45, a. 3). The Christian seeks not only union with divine Wisdom but also practical ways to live wisely. Perhaps the following suggestions can elicit from others ways to live wisely under the guidance of the Holy Spirit.

1. Develop docility to the Holy Spirit, not as some abstraction but as Love, as in God is love (1 Jn 4:16) for love is a kind of wisdom. The Eucharistic Prayers of the Mass model this request: "Make holy, therefore, these gifts we pray, by sending down your Spirit upon them like the dewfall, so that they may become for us the Body and Blood of our Lord Jesus Christ" (Eucharistic Prayer II). This is the first *epiclesis*, that is, a calling on the Holy Spirit to bring about this presence of Jesus. A second *epiclesis* prays for unity as the Body of Christ: "Humbly, we pray that, partaking of the Body and Blood of Christ, we may be gathered into one by the Holy Spirit" (Eucharistic Prayer II). We live wisely when we are

guided by the Holy Spirit and when we resemble Christ, "the wisdom of God" (1 Cor 1:24).

2. Remember when one had to be present at the offertory, the consecration, and Communion to fulfill one's Sunday obligation? Did that not make the Liturgy of the Word a second-class citizen? How that perception has changed when the Liturgy of the Word is presented as an event that forms the assembly into a wisdom community, not a private, individual experience. We have been created in the image and likeness of a God who exists in a loving relationship of Father, Son, and Holy Spirit. Without this Trinitarian model and pneumatological inspiration, the community may merely tote the barge rather than let the delightful breeze of the Holy Spirit fill the sails of the community with loving impulses of wisdom.

3. If the Christian community is to become wise, each member is called to develop a growing and personal loving relationship with Jesus Christ, who is the Wisdom of God, whose Father loves humans with the same lavish love that the Father has for the Son (Jn 17:23). Knowledge of the other grows personal relationships while mutual love means that friends actually exist in one another. Paul models such a relationship: "For I decided to know nothing among you except Jesus Christ and him crucified" (1 Cor 2:2). It is the Holy Spirit who brings about mutual presence with Jesus.

4. Like Solomon, one needs to bring to prayer a *leb somea,* a listening heart, so that one can be about the Father's

business rather than enmeshed in idle individualism. To listen quietly for the inspiration of the Holy Spirit is not the same as waiting to hear words or voices but rather to be lovingly attentive to the presence of Jesus Christ. At the liturgy that means that conscious, active, and full participation makes one attentive to the work of the Holy Spirit who as the Love between the Father and Son is also the Spirit who binds one to the Lord.

5. Augustine called love of God and love of neighbor twins, and the wisdom of the tradition says that love of God is tested by growth in love of neighbor. This wisdom Teresa of Jesus knew well; in fact, she says, "I cannot doubt this."[42] Mere talk about mysticism and contemplation is just so much fluff if we Christians do not strive to grow in love of neighbor that expresses itself especially in service of the neighbor in need who lacks food, drink, clothes, health, or freedom (Mt 25:31–46).

6. The Christian community in the West would be wise to ponder more than it has the wisdom of Eastern Christianity, which insists that we become like our maker when we grow in love, so deeply in love with God that this love of God colors everything else in our lives. This transformation in God through love (à la John of the Cross) is what the East calls deification or divinization.

To grow in wisdom is to live a continual Advent. Advent is not only a season of the year but also an ongoing contemplative posture before the Father, Son, and Holy Spirit. The first O Antiphon in Advent is a prayer for all seasons: "O Wisdom, who has come forth from the mouth of the

Most High, reaching from end to end, arranging all things mightily and sweetly, come teach us the way of prudence." This antiphon is a call to drink deeply of the wine of holy wisdom. In the same spirit of Advent, the second stanza of the Advent hymn "O Come, O Come Emmanuel" captures an age-old desire to become wise with God's Wisdom.

O come thou Wisdom from on high,

Who orders all things mightily;

To us the path of knowledge show,

And teach us in her ways to go.[43]

## Notes

1. Thomas Aquinas, *Summa contra gentiles*, 1.2.1.

2. Aristotle, *Metaphysics*, A.1.

3. David F. Ford, *Christian Wisdom: Desiring God and Learning to Love* (Cambridge: Cambridge University Press, 2007).

4. Roland E. Murphy, *The Tree of Life: An Exploration of Biblical Wisdom Literature*, 3rd ed. (Grand Rapids, Mich.: Eerdmans, 2002), 103–4.

5. Gerhard von Rad, *Wisdom in Israel* (Nashville: Abingdon, 1972).

6. Keith J. Egan and Craig E. Morrison, eds., *Master of the Sacred Page: Essays and Articles in Honor of Roland E. Murphy, O.Carm., on the Occasion of His Eightieth Birthday* (Washington, D.C.: Carmelite Institute, 1997), 42.

7. Raymond E. Brown, *Reading the Gospels with the Church: From Christmas through Easter* (Cincinnati: St. Anthony Messenger Press, 1996), iv.

8. Murphy, *Tree of Life*.

9. Ibid., 1.

10. Roland E. Murphy, "The Listening Heart," in *Biblical People as Models for Campus Ministry*, ed. M. Galligan-Stierle et al. (Dayton, Ohio: Catholic Campus Ministry Association, 1988), 47–56.

11. The Latin is *verbum sapienti satis est.*

12. Murphy, *Tree of Life*, 133.

13. Ibid., 147.

14. Elizabeth A. Johnson, *Quest for the Living God: Mapping Frontiers in the Theology of God* (New York: Continuum, 2008), 294.

15. Thérèse of Lisieux, *The Story of a Soul: The Autobiography of Saint*, trans. John Clarke, 3rd ed. (Washington, D.C.: ICS Publications, 1996).

16. Robert L. Wilken, *The Spirit of Early Christian Thought* (New Haven, Conn.: Yale University Press, 2003), 96–97.

17. Raymond E. Brown, *The Gospel according to John* (i–xii), Anchor Bible, vol. 29 (Garden City, N.Y.: Doubleday, 1966), CCXXII.

18. Elizabeth A. Johnson, "Jesus, the Wisdom of God," *Ephemerides Theologicae Lovanienses* 61 (1985): 284 (citing Brown, *Gospel according to John*, CXXIV).

19. Constance FitzGerald, "Transformation in Wisdom: The Subversive Character and Educative Power of Sophia in Contemplation," in K. Culligan and R. Jordan, eds., *Carmel and Contemplation: Transforming Human Consciousness*, 281–358 (Washington, D.C.: ICS Publications, 2000).

20. Johnson, "Jesus, the Wisdom of God," 261–294.

21. Johnson, *Quest for the Living God*, 105.

22. *The Wisdom of the Desert*, trans. Thomas Merton (New York: New Directions, 1960).

23. Douglas Burton-Christie, *The Word in the Desert* (New York: Oxford University Press, 1993), 144–46.

24. *John Cassian: The Conferences*, trans. Boniface Ramsey (New York: Paulist Press, 1997); *John Cassian: The Institutes*, trans. Boniface Ramsey (New York: Newman Press, 2000).

25. David Knowles, *The Monastic Order in England: A History of Its Development from the Times of St Dunstan to the Fourth Lateran Council*, 2nd ed. (Cambridge: Cambridge University Press, 1963), 11–12.

26. M. H. Vicaire, *Saint Dominic and His Times* (New York: McGraw-Hill, 1964), 43.

27. Jean-Pierre Torrell, *Saint Thomas Aquinas*, vol. 1, *The Person and His Work*, trans. Robert Royal (Washington, D.C.: Catholic University of America Press, 1996), 15.

28. Kees Waaijman, *The Mystical Space of Carmel: A Commentary on the Carmelite Rule*, trans. John Vriend (Leuven, Belgium: Peters, 1999). See notes in this volume for references to Cassian's writings.

29. Otger Steggink, *La Reforma del Carmelo Español* (Rome: Institutum Carmelitanum, 1965), 357.

30. "The Liber de Institucione et perculiaribus gestis religiosorum Carmelitarum . . . ," ed. Paul Chandler (unpublished PhD diss., Centre for Medieval Studies, University of Toronto, 1991), xcxv.

31. Augustine, *The Confessions*, trans. Maria Boulding (Hyde Park, N.Y.: New City Press, 1997), 9.10.23–24.

32. *The Augustine Catechism: The Enchiridion on Faith, Hope, and Love*, trans. Bruce Harbert (Hyde Park, N.Y.: New City Press, 1999), 33.

33. Teresa of Ávila, *The Way of Perfection*, in *The Collected Works of St. Teresa of Ávila*, vol. 2, trans. Kieran Kavanaugh and Otilio Rodriquez (Washington, D.C.: ICS Publications, 1980), 28.2.

34. This translation of Ps 94:11 is from the NRSV.

35. See Yves Congar, *I Believe in the Holy Spirit*, trans. David Smith (New York: Crossroad, 1997), 1:9–12.

36. John of the Cross, *The Living Flame of Love*, in *The Collected Works of St. John of the Cross*, trans. Kieran Kavanaugh, O.C.D., and Otilio Rodriguez, O.C.D. (Washington, D.C.: ICS Publications, 1991), 3.46.

37. Reginald Garrigou-Lagrange, *The Three Ages of the Interior Life*, trans. M. T. Doyle (St. Louis, Mo.: Herder, 1947–1948), 313.

38. Teresa of Ávila, *The Interior Castle*, in Kavanaugh and Rodriquez, *Collected Works*, vol. 2, 3.2.10, 4.1.4.

39. Etienne Gilson, *Wisdom and Love in Saint Thomas Aquinas* (Milwaukee: Marquette University Press, 1951), 5.

40. John of the Cross, *The Spiritual Canticle*, in *The Collected Works of St. John of the Cross*, trans. Kieran Kavanaugh and Otilio Rodriguez (Washington, D.C.: ICS Publications, 1991), 29.3.

41. John Paul II, apostolic letter *Novo millennio ineunte*, heading to no. 58.

42. Teresa of Ávila, *Interior Castle*, 5.3.8.

43. Johnson, *Quest for the Living God*, 104.

# From Impasse
# to Prophetic Hope:
## *Crisis of Memory*

CONSTANCE FITZGERALD, O.C.D.

IN AN EARLIER WORK I LOOKED at John of the
Cross's teaching on the dark night,[1] including the traditional signs marking the passage from meditation to contemplation, through the lens of impasse and applied it to
personal spiritual growth as well as to one's relational life,
the development of society and culture, and the feminist
experience of God.[2] That insight provided a hermeneutical key for many and began changing the perception of the
multiple impasses—relational, ecclesial, societal, political,
ethical, scientific, economic, environmental, and cultural—
which engage people today.[3] That it continues to elucidate
contemporary experience, prompt new questions, raise radical challenges, and open up fresh avenues of investigation
underlines how much the great apophatic mystical traditions of Christianity are a promising source of wisdom and
guidance for theology and spirituality.

Now I want to investigate a deeper experience of dark
night, what the Carmelite mystical doctor, John of the

Cross, calls the purification of memory,[4] because currently impasse seems centered in great part in memory and imagination, in the conflict between the past and the future. In the first and longest section, I want to reflect on the central importance of memory as well as the limiting and destructive power that memories hold. In that context, I hope to interpret what John of the Cross means by "purification of memory" and then draw briefly on the work of Miroslav Volf and Beverly Lanzetta to illustrate it. Second, I want to point to the goal of this process of purification of memory for John: prophetic hope that expresses itself in what I call "the prayer of no experience," which I will attempt to describe. Finally, I want to suggest that in this utterly silent *prayer*, a radically new "self" is being worked on and shaped, a dispossessed "self" truly capable of living and loving in a way that realizes more fully our relational evolution and synergistic existence in the universe. My treatment of the self and the evolution of consciousness may be the most perplexing aspect of this study—one where more theological reflection in dialogue with the experience of others is needed.

This presentation of an experience of more profound impasse and deeper contemplative growth is integrally connected to my earlier interpretation. Although my exploration raises its own disturbing questions, I hope it will offer a significant contribution to theological reflection and spiritual experience at a time when polarization, suspicion, denouncement, investigation, silencing, alienation, anger, cynicism, and sadness divide our church, and when our country is rocked with economic suffering precipitated by years of wrongdoing and greed; our political process is driven by a cruel bipartisanship that endangers the common good; our Earth is menaced with global warming and ecological distress that threaten all planetary life with eventual extinction; the religions of the world are plagued with extremism and age-old distrust that fuel war and terrorism; and the people of the world are abused with violence, slavery, and deprivation too great to measure. We are encumbered by old assumptions, burdened by memories that limit our horizons and, therefore, unfree to see God coming to us from the future. Slow to deal with different levels of complexity of consciousness[5] or to tolerate ambiguity before the Holy Mystery of our lives, the institutional church, it seems to me, is immersed in an impasse, a crisis of memory, which only a continuing openness to contemplative grace and purification can transform.

## Purification of Memory

We are a people of memory. Central to our Christian identity is the memory of the life, death, and resurrection of Jesus; as church, we understand our authenticity as historically derived and see ourselves as guardians of a sacred tradition we dare not forget. Nonetheless, it is no naïve accident that John of the Cross writes at such length on the *purification* of memory in the third book of *The Ascent of Mount Carmel* (1–15) and throughout the second book of *The Dark Night*. Nor is it any wonder that this is such a misunderstood and even dangerous part of his teaching, considering his counsel both to draw the memory away from its "props and boundaries" and to "forget" both wrongs suffered and good experienced.[6]

Let me sketch in my own words the basic dynamics in this process of purification. In the deeper reaches of a contemplative life, a kind of unraveling or loss of memory occurs that can be more or less conscious. Then one's usual way of harboring memories is incapacitated (see N 2.3.3; 8.1–2). A person's past becomes inaccessible as a basis for finding meaning. The experience seems to be not so much an *emptying* of memory, as John describes it, as an unraveling or delinking of it. A person continues to have memories of the past, and may be bombarded with them, but they are somehow uncoupled from the self. Their significance is altered. Memories do not mean what one thought they did. In a mysterious way there is a cutting off of both past and memory that is inimical to one's personhood. The capacity one loses is the ability to "re-member," that is, to "member" again, bringing past elements together, forward to the present, and reconstructed into a newly relevant whole. When memory is "de-constructed" in the dark night, the past can no longer weave its thread of meaning through the person's lived experience into the future. Past, present, and future do not fit together. What one remembers, how one remembers, and how long one remembers is called into question. The past can seem a mockery or an illusion; the psychological and intellectual structures that have supported or held us together over a lifetime, "the beacons by which we have set our course,"[7] and the certainties on which we have built our lives are seriously undermined or taken away—not only in prayer but also in and by life, and a profound disorientation results. This is keenly felt as a loss of authenticity, truthfulness, and even identity. On a very fundamental level our selfhood—who we are—is threatened (N 2.9.5; 2.9.7). While I have attempted to describe this experience, it has many different faces and is a frightening and seriously destabilizing, liminal experience, leaving a person undone, silenced. How long this turmoil in the memory will last depends on the extent to which one's past encumbers God's approach.

So much that fills our memory blocks this coming of God in love toward us. For John of the Cross, the human person is seen as an infinite capacity for God.[8] As long as one is preoccupied with filling the great *caverns* of the mind, heart, memory, and imagination with human knowledge, loves, memories, and dreams that seem to promise complete satisfaction, or at least more than they can ever deliver, the person is unable to feel or even imagine the vast hollowness one is. Only when one becomes aware of the illusory and limiting character of this fullness in the face of the breakdown of what/whom we have staked our lives on, the limitations of our life project and relationships, the irruption of our unclaimed memories, and the shattering of our dreams and meanings, can the depths of hunger and thirst that exist in the human person, the infinite capacity, really be experienced.[9] Therefore, only when the great cavern of the memory is enfeebled by its obsession with the past—past pleasure and past pain—debilitated by its unforgettable suffering over losses and evil inflicted, limited by its inability to come to terms with a complex world, constricted by its need to organize images or to understand and unsay inherited constructs, can the great void of yearning for God really be admitted. Although triggered by the intimately close presence of the divine,[10] the meaning of this profound pain is hidden from our rational understanding, initially even our spiritual intuition. But for John of the Cross, this experience signals that the memory is being deconstructed or dispossessed in a redemptive movement whereby the incredibly slow appropriation of theological hope gradually displaces all that impedes new vision, new possibility, the evolution of a transformed self that is freed from bondage to its confining or destructive past. Crucial to any personal appropriation of hope is the ability to read the signs of what is going on so as to remain with the unfolding process.

## The Ambiguity of Memory

Why is this so difficult? Memory is a complex and ambiguous power. Multiple distinctions need to be made. Consider, for example, the distinction between the personal healing of memories and corporate processes of reconciliation; the distinction between memory as dangerous in the sense that liberation theologians speak of the dangerous memory of Jesus Christ and memory as dangerous in the destructive sense; the distinction between history and memory; or the biblical and liturgical meaning of memory where past, present, and future come together. Here I will focus on only one aspect of the ambiguity of memory in light of John of the Cross's treatment of purification of the memory.

Our memories have made us who we are, spiritually and humanly. No-memory makes authentic human relationship virtually impossible and robs us of our identity. I cannot forget the pain of the husband of an Alzheimer's patient, who in despair said of his wife, "She has only the present. To have only the present—that is hell." As Yale theologian Miroslav Volf suggests, however, in *The End of Memory: Remembering Rightly in a Violent World*, what we remember, what others including our culture remember with us and for us, how we remember, and how we weave these memories together into the fabric of our lives matters decisively in shaping our identities.[11]

The difficulty is that memories can lead us to either healing and empathy or hostility and destruction. On the one hand, the human community is saturated with the injunction to remember—not only its triumphs of courage but also and especially the unspeakable horrors of holocaust, genocide, slavery, rape, ethnic cleansing, torture, and abuse precisely so that they never occur again. On the other hand, "the human race as individuals and tribes, at this very moment, is in huge measure bound to the past, to memory, in debilitating and destructive ways."[12] Remembering wrongs suffered seems indispensable to healing, we are told, and is often a means of constructing and consolidating a community that tells the same narrative of anguish; and the memory of past injustices can certainly engender empathy, solidarity, and justice for others who are oppressed. However, some victims of such evil, precisely because they remember their own victimization in the past, personally or as members of a persecuted, marginalized group, can feel justified in perpetrating violence, hatred, oppression, and even ethnic cleansing in the present. "So easily does the protective shield morph into a sword of violence" that can last for generations, as Volf reminds us.[13]

Conscious of the horrendous evil inflicted upon him and the Jewish people, Elie Wiesel, that eloquent survivor of the holocaust, is well aware of the ambiguity of remembering. As deeply as anyone, he knows the pain of memory and the desperate "need of many victims to wipe from their memories all traces of days that are blacker than nights,"[14] just as he realizes how clinging to the dead can diminish our capacity to live and to love in the present and for the future. He reflects on the effect of the negative use of memory throughout history—as illustrated in Bosnia, "that tormented land" where, he writes, "it is memory that is a problem. It's because they remember what happened to their parents or their sister or their grandparents that they hate each other."[15] While acknowledging the need to redeem memories, still "this passionate prophet of memory" can only continue crying out with glaring, powerful consistency one message: *Remember!*[16] He can go no further.

The litany of experiences which cultural critics and survivors, psychologists and historians, theologians and novelists do not want us to forget has given birth to trauma theory, mimetic theory, nonviolent theory, feminist theory and theology, and theologies of healing aimed at redeeming memory.[17] All of this (including current neurological research on editing memory) has clouded the lens through which I look at John of the Cross's teaching. Suspended in an intellectual impasse, I struggle to hold in tension both the power of memory and the importance of history in giving us context, on the one hand, *and* on the other hand, the need to forget and be open to the radical transformation of the self and the memory. I ask how we can remember and forget at the same time. I wrestle with remembering anew so that we can tell the narrative differently, and I wrestle with forgetting when forgetfulness and silence are dangerous, for example, for women who are lower in the social hierarchy, or for those who come out of a heritage of slavery whose potential for being forgotten has been greater than for most. I strive to be faithful to and in solidarity with those who continue to remember indescribable violation, and at the same time I am receptive to the transforming power of hope that deconstructs memory and to the fathomless Mystery coming to us from the future. I suggest that in this impasse, psychology and the social sciences do not take us far enough. We need the insights of theologians and mystics.

## Interpretations of John of the Cross in the Contemporary Context

I turn to the example of John of the Cross's life and his mystical texts on dispossession in the memory to understand how they function for personal and communal transformation. Abused for months in a cold, dark prison cell, humiliated, starved, beaten regularly in the refectory by the other friars, and *brainwashed* to persuade him to repudiate Teresa of Ávila and the Carmelite Reform, he was saved from certain death only by a daring escape. Clearly John could have been embittered or destroyed by the experience and never moved beyond it. Instead, this sixteenth-century Carmelite offers us a mystical inheritance and a provocative challenge.

Almost five centuries later, in his masterful study *The End of Memory*, Miroslav Volf describes a similar process.

He delineates the complex, poignant process whereby he passed from the destructive, confining memory of his intense, dehumanizing interrogation and severe psychic battering in communist Yugoslavia to a realization that the ability to let go of the memories of the evil inflicted by Captain G., his tormentor, would come about only as "a gift of God to the transformed self," a proleptic experience of the new "world of love" to come.[18] Volf's genius lies in his psychological, theological, cultural, and spiritual analysis of the deliberate steps involved in his own concrete embodiment of exactly what John of the Cross calls the purification and transformation of memory and Volf's conviction that he would "squander his own soul" if he failed to follow the path toward which Christ called him, if he did not surrender to the redeeming process in all its pain and ambiguity. As he works meticulously through issues of memory and identity, Volf probes the obligation to remember truthfully as a prerequisite for achieving justice for the wronged and the need to remember therapeutically so that wrongs suffered can be integrated into a new narrative and the grip of the past on one's identity, broken; as he wonders repeatedly how long one must remember and when, if ever, one can forget, he exposes the severe displacement and the impasse this purifying experience causes.

While it is impossible to synthesize here Volf's careful theological development, he concludes that through the memory of the Passion of Jesus, God will purify his memory of wrongs suffered since his identity as a Christian stems not from the evil done to him, or from his own false innocence whereby he might justify himself, but from his being beloved of God notwithstanding any sin. So his overriding spiritual intuition anticipates a time when evil suffered will "not come to mind," will be "forgotten," because both wronged and wrongdoer will be forgiven, reconciled, transformed, and immersed in the love God.

If we turn to the night of memory in women's spiritual experience for other examples, we see a multifaceted picture. First, when the purifying touch of secret Wisdom awakens out of numbness a woman's deeply abused humanity, she, first of all, *remembers*.[19] Here again, multiple distinctions are needed. Women's experience of chattel slavery or sexual and physical abuse cannot be compared to privileged women's experience of social or ecclesial marginalization. But in any form of systemic injustice, the woman, like Volf, *remembers*: with extraordinary poignancy she remembers all the acts of inequality, dismissal, inferiority, subordination, violence, subjugation, and silencing, all the disfiguring assumptions that the dominant culture of patriarchy or the majority race or class has projected and continues to inflict on her. Even more, she becomes painfully aware of all the past emotion, passion, and feelings associated with these acts that have left her so intensely wounded. Because so many women forget on purpose, or for unconscious reasons fail to see, the initial step of purification is *remembering*, and this remembering is a miracle of contemplative grace. Failing to understand the *spiritual* process underway, many go no further.[20]

Only very gradually, under the influence of hidden Sophia drawing a woman deep into herself and her own body memory, does the painful unraveling of her social constructedness, previous spiritual experience, and past dependencies and loves, successes, and failures yield to the dark, mysterious, hidden, purifying embrace of intimate divine love effecting woman's radical unsaying of "all the images, understandings and memories that do not name her" or her God.[21] At its nadir this is the experience of the empty tomb, "where the 'follow me' of Jesus comes from a voice which has been effaced,"[22] and from where woman will rise to see herself affirmed in the beauty of divine Wisdom.[23] With powerful intensity and considerable clarity, Beverly Lanzetta is, I believe, describing this night of memory in her work *Radical Wisdom: A Feminist Mystical Theology*, on which I have drawn here, when she discusses the *via femina* of contemporary woman related to the contemplative prayer development of Teresa of Ávila. Because this radical emptying out[24] of woman's constructed selfhood is so profoundly united with the kenosis of Jesus,[25] this dispossession in the feminine memory effects a solidarity that reaches far beyond the personal into the communal, into the souls of all women, and then deep into the human spirit.[26]

Although I have dwelt on traumatic memories at some length, it is equally important to recall that John extends memory's forfeitures particularly to spiritual gifts and consolation, to human achievements and natural endowments, and to one's carefully achieved selfhood. The most critical remnant of one's former experience/knowledge of God, as well as one's perceived wholeness to which one had been clinging without realizing it, is taken away. One successful, contemporary, American woman's poignant description of her experience of purification of memory witnesses to this.

Largely unencumbered by projections of inferiority and subordination, she writes in her journal,

> It is as if I have been robbed profoundly, precisely of the comforting, assuring memory of presence, which is so vital to my self-identity, as it is informed by my past. I no longer own or possess my interior memories of my past (even in some exterior ways). If, like a person with amnesia, I were a complete blank, I would not suffer so. In this way, memory is not exactly "lost." Instead, it is numbed. I remember just enough to be in pain. I still know that I once knew (or thought I knew) God. I still know that I once found meaning and mission in the sense of God's presence and love. I know this but I can no longer connect it with myself. Everything has been de-linked. When I sit for a time of purported prayer, I only feel loss. What I thought I had, now seems like a lie, an illusion. I have been emptied of all claim to authenticity for all that I have lived. I search for a word meaning *to take away the essence of, radically*. The hollowing out is so deep that by its essence it highlights that there are deeper and deeper levels that have not been touched. The only light that is given by this experience shines on the seemingly infinite levels of emptying that are waiting to happen. I find myself wondering how the little acorn of a person I am can possibly have these infinite levels to be emptied. With such a radical process underway within me, how is it possible that something of myself remains? I feel like a shell of a person.[27]

And I am dispossessed in other ways too. My health has been taken away. My considerable financial resources are seriously threatened—this is part of the loss of my past. All that I have accumulated, all the tangible signs of the life I once led, are being ground into dust. This vanishing of the product of my work and life removes another layer of evidence for the successful life I once lived. There is no proof, even exterior, of what once was. For years I have known that my intellectual strength has been an ability to use memory to make associations between concepts, to piece things together to reach good and sometimes insightful conclusions. This part of me seems dead at the moment. Still, it is curious to me that throughout this time I have been able to be productive, to work effectively and to concentrate. In my everyday life, I have energy and ability. And so I know at least that this experience is not depression.

The journal concludes,

As I continue living through this, I have been shown the possibility that this memory unraveling is perhaps a necessary step to true hope. Because the experience denies my past, I have nothing to project on to God for the future or even the present. I experience a poverty that could lead me to hopelessness—to expect nothing of the future because the thread of my past has unraveled, and I no longer have a context for my life.[28] Here the competing directions are despair or a true hope, a hope that is independent of me and my accomplishments, spiritual or otherwise.[29]

## Birth of Theological Hope

Many would see only destruction or psychological illness at work in this woman's life, and the experience of contemplative purification can resemble dark psychological states like depression, so destructive of the self. But Denys Turner, reflecting on depression and dark night, makes an important distinction. While both are malaise of the self, the prognosis is different. The final outcome the depressed person hopes for in therapy or treatment is the restoration of the self that has been lost, albeit a more mature one. "The dark nights on the other hand are entered into as loss of that same self, for in that consists their pain, but the hope it [the self] acquires is of the non-recovery of that selfhood in any form for what is lost in the passive nights was never the self at all, but only an illusion all along."[30] The selfhood that is lost will never be regained and therein lies its hope. In this purification, the annulling of the memories, we are being dispossessed of the autonomous self, our achieved selfhood put together over a lifetime.

John of the Cross does, in fact, make sense of the experience, the purification of the memory, by linking it to theological hope, and this is what I want to emphasize. The cavern of the memory is filled and cluttered with the past— its graces and achievements, its experiences too many and varied to recount. The impotence or muting of this past, authored by the hidden inpouring of God, is precisely the condition that makes hope in the strictly theological sense even possible.[31] As memory slowly becomes a silent space, what very gradually takes over is true theological hope.[32]

Activated by divine presence, hope is essential to purification. Without it there is no purification, only suffering. When the emptiness of the memory on the level of affectivity and imagination becomes a deep void of yearning, it is hope that opens up the possibility of being possessed by the infinite, unimaginable, incomprehensible Mystery of love that is so close. John describes it this way: "Hope empties and withdraws the memory from all creature possessions, for as St. Paul says, hope is for what is not possessed. It withdraws the memory from what can be possessed and fixes it on what it hopes for. Hence only hope in God prepares the memory perfectly for union with [God]" (N 2.21.11). I believe we can clarify the relationship between memory's deconstruction and theological hope by drawing new insights from the developing theology of evolution, which has been notably synthesized by Templeton scholar John Haught. Building on the work of Karl Rahner, Paul Tillich, Pierre Teilhard de Chardin, and others, Haught speaks compellingly of a "metaphysics of the future":

> A metaphysics of the future is rooted in the intuition, expressed primordially in the biblical experience, . . . that the abode of ultimate reality is not limited to the causal past nor to a fixed and timeless present "up above." Rather it is to be found most characteristically in the constantly arriving and renewing future. We need a vision of reality that makes sense of the most obvious aspects of life's evolution, in particular the fact that it brings about new forms of being. . . . [This] alternative view of reality . . . is a metaphysics that gives priority to the future rather than to

the past or the present . . . and is rooted deeply in the experience that people have of something that to them is overwhelming and incontestably real, namely, what might be called metaphorically the "power of the future." Of course, it is perhaps only by adopting the religious posture of hope that they have been opened to the experience of this power.[33]

Haught would say that this "power of the future," which grasps us and makes us new, might be called "God," who is always alluring us forward from a future that comes to meet us.[34]

Before memory is purified, we can thwart our encounter with the future, without even realizing it, by relying on the images that memory has saved for us—images of our past, joyful or sad, pleasant or unpleasant, fulfilling or detrimental. We project these images onto our vision of the future; we block the limitless possibilities of God by living according to an expectation shaped, not by hope, but by our own desires, needs, and past experiences.[35] Dutch Carmelite theologian Kees Waaijman and his colleagues remind us that we have the mistaken notion that we are completely open to the reality around us, whereas we necessarily trim back any new impressions to the images we already carry within ourselves and that provide us with something secure to hold onto. "However much we may open ourselves in self-forgetfulness to the other reality that reveals itself to us, in fact, we do not get beyond the reduction of the other to that which is ours."[36] Bringing a preunderstanding to every dream, we are condemned, without memory's purification, to a predictable and even violent world.[37]

Miroslav Volf's experience led him to the conclusion that if he continued to let the stored impressions of wrong-doing define him, he would take on a distorted identity that would be frozen in time and closed to future growth.[38] Given that the memory of his abuse kept metastasizing itself into his anticipated future, he realized he could not permit his communist interrogator to define the boundary of his expectations forever. Grasped by hope in "Jesus Christ [who] promises to every person a new horizon of possibility, a new world freed from all enmity, a world of love," and believing that those new possibilities for the Christian are defined by that promise and not by past experience or worn out assumptions, Volf was able to open himself to the flame of God's presence; he was able to receive a new identity defined by God's love. Now, as a consequence of God's gift to him of self-transcendence, evil suffered would "not-come-to-mind." In Christ he would live into a future beyond imagining.[39] With his memories undone and absorbed by the fire of contemplative love, he would find the way past the limits of his experience to the truth that has no borders, the meeting that exists beyond his perceptions.

This dynamic of being able to yield unconditionally to God's future is what John of the Cross calls *hope*, a hope that exists without the signature of our life and works, a hope independent of us and our accomplishments (spiritual gifts or ordinary human achievements), a hope that can even embrace and work for a future without us. This theological hope is completely free from the past, fully liberated from our need to recognize ourselves in the future, to survive, to be some-one. When we are laid flat by the deconstruction/silencing of our memory, it is hope that is very gradually taking over the operation of the memory/imagination, hollowing out a place for the "power of the future," for the coming of the Impossible.[40] For hope to extend itself this far by perpetual expectation into the realm of the Invisible and Incomprehensible, its movement will have to be purified of all forms of self-preservation, all efforts to preserve one's selfhood as it is. David F. Ford clarifies this further: "Hope does not desire anything for itself. It does not return to itself but rather remains with that which is hoped for."[41] The key insight here is that it is the limited self constituted by the past that needs to yield to the transforming power of God's call into the future.

If this freeing process of purification or forfeiture were up to us we would not, could not, accomplish it. To attempt to unravel one's memory outside of this understanding, unprecipitated by the burning presence of the divine, is absolutely destructive and unhealthy, but this purification overtakes us in the events of our lives and God works with us in the depths of these occurrences. When, for example, theologians are placed under suspicion or silenced, when their work is rejected, or when their identities as Catholic theologians are threatened, questioned, or denied, they undoubtedly experience such dispossession. But however this undoing occurs, it is inevitably accompanied by forfeiture in our spiritual lives and prayer, in all that concerns God. (John calls this the "supernatural memory.") The memory of all our spiritual experiences, above all, creates a pattern of expectation that must yield to the unknown Mystery. And so we experience a draining off of any spiritual meaning in prayer, in our feelings about God, and in our experience of liturgy and church. The inadequacy of theology looms large or even worse seems like an empty shell, and all this seems irreversible.

You can see what a radical call this is. Those who answer it must be prepared to leave so much behind, to stop cling-ing to a security that has been taken away. Perhaps those who finally understand and give their lives over to the dis-mantling of the archives of memory by accepting the gift of hope eschew keeping a death grip on what has given them assurance of their value and place in the church.

## Prophecy and Prayer of No Experience

The profound and painful purification I have been outlining really does change a person's memory. This dark passage does have an arrival point: prophecy. Obsession with the past gives way to a new undefinable sense of relatedness or intimacy, an experience of ultimate assurance, and this conversion releases creativity and most importantly freedom for the limitless pos-sibilities of God, for hope. This freedom, this posture of hope, is really prophecy, for it enables people to reveal the vision of a different kind of future than the one we want to construct from our limited capacities. Such individuals become proph-ets when they show the way, when they are willing to stand on the horizon so that all can see this future, God's future.

It is tempting to envision this emergence from the dark night, this dawn, as a time of wondrous consolation and light, marked by the constant sense of God's presence and highlighted with ecstatic experiences of delight in union with God. But while John of the Cross acknowledges that there may be ecstatic delight, he hints, and I believe, that the actual day-to-day experience in dark night's dawn may be quite different. Perhaps we need to consider anew what we mean by spiritual ecstasy. Perhaps a spiritual ecstasy, in our day, might be defined as any moment when we fully and truly step out of, or are impelled beyond, ourselves.[42]

In fact, from what I have witnessed in spiritual direction and other conversations, openness and freedom in the liberated memory is experienced not so much as consolation but as a profound peace in the silent unknowing and in the dark empty space of encounter with God, the truly Other, an emptiness that is content not to seek fulfillment in its own time. I call this prophetic hope, which "expresses" itself in what I have named the *prayer of no experience*. The depth and prevalence of such prayer begs for interpretation and meaning.

Very often after years of trying to pray and live faithfully, after receiving precious graces, consolations, and insight, persons experience not presence but *nothing*, silence, in their prayer. Many mature, dedicated, seasoned religious people who pray steadfastly and work courageously in the church describe this phenomenon. They report that there is absolutely nothing discernible going on when they pray and yet they do need prayer; they are faithful to it and actually spend considerable time in silent *there-ness*. But the only experience is *no experience*, the silent place. This is not, I am convinced, the normal season of dryness that earnest people pass through in early prayer development. It is not the loss of enjoyment, pleasure, contentment, and sensitivity in life, prayer, and ministry, that transitional purification that "dismantle[s] the whole apparatus of sensory ego-compensation."[43]

Though we would probably see these individuals, *pray-ers of no experience*, as remarkably self-possessed and loving, ministerially effective, and at the height of their vocational or scholarly achievements, they realize, without dramatization, that they do not quite know who they are anymore. This is not an identity crisis of the young, or not so young, adult, or of those who have never discovered themselves, authored their own lives, and borne their own responsibility. It is not even a midlife crisis with its bid for freedom in sometimes irresponsible escape or heedless self-realization. It is far deeper than these. On one level these persons no longer know what they believe. But on a more profound level, they walk in faith, accustomed to doubt and inner questioning yet possessed by a hope that is wordless and imageless in its expectation of "what eye has not seen nor ear heard." They are marked by a certain serenity of spirit indicative of the degree to which this dark theological faith has gripped the intellect and pure theological hope has filled the memory obscuring and emptying them and guiding the person toward the "high goal of union with God" (A 1.4.1). While they theoretically, academically, and responsibly maintain a hold on their theological underpinnings and remain faithful to their religious tradition and liturgical life, they realize experientially that none of us is meant to know who God is, but only who/what God is not. These people have perhaps made the conclusive passage from extreme desolation of spirit where they felt abandoned by or distant from God to the love opened to them by fathomless Mystery, and this is why I think they are on the dawn side of the dark night of the spirit, perhaps the first stage of a truly transformed consciousness. I suggest these prophets of hope are *being worked on*, transformed by love, in profound silence.[44]

Looking through this lens of silence/emptiness, we see that, in fact, these prophets of hope have been able to move beyond the "self of experience" that blocked any true encounter with the Other. Such an encounter requires an "empty space from which the self has withdrawn"—and this is true in the most radical degree if we are to encounter God, who is the most absolute Other to us.[45] To have "no experience of selfhood" may in fact be the singular hallmark of a transformed self. *No experience pray-ers* are exhibiting in themselves the presence of a purely passive power, a capacity to be attracted by the Future,[46] and a movement toward God in love-filled hope no longer grounded in the need to possess, to enjoy, or to dominate by words, memory, or understanding. This is the ultimate silence, the ultimate empty space, and may very well be one kind of ecstatic experience of union. Karl Rahner understood this: "There is no such thing either in the world or in the heart, as literal vacancy, as a vacuum. And whenever space is really left—by death, by renunciation, by parting, by apparent emptiness, provided the emptiness that cannot remain empty is not filled by the world, or activity, or chatter, or the deadly grief of the world—there is God."[47]

## Dispossession of Self

I believe a dispossession of selfhood is being actualized in this silent *prayer of no experience*,[48] and I suspect it has a specific prophetic purpose. This is in keeping with my years of sitting with John of the Cross and hints at what I have learned in the intervening time between the writing of "Impasse and Dark Night" and this essay. It is my strong suspicion that the *prayer of no experience*, effecting an essential change in selfhood, may be emerging with such frequency as a response to a world driven by selfishness and self-concern. Any hope for new consciousness and a self-forfeiture driven by love stands opposed by a harsh reality: we humans serve our own interests, we hoard resources, we ravage the Earth and other species, we scapegoat, we make war, we kill, we torture, we turn a blind eye to the desperation and needs of others, and we allow others to die. We simply are not evolved enough to move into a different future from which God comes to us. Our ability to embody our communion with every human person on the Earth and our unassailable connectedness with everything living is limited because we have not yet become these symbiotic "selves." We continue to privilege our personal autonomy and are unable to make the transition from radical individualism to a genuine synergistic community, even though we know intellectually we are inseparably and physically connected to every living being in the universe. Yet the future of the entire earth community is riding on whether we can find a way beyond the limits of our present evolutionary trajectory.

I am aware of the discomfort my insistence on dispossession of self might evoke in many of you who rightly ascribe to the principle of personal autonomy and the value of the individual. I am not denying the necessity of growing to healthy autonomy or the danger of a selflessness that is unwilling or unable to achieve a strong agency. I value the life's work of very fine scholars, many of them women who, at the end of modernity, have tried so hard and so successfully through their scholarship and advocacy to claim agency for all women and for disenfranchised groups. But our *present* situation in the world does not allow us to stop at the call for or to cling unreflectively to the idea of such individual autonomy. For if there is any insight that we have gained from postmodernity, it is that radical interdependence can, must, and indeed does coexist with individuals' power to act. Then, what I am suggesting in this essay speaks of a useful and necessary dispossession that does not deny or stand as obstacle to mutual relationship of persons and community.

The transformation taking place in the *prayer of no experience* opens into a profoundly different realm for which we do not have adequate words: the deconstruction of even healthy forms of autonomy that no longer represent the deepest possibilities of individuals themselves and humans with God or the radical need of the human community for a deeper synergy. What this prayer predicts as possibility for what the human person and the human community are to become is far beyond what a coalition of strong-willed, autonomous, right-thinking, ethical people can ever achieve on their own. I know that with this formulation I have gone into a dangerous space where language fails me and impasse confronts me.

If the process underway in the *prayer of no experience* is silently dispossessing us of our possessive selfhood, might this forfeiture amount to an evolutionary leap toward selflessness? Though we are inclined first to understand John Haught's observation that evolutionary reality brings about "new forms of being" as pertaining just to physical forms, surely we are aware on further consideration that evolution is not so confined. This we know from the emergence of consciousness, our latest evolutionary leap. And analogously if our consciousness develops, then Edith Stein's assertion as early as the 1930s that the human *spirit* evolves too must be true, as must Pierre Teilhard de Chardin's speculation that the next evolutionary stage would be concentrated precisely in the realm of spirit (mind) or consciousness, his "noo-sphere." His understanding of this next phase reflects his awareness of the interdependence of the spirit and the body for mutual development. Thus, the hypotheses of these great thinkers make me bold to contend that this prayer, expres-sive of a prophetic hope, is an important contemplative bridge to a new future, to the transformation or evolution of consciousness, and through these *pray-ers of no experience* the human person is being changed radically.[49]

Reaching beyond the horizon of present expectation and imagination, and willing to go beyond the boundaries of their lives/selves to make an irrevocable passage into a new place, a new way of "being" in the universe, these prophets of hope stand open to receive the unimaginable future to which God is alluring us; moreover, they actually serve as the doorway to it. Emmanuel Levinas, the twentieth-cen-tury philosopher and, like Edith Stein, an early disciple of Edmund Husserl, understood this movement. Levinas ulti-mately moved beyond ontological philosophy to emphasize the primacy of the ethical relationship with the Other. In this passage he appropriates radical self-dispossession and locates prophecy precisely in the silent eschatology of profound theological hope:

> What comes to mind is the statement of Leon Blum who, imprisoned in a Nazi camp, wrote: "We work *in* the present, not *for* the present." Genuine dedication in working does not seek the applause of one's own time. It devotes itself in dark trust to "a time which lies past the horizon of my time." Surfacing here is the eschatological meaning of "some work." Our work in this age is fragmentary, part of a whole we cannot take in from where we sit. It is only a completely naked faith which knows that this "some" is bound up with a body of the Messiah I can neither conceive nor organize. By disinterestedly stepping outside of myself in work I exercise myself in darkly trusting the End. As worker I abandon the prospect of "personally experiencing the outcome" of my work. This work is essentially prophetic: it works "without entering the Promised Land." This prophetic eschatology is free: delivered from the snares of calculation, delivered from the nihilism of uncommitted game-playing and waste. And stronger: in dark trust discerning a triumph "in a time without me. . . ." The prophetism of this work is located precisely in this eschatology without hope for myself. . . . Really working exceeds the boundaries of one's own time. It is action for a world that is coming, action which surpasses this time, action in which I surpass myself, and in which the yearning for an epiphany of the Other is included.[50]

I want to leave before us in our sad, conflicted church this image of the self-dispossessed prophet whose face is turned in radical hope toward the God coming from the future. When such prophets overstep the horizon of their own time, their own life, in work, in words, in scholarship, in teaching, in ministry, and in who they are as people of silent prayer, not only are they themselves reborn on the other side of the boundary, but also they are also carriers of the evolution of consciousness for the rest of humanity. We can hope that as more and more people make this dark passage to prophecy, this movement of the human spirit will "selectively activate genetic potentials" different from those operative in our present selfhood.[51] As a result, a critical mass will be generated that will lead all humanity across the frontier into the new epoch that is trying to be born. Only our unpurified memories prevent us from imagining a future in which our descendants are not like the human beings we know ourselves to be.

Like another Carmelite, Edith Stein, whom I mentioned earlier and who died with her people in the extermination camp at Auschwitz, betrayed by the state to which she had vowed a total commitment in her youth, I am suggesting the powerful influence of a *spiritual* generativity. The evolution of spirit or consciousness of which Stein speaks happens not just or mainly through a physical propagation but through a spiritual one in which people "bear fruit by virtue of the atmosphere which radiates from them on their environment and . . . also by means of the works which they produce in common and through which they propagate their spirit."[52] This idea of spiritual generativity may sound far-fetched or ungrounded until we consider what scientists are discovering and speculating about the true nature of our world. For example, as long ago as 1982 it was reported that under certain circumstances sub-atomic particles such as electrons are able to instantaneously communicate with each other regardless of the distance separating them, whether an inch, 100 feet, or 10 billion miles apart. Scientist David Bohm's explanation is that there is a deeper and more complex level of reality than we experience, an "implicate order or unbroken wholeness" from which all our perceived reality derives.[53] If such a fabric of interconnectedness exists in nature, it is no stretch of the imagination to apply it to consciousness. Genuine contemplatives have testified to this long before scientists.[54]

In a time of unraveling in the church, when past, present, and future do not seem to hold together in a promising continuity and when we stand perhaps at the cusp of an evolutionary breakthrough, we do not know how our work will be used or if it will be accepted or appreciated, nor can we ascertain what benefit it will bring to the church, religion, American society, or the earth community, now or in a farther future. But I am sure, from my years of keeping company with John of the Cross, that in the personal and communal crisis of memory going on, we are being offered, we are being given hope for ourselves and humanity—profound, radical theological hope—in a God who is coming anew and calling us forward. We must witness to this in our lives, our work, our scholarship, even in betrayal and suffering.[55] From within the mystical tradition, we are being challenged to be contemplatives willing to be stretched beyond ourselves toward a new epiphany of the Holy, incomprehensible Mystery. Let us be prophets of hope!

## Notes

1. I am grateful to Sue Houchins, Brian McDermott, and Mary Catherine Hilkert for their generosity in reading my essay and offering valuable criticism and suggestions, to Leah Hargis for her help with endnotes, to Frances Horner who worked with me on an earlier text, and to Shawn Copeland for her generous response. This essay was previously published in *Proceedings of the Annual Convention* (*Catholic Theological Society of America*) 64 (2009): 21–42.

2. Constance FitzGerald, "Impasse and Dark Night," in *Living with Apocalypse*, ed. Tilden H. Edwards (San Francisco: Harper and Row, 1984), 93–116. Article can also be found in *Women's Spirituality: Resources for Christian Development*, ed. Joann Wolski Conn (Mahwah, N.J.: Paulist Press, 1986), 287–311. Belden Lane first introduced me to "impasse situations" in his essay "Spirituality and Political Commitment: Notes on a Liberation Theology of Nonviolence," which appeared in *America* 144, no. 10 (March 14, 1981): 197–202.

3. See, for example, Sandra Schneiders, *Finding the Treasure: Locating Catholic Religious Life in a New Ecclesial and Cultural Context* (Mahwah, N.J.: Paulist Press, 2000), 153–83; Nancy Sylvester and Mary Jo Klick, *Crucible for Change: Engaging Impasse through Communal Contemplation and Dialogue* (San Antonio: Sor Juana Press, 2004); Beverly J. Lanzetta, *Radical Wisdom: A Feminist Mystical Theology* (Minneapolis: Fortress, 2005); Kristine M. Rankka, *Women and the Value of Suffering* (Collegeville, Minn.: Liturgical Press, 1998), 218–22; Bruce H. Lescher, "Spiritual Direction: Stalking the Boundaries," in *Handbook of Spirituality for Ministers*,

ed. Robert J. Wicks, vol. 2 (New York: Paulist Press, 2000), 324; Mary Catherine Hilkert, *Naming Grace: Preaching and the Sacramental Imagination* (New York: Continuum, 1997); and M. Shawn Copeland, *The Subversive Power of Love: The Vision of Henriette Delille* (Mahwah, N.J.: Paulist Press, 2009).

4. John of the Cross, *The Ascent of Mount Carmel*, in *The Collected Works of St. John of the Cross*, trans. Kieran Kavanaugh and Otilio Rodriguez, rev. ed. (Washington, D.C.: ICS Publications, 1991), 3.2.2–3. Unless otherwise noted, all references to the writings of John of the Cross are taken from this volume. For abbreviation key, see front matter in this book.

5. See Robert Kegan, *In Over Our Heads: The Mental Demands of Modern Life* (Cambridge, Mass.: Harvard University Press, 1994), 312–16.

6. "It must strip and empty itself of all this knowledge and these forms and strive to lose the imaginative apprehension of them" (A 3.2.4). See also A 3.2.2–4; 3.3.2–6.

7. Hein Blommestijn, Jos Huls, and Kees Waaijman, *Footprints of Love: John of the Cross as Guide in the Wilderness* (Leuven, Belgium: Peeters, 2000), 74.

8. F 3.18–22. Constance FitzGerald, "Transformation in Wisdom: The Subversive Character and Educative Power of Sophia in Contemplation," in K. Culligan and R. Jordan, eds., *Carmel and Contemplation: Transforming Human Consciousness*, 281–358 (Washington, D.C.: ICS Publications, 2000), 351n46.

9. For a more extensive interpretation of the process of purification in John of the Cross, see FitzGerald, "Transformation in Wisdom," 303–25.

10. This intimately close presence of the divine John of the Cross calls infused contemplation, dark night, an inflow of God, secret Wisdom, mystical theology, and loving knowledge. See N 2.5.1–2, 2.17, and A 2.8.6. Another relevant text is N 1.10.6 where infused contemplation is, according to Kieran Kavanaugh, mentioned for the first time and equated with "dark and secret contemplation" and "secret and peaceful and loving inflow of God."

11. Miroslav Volf, *The End of Memory: Remembering Rightly in a Violent World* (Grand Rapids, Mich.: Eerdmans, 2006), 25. See also Elizabeth A. Johnson, *Friends of God and Prophets: A Feminist Theological Reading of the Communion of Saints* (New York: Continuum, 1998), 164–65.

12. Brian McDermott, unpublished homily given at Baltimore Carmel, January 18, 2009.

13. Volf, *End of Memory*, 27–33.

14. Elie Wiesel, *Forgotten* (New York: Schocken, 1992), 297.

15. Elie Wiesel and Richard D. Heffner, in *Conversations with Elie Wiesel*, ed. Thomas J. Viincigoerra (New York: Schocken, 2001), 144–45.

16. Volf, *End of Memory*, 34; see 24–34. Volk reminds us that fifty years after the terrible Kristallnacht, Elie Wiesel spoke these words in the German Reichstag: "We remember Auschwitz and all that it symbolizes because we believe that, in spite of the past and its horrors, the world is worthy of salvation and salvation, like redemption, can be found in memory" (ibid., 19).

17. See, for example, Rene Girard, *Violence and the Sacred*, trans. Patrick Gregory (Baltimore: Johns Hopkins University Press, 1979); Rene Girard, *The Scapegoat*, trans. Yvonne Freccero (Baltimore: Johns Hopkins University Press, 1986); Flora Keshgegian, *Redeeming Memories: A Theology of Healing and Transformation* (Nashville: Abingdon, 2000); Judith Lewis Herman, *Trauma and Recovery* (New York: Basic Books, 1992); and Jon G. Allen, *Coping with Trauma*, 2nd ed. (Arlington, Va.: American Psychiatric Publishing, 2005). See also Johnson, *Friends of God*, 141–70, for the importance of memory in reclaiming women's lost history and rectifying their distorted and silent history.

18. Volf, *End of Memory*, 146–47.

19. See John of the Cross's *Living Flame of Love* (F 2) for "purifying touch"; see also FitzGerald, "Transformation in Wisdom," 308–18, 326–27.

20. I suggest that without an understanding of spiritual development, psychotherapy will have limited and inconclusive results.

21. Lanzetta, *Radical Wisdom*, 132–35. I appreciate Lanzetta's insights, which I have integrated with my own in the preceding section. I believe woman's experience, "via femina," she describes *is* the dark night purification of memory that John of the Cross develops, even though Lanzetta appears to think "via femina" is something beyond John's (male) descriptions. She seems to suggest, however, that it is Teresa's experience. When Teresa says a specific experience of loneliness and suffering is "beyond" everything she has written, she is referring to her *Life* but not to the *Interior Castle*, which she wrote about fifteen years later. When she wrote the *Life*, she had not experienced the spiritual marriage or the darkness preceding it. See Constance FitzGerald, "Discipleship of Equals," in *A Discipleship of Equals: Towards a Christian Feminist Spirituality*, ed. Francis A. Eigo (Villanova, Pa.: Villanova University Press, 1988), 63–97.

22. See Natalie Zeman Davis, "The Quest of Michel de Certeau," *New York Review of Books*, March 15, 2008, 57–60.

23. In *The Spiritual Canticle*, John of the Cross describes the movement from purification of the memory to its transformation when he writes, "[God] fills her memory with divine knowledge, because it is now alone and empty of all images and fantasies" (35.5). Such transformative self-donation on the part of God embraces the loved one in the beauty of divine Wisdom, in whom the person beholds, as in a mirror her own beauty. Subverted definitively is the confining, hoarding, colonizing power of memory and past assumptions in an affirmation that spirals to seemingly endless degrees of mutual appreciation singularly determined not by the self-possession of the loved person but by the beauty of Wisdom whose depth and breadth of feeling can gather every absurdity and contradiction into an ever expanding pattern of beauty. John sings, "Let us rejoice, Beloved, and let us go forth to behold ourselves in your beauty . . . that I be so transformed in your beauty and we be alike in beauty possessing then your very beauty . . . in such a way that each looking at the other may see in each other their own beauty, since both are your beauty alone" (36.5).

24. Although I have largely avoided John's language of "emptying" the memory, this experience really is an *emptying* out of memory.

25. For John of the Cross, Jesus Christ is the pattern of the Dark Night; see A 2.7.2–8.

26. In *The Subversive Power of Love*, 49–67, M. Shawn Copeland shows what I am describing as exemplified in Henriette Delille. For further explication of solidarity in difference, see also Johnson, *Friends of God*, 175–80, who also references M. Shawn Copeland, "Toward a Critical Christian Feminist Theology of Solidarity," in *Women and Theology*, ed. Mary Ann Hinsdale and Phyllis Kaminski, Annual Publication of the College Theology Society 40 (Maryknoll, N.Y.: Orbis, 1995), and "Difference as a Category in Critical Theologies for the Liberation of Women," in *Feminist Theology in Different Contexts*, ed. Elisabeth Schussler Fiorenza and M. Shawn Copeland (London: SCM Press, 1996), 143.

27. N 2.5–6.

28. N 2.9.7.

29. From a private spiritual journal shared with me.

30. Denys Turner, "John of the Cross: The Dark Nights and Depression," in *The Darkness of God: Negativity in Western Mysticism* (Cambridge: Cambridge University Press, 1995), 244; see also 226–51.

31. For a clearer understanding of the meaning of theological hope in John of the Cross, consult Karl Rahner's "On the Theology of Hope," in *Theological Investigations*, vol. 10, *Writings of 1965–67*, 2, trans. David Bourke, 242–59 (New York: Seabury, 1977).

32. Focusing on hope, John of the Cross explains in *The Ascent of Mount Carmel*, "Hope puts the memory in darkness and emptiness as regards all earthly and heavenly objects. Hope always pertains to the unpossessed object. If something were possessed there could no longer be any hope for it. St. Paul says to the Romans: 'Hope that is seen is not hope, for how does a person hope for what is seen— that is, what is possessed?' As a result this virtue also occasions emptiness, since it is concerned with unpossessed things and not with the possessed object" (A 2.6.3). See Blommestijn, Huls, and Waaijman, *Footprints of Love*, 71–73. I am indebted to the authors' treatment of the purification of memory and specifically here to

hope. These Dutch Carmelite scholars have been working with the purification of memory in John as I have.

33. John F. Haught, *God after Darwin: A Theology of Evolution* (Boulder, Colo.: Westview, 2000), 88–89.

34. Ibid., 90.

35. John writes, "The spiritual person must continually bear in mind the following precaution; he [sic] must not build up an archive of impressions in his memory of all the things he hears, sees, smells, and touches. On the contrary, he must immediately forget them and, if necessary, apply as much energy to forgetting them as others do to remembering them. He must do this in such a way that no communication or idea of these things remains in his memory. He must act as if these things did not exist in the world. Thus he leaves the memory free and unencumbered and unattached to any earthly or heavenly consideration. He then arrives at a state such that it would appear as though he had no memory. He must freely let it sink into oblivion as a hindrance" (A 3.2.14). John further explains, "God displays no form or image that can be encompassed by the memory. Hence also the memory, when it is united with God, is without form or image. . . . Our everyday experience in fact also teaches us this. The memory is devoid of all images and imbued with the supreme good. It has completely forgotten everything and no longer remembers anything. For union with God empties the imagination and sweeps out all forms and communications, and elevates it to the supernatural" (A 3.2.4). The translations of these two texts are taken from *Footprints of Love*. I am grateful to Blommestijn, Huls, and Waaijman for their articulation of this experience; their thought is so close to my own (see 71–73).

36. Blommestijn, Huls, and Waaijman, *Footprints of Love*, 90.

37. Coming from another tradition, Christopher Bamford articulates even more explicitly how the archives of our images block an authentic encounter with the Other, or any vision for the future. Commenting on Meister Eckhart's instruction on detachment, he says, "By images Eckhart means the contents of consciousness: the finished fixed forms—past thoughts and memories—which we take to be the world but which in fact are not the world in

its immediacy and present-ness, but only our own past, our own habits and fixed tendencies. Immured within these images, we feed upon ourselves and take our self-feeling for the world. These images interpose themselves between us and the world, breaking the continuum of being, and making any true meeting or knowledge impossible." Christopher Bamford, "Washing the Feet," *Parabola* 10, no. 3 (1985): 67.

38. See Volf, *End of Memory*, 12. According to Volf, whether memories multiply pleasure or replicate pain, they cut us off from the future (21).

39. Ibid., 81–83, 145–47.

40. John explains, "None of the supernatural forms and ideas that can be received by the memory is God, and the soul must empty itself of all that is not God in order to go to God. Consequently, the memory must likewise dismiss all these forms and ideas in order to reach union with God in hope. Every possession is against hope. . . . As St. Paul says, hope is for that which is not possessed (Heb. 2.1). In the measure in which the soul becomes dispossessed of things, in that measure will it have hope, and the more hope it has the greater will be its union with God, for in relation to God, the more a soul hopes the more it attains hope" (A 3.7.2). See Blommestijn, Huls, and Waaijman, *Footprints of Love*, 71–73, 79–82.

41. David F. Ford, *Self and Salvation, Being Transformed* (Cambridge: Cambridge University Press, 1998). In *Darkness of God*, Denys Turner writes in similar fashion: "As memory we are dispossessed by hope of any power to construct for ourselves an identity of our own" (246).

42. I am not alone in this interpretation: "In the state of ecstasy," Kees Waaijman and his colleagues suggest, "we are beside ourselves and become strangers and pilgrims who no longer feel at home anywhere and lose our footing" (Blommestijn, Huls, and Waaijman, *Footprints of Love*, 127).

43. Turner, *Darkness of God*, 236.

44. Commenting on "in solitude he guides her, he alone," John explains that "the meaning of [this line of *The Spiritual Canticle*

poem] is not only that he guides her in her solitude, but it is *he alone who works in her* without any means. This is a characteristic of the union of the soul with God in the spiritual marriage: *God works in and communicates himself to her through himself alone*, without using as means the angels or natural ability, for the exterior and interior senses, and all creatures, and even the soul herself do very little toward the reception of the remarkable supernatural favors that God grants in this state" (C 35.6).

45. Blommestijn, Huls, and Waaijman, *Footprints of Love*, 122.

46. "And the memory, which by itself perceived only the figures and phantasms of creatures, is changed through this union so as to have in its mind the eternal years" (F 2.34.4), and "its memory is the eternal memory of God" (F 2.34.7).

47. Quoted in Daniel O'Leary, "Space for Grace," *Tablet*, November 18, 2006.

48. "The soul is dead to all that it was in itself" (F 2.34.7).

49. What is remarkable in the final section of *The Spiritual Canticle* is the progressive character of transformation and, even more surprising, the differing meanings John ascribes to these almost infinite *transformative* possibilities. The history of these stanzas reveals that in the freer, more passionate and daring first redaction of the canticle commentary (1584), John situates his marvelous expectations for *continuing transformation* this side of death with only minor gesturing to eternity. In the second, more theologically refined redaction written a year or two later (1585–1586), probably with an eye on the Inquisition, his great hope sees these same transformative consequences taking place largely over the horizon of death. My intuition favors John's first, more spontaneous and "dangerous" explanation in what is known as canticle A. What I want to note in these mystical texts is John's testimony that silent contemplative union, the *prayer of no experience*, radically changes a person and opens into truly new possibilities, new vision, and a vast, bottomless, and incomprehensible Future toward which hope reaches and love gives. John writes: "This thicket of wisdom and knowledge of God is so profound and vast that, for all the soul may know thereof, she can ever enter farther still, so vast is it, and so

incomprehensible are its riches (A 35.5–6). . . . There we shall enter and be transformed in the transformation of new knowledge and new acts and communications of love. For although it is true that the soul, when she says this, is already transformed . . . in this wisdom . . . it does not therefore follow that she cannot in this estate have new enlightenments and transformations of new kinds of knowledge and divine light" (A 37.5).

50. Adriaan Peperzak, *Het Menselijk Gelaat* (The human face) (Bilthoven, Netherlands: Amboboeken, 1971), 172–73. This is a collection of articles on Emmanuel Levinas. The Levinas text may be found in English in Kees Waaijman, *The Mystical Space of Carmel: A Commentary on the Carmelite Rule*, trans. John Vriend (Leuven, Belgium: Peters, 1999), 209–10. Although Waaijman seems to give this as a direct quote, the quotation marks within the text make it ambiguous. Certainly Levinas discusses these thoughts in "Meaning and Sense," in *Emmanuel Levinas: Basic Philosophical Writings*, ed. Adriaan T. Peperzak, Simon Critchley, and Robert Bernasconi (Bloomington: Indiana University Press, 1996), 33–64.

51. In an editorial, "Human Nature Today" in the *New York Times* for June 26, 2009, columnist David Brooks, paraphrasing the thought of Sharon Begley, writes, "The first problem is that far from being preprogrammed with a series of hardwired mental modules, as evolutionary psychologist types assert, our brains are fluid and plastic. We're learning that evolution can be a more rapid process than we thought. It doesn't take hundreds of thousands of years to produce genetic alterations. Moreover, we've evolved to adapt to diverse environments. Different circumstances can *selectively activate different genetic potentials*. . . . Human nature adapts to the continual flow of information—adjusting to the ancient information contained in genes and the current information contained in today's news in a continuous, idiosyncratic blend." See Sharon Begley, "Don't Blame the Caveman," *Newsweek*, June 30, 2009. Is it not even more likely that the spiritual process of transformation effects profound adaptation?

52. Edith Stein, *Finite and Eternal Being*, trans. Kurt F. Reinhardt (Washington, D.C.: Institute of Carmelite Studies, 2002), 266.

53. David Bohm, *Wholeness and the Implicate Order* (Abingdon, UK: Routledge, 2002).

54. See, for example, John of the Cross's *Living Flame*: "The soul feels its ardor strengthen and increase and its love become so refined in this ardor that seemingly there flow seas of loving fire within it, reaching to the heights and depths of the earthly and heavenly spheres, imbuing all with love. It seems to it that the entire universe is a sea of love in which it is engulfed, for conscious of the living point or center of love within itself, it is unable to catch sight of the boundaries of this love" (2.10); see also Teresa of Ávila, *The Book of Her Life*, in *The Collected Works of St. Teresa of Ávila*, trans. Kieran Kavanaugh and Otilio Rodriguez, vol. 1, rev. ed. (Washington, D.C.: ICS Publications, 1987), 40.10.

55. Building on Walter Brueggemann's work on the prophetic imagination, Mary Catherine Hilkert in *Naming Grace* (81–84) describes the task of the prophetic preacher and the prophetic community as that of not only giving language to people's pain and grief in a time of impasse like ours but also focusing on the coming of God, the reign of God, and the rekindling of hope.

# The Wisdom of "Work" in the Carmelite Rule

KEES WAAIJMAN, O.CARM.

TRANSLATED BY SUSAN VERKERK

IF THERE IS WISDOM HIDDEN in the Carmelite Rule, which reflects both the insights of St. Albert, the giver of the Rule, and the experiences of the lay hermits in the Carmel mountains, then we probably encounter it in its most condensed form in the chapter (or number[1]) on work.

Of course, wisdom lies nestled within other parts of the Rule. Indeed, it is a sign of wisdom that Albert situates the lay hermits' form of life (nos. 3–21) within the framework of the imitation of Christ; for this is the entry into union with God, which at the same time progresses with purity of heart (no. 2). In the conclusion of his letter (nos. 22–23), Albert wisely asks the men dwelling on Mount Carmel to remember this. In this way, the form of life of the lay hermits is not isolated from the many routes along which people travel as they search for God. It is also a sign of wisdom to link together both the personal and the community spirituality of the lay hermits (nos. 10–15), a point that on the basis of their own experience they had expressly requested. In this way, two essential dynamics of human existence—the strengthening of the self and justice for the other—are brought into balance with each other, and both are held together in the same Source. Furthermore, it is a sign of wisdom to link this combined action to a great sensitivity both for the place where each and all live (nos. 5–10) and for the fundamental dynamic of coming together on organizational, liturgical, economic, communicative, and spiritual levels (nos. 4 and 12–15). Finally, wisdom appears in the admonitions about fasting and abstinence, which bear on the welfare of our body's immune system (nos. 16–17). All these are signs of wisdom.[2]

In my opinion, however, the greatest wisdom is contained in the four numbers of the Rule (nos. 18–21) that describe the transformation in God, with work placed at the very center of the process. Purely from a quantitative perspective, these sections make up more than half of the actual *formula vitae*. The Formula of Life consists of 857 words. Of these, 455 words are dedicated to the transformation in God's attributes (nos. 18–19) that is exercised and preserved through working in silence (nos. 20–21). Chapter 20 on work, which contains 146 (32 percent) of the 455 words, plays an essential role in this perspective on transformation. Work is inwardly linked with God's attributes, which must clothe the lay hermits, and with the silence that, in the cultivation of justice, must permeate work (nos. 21). The placing of the chapters on "the armor of God" and work (nos. 18–20) between, on the one side, the continuation of fasting and abstinence, which builds up the immune system (nos. 16–17), and on the other side, the silence that makes this work hopeful and just (no. 21) helps to ensure that

Carmelite spirituality stands with both feet on the ground and is not estranged from the everyday life that Carmelites, as lay hermits, are called to live.

In this contribution I adhere closely to the text of the Rule of Carmel, following closely what it says about work (no. 20). In doing this, it is not my intention to lock up the text in itself or in historical reconstructions. On the contrary, while I endeavor to remain loyal to the text and its historical setting, I wish to explore the spaciousness of the Rule by (1) situating work within the whole of the form of life; (2) reading the text against the background of Scripture and the history of Christian spirituality; (3) discussing its relevance for those who are searching for God in their daily life and work; (4) indicating points of contact for interreligious and interspiritual conversation; and (5) last but not least, searching for the wisdom that hopefully lies hidden in the Rule.

## The Rule's Basic Instruction about Work

Some work

must be done by you.

Albert requires only five Latin words to tell the Carmel dwellers what is expected of them: "*Aliquid operis semper faciendum est.*"[3] The rest is explanation, illustration, and reflection. Even though the instruction is short, it is well worth attending to some of the words and phrases in order to get a sharper picture of its purpose.

## Some Work

This literally translates as "something" (*aliquid*), which can be considered under the category of works (*opera*).[4] This category is at the same time defined and undefined. It is undefined because the type of work the "something" is about is left blank. Moreover, Albert probably chose the plural "works" to indicate to the lay hermits in the mountains of Carmel that they could undertake a range of different works and not restrict themselves to one type of work.[5] Nicholas the Frenchman, who lived on Mount Carmel not long after the Rule was written, understood working to involve both spiritual activities (reading, meditation, prayer, etc.) and physical work (copying codices, agriculture, etc.).[6] When we look closely at the Rule, the following works appear: cooking (see no. 7); welcoming visitors and caring for guests (see no. 9); allocating goods (no. 12); keeping livestock and poultry (see no. 13); transporting (no. 13); building (no. 14); and caring for the sick and frail (see nos. 16–17). New works were added over time: missionary work (see no. 17); caring for souls, studying, educating, and so forth. Anyone who surveys the range of work carried out by the tens of thousands of men and women who have solemnly taken the vows of the Carmelite Rule can only conclude that "some work" is indeed undefined.[7]

At the same time, however, the "something" of work can be given a basic definition, because to work means to be engaged in something with attention and concentration. Whether it concerns working the land, manufacturing implements, constructing and renovating buildings, caring for animals, exploring texts, copying a codex, or any form of the care of souls, working requires this: attention and concentration. The acting person is drawn, already occupied, into the doing [*facere*] of the work, and through this withdraws his or her gaze from both self and other. The one who works is woven into the movement of the work. As the Dutch poet Gerrit Achterberg so strikingly writes about one of the works of Jesus: "Jesus wrote with his finger in the sand / . . . We do not know what he wrote, / He himself had forgotten it, / submerged in the words of his hand."[8] In the process of writing, Jesus was submerged in his doing. This doing forms a personal element, an individual web, which neither viewer nor doer is able to understand. Achterberg writes, "We do not know" and "He himself had forgotten it." Praxis weaves its own element. However, this does not mean that the activity is locked up within itself. On the contrary, praxis unfolds itself in its own space and openness—in its own wisdom.

## By You

"Some work" receives a new definition by the fact that the work must be done "by you." When work must be done "by you" (plural), the social dimension of work comes into view.[9] Four aspects flow directly out of the fact that Albert is addressing himself to a community.

First, from the moment the hermits become part of a community, their work, irrespective of how different it is from that of the others, becomes part of the work of the community.

Second, it is inevitable that the community, implicitly or explicitly, approves the nature of the work and determines in one way or another whether this concrete work is viable, authentic, sound, and meaningful. Work that transgresses moral borders will sooner or later be exposed to the critical judgments of the community.

Third, the different activities call for a mutual harmonization. Thus, number 21 also talks of the need for some communication. This number on silence is explicitly concerned with the cultivation of justice through appropriate mutual companionship. In this way, number 12 on the community of goods will not fail to exercise its influence: no one keeps something only for him- or herself. Instead, in work as in all things, each shares and allows everything to be communally held.

Finally, the community will also give feedback on the amount of work being done. The number about the weekly chapter (the prescribed gathering in common of the hermits, or of monastics and religious) speaks clearly about the "excesses and shortcomings of the brothers where such are detected in someone" (no. 15). We can infer from the stories about hermits elsewhere in the Holy Land that excesses concerning work are not fictitious. This may even have driven Albert to speak restrictively when he wrote about "*some* [*aliquid*] work."[10] Later, yet another aspect of the nature of the community's work will be explored, when Albert promotes St. Paul as someone who undertakes work "so as not to be a burden to any of you" (no. 20).

## Must Be Done

In the instruction about work, the phrase "must be done" links both formally and in depth with the chapters concerning the armor of God (nos. 18–19).

Formally, the instruction about work (no. 20) connects with the chapter on the armor of God (no. 19) because both numbers are presented in the Latin gerundive (a form expressing a sense of obligation with passive meaning): must be girded, must be protected, must be fastened, must be taken, must be put on, and must be done. Through this use of the gerundive form, the Rule tells us how we are to respond to the trials and tribulations that will inevitably cross our path, so that they become forces for good, for wholeness.

Further, these two numbers (19 and 20) are linked together on a deeper level by the words "And whatever activity must be done by you [*agere*], let it be done [*fieri* is the passive of *facere*] in the Word of the Lord." Obviously in relation to the activities which must be done, *fieri* encompasses more actions than just "some work." But in each situation, what all these activities have in common is that they "must be done," that is, they must be attentively undertaken. Everything must be done "in the Word of the Lord." That Word is not only the written word or the spoken word but also the Word in which everything is created (Gn 1; Ps 33:6, 9; Ps 119:89–100; Jn 1) and in which the promise of the final fulfillment is carried (Is 40:6; Is 41:4). All work, irrespective of what it is, must situate itself in the all-encompassing speech of God that continues through time and looks forward to the final fulfillment. Whatever the Carmelite does, he or she must practice listening to the foundational movements of God's Word, which means listening in hope and silence, in order to see.

# Work as the Soul's Protection against Evil

> . . . so that the devil finds you always occupied
> so that he will be unable to find an entry
> into your souls. (no. 20)

After Albert has stated his ultra-short instruction about work, in three steps he then draws us further into the meaning of work. The first step concerns the psychological level (your souls) and is apotropaic in nature: work wards off the influence of the devil. By means of two linked subclauses (so that . . . so that . . . ), Albert names the immediate consequence of doing "some work." Without doubt, the second clause is subordinate to the first, but because both are so connected and in parallel (i.e., the words "so that" and "to find" appear twice; and "occupied" and "unable to find an entry" denote the parallels), the whole of the phrase creates the impression of a climax.

## The Devil

The subject of the two inferred subclauses is the devil. We come across the devil at the beginning of number 18. The first time, he is implicitly present when Albert, recalling the suffering of Job, calls the human situation on Earth a trial. Anyone who is well versed in the Bible knows that it was Satan who, with God's consent, tested Job. The second time, he is named explicitly as "your adversary the devil" who prowls around like a roaring lion looking for someone to devour. The third time he appears, the scoundrel is an archer who shoots fiery arrows at the Carmel dweller—arrows only the shield of faith can withstand (no. 19).

Within the Christian faith, the devil plays the role of one who obstructs the God-human process of transformation.[11] This obstructer is designated in various ways: the devil (who tangles up), Satan (who hinders), corrupter, adversary, the unfriend, wicked person, dragon, snake, lion, and so forth. The desert monks, and the traditions that stemmed from them, saw the devil as the cause of all ambiguity, affliction, and vice, and therefore as the adversary, who in the spiritual life must be resisted.[12] Even so, the influence of the devil was restricted. After all, he is a creature created by God, just as we are, and his afflictions are permitted by God so that we will grow in spiritual aptitude. Such a process is evidenced in the lives of Abraham, Job, Jesus, Anthony, and so many other spiritually mature people. Moreover, fundamental for Christian spirituality is that the destructive power of the devil was vanquished in Jesus Christ. Ascetic exercises (including work) and discerning the spirits are effective methods for seeing through and challenging the afflictions that deceive us. Important for our study is the fact that the devil exercises his influence only from the outside and is not, in advance, already within us.[13]

## Finds You Always Occupied

The Rule opts to see the devil as one who is outside, prowling restlessly around, looking for some place that will provide an entry into the soul. But when the lay hermit is always working, then the devil finds that person always occupied. The door is padlocked, just as water is unable to penetrate a bird's feathers when they are greased. "Some work" and being "always occupied" illuminate both sides of the coin; only the perspective is different. What is seen by the Carmel dweller as "some work" is seen from the devil's perspective as finding someone occupied. "Work" works through itself: *ex opere operato*. Working is in itself apotropaic—just as the destroyer is unable to enter the houses of the Israelites to strike them down when the doorposts are sprinkled with blood (Ex 12:22–23). From the perspective of demonology, work is effective. Hence the use of the two consecutive subclauses.

## So That He Will Be Unable to Find an Entry

From the consequence of doing some work, another consequence appears, namely, that it will be impossible for the devil to find an entry anywhere into those who dwell on Mount Carmel. Albert himself followed the Rule of the Canons Regular, and it is possible that in writing to the Carmelites, some echo of this was being played out.[14] Chapter 25 of the Canons' Rule points out that no one may find an entry (*adytum inveniat*) through which he or she can enter the cloister (*ingredi*). Thus, the two consecutive subclauses can be read as a climax and spelled out in the following way: the devil finds Carmel dwellers always at work and always occupied, so occupied in fact that he can find no place to enter the soul. The repetition of the verb "to find" strengthens this climax and can be spelled out thus: even though the devil roams around and searches, he finds no way in, he is unable to find an entrance. Therefore, the lay hermit keeps the devil at arm's length—at a spacious distance.

## Into Your Souls

The devil is strongly attracted to the soul. He directs much of his searching toward it. Work is a sufficient defense against this attack. This conceptual universe finds its basis in the spiritual anthropology that traditionally finds its central point in the soul (in Hebrew *nefesh*, Greek *psuché*, and Latin *anima*).[15] Essential to this is that the soul exists as a vulnerable internal space that becomes visible on the outside in relation to its surroundings. This inner space is needy and sensitive. In this space life stirs, is warm-blooded, breathes, and moves. It is in this space that the self moves toward the light. Here lives our soul's longing for the other whom we carry within us. Here our devotion grows along with the gift of self. This space within is vulnerable, and when the soul is confronted with external influences, which it must resist, this vulnerability becomes visible.

At this point, what also emerges is the need of the outer side—the external soul. This external side of the soul, the so-called fleshly soul, comes piercingly into view in the book of Job. Satan has stripped Job of his livestock, his servants, and his children (Job 1:13–19). However, this is not enough for him. He wants more. He wants Job's soul. Why? Because only when Job is attacked in his own soul will it be shown if Job truly fears God (Job 1:8; 2:3). Satan's standpoint is clear: "A skin for a skin! Everything that someone has he will give for his soul!" (Job 2:4).[16] God accepts Satan's standpoint.

It is indeed reasonable that the price is costly, as it involves testing Job to find out if he truly fears God: "Here, he is in your hand. But spare his soul" (Job 2:6). The writer is playing here with the two-sidedness of the soul. Satan only sees the external soul (possessions, servants, children, body) and particularly desires to impact on this layer. On this point, God gives the tester free reign, but as for the inner side of the soul, Satan must leave that alone. This is reinforced later in the story. Job's external soul is tested further, but his inner soul remains resilient against the onslaught.

This biblical anthropology shows clearly what Albert has in mind: he regards the doing of "some work" as a buffer that acts at a psychosomatic level. Attentive and concentrated working is apotropaic in relation to that which is destructive to us, that which deceives us. However, this shield against the undermining of life is, in a paradoxical way, open and susceptible to the bestowing of life. The soul is like our skin: it keeps at bay those things that can infect us while at the same time, because of its porosity, it allows in those things that give life: light, sound, food, and love. It is wise of Albert to give the lay hermits the stringent advice "to do some work," because it offers the opportunity for attentive and concentrated activity that, in turn, supports our psychosomatic immune system. By not prescribing the type of work, Albert opens up possibilities for a multitude of people. Also in this way, the "skin" of the community can develop its different specialties (seeing, hearing, touching, holding, walking, tasting, etc.) that can be important for the survival of the community. Thus, we are brought to the next layer of work: the community dimension.

## Work Builds Up the Community

> In this matter you have both the teaching and example
> of the blessed apostle Paul,
> in whose mouth Christ spoke
> and who was appointed and given by God
> as preacher and teacher of the nations
> in faith and truth.
> If you follow him, you cannot go astray. (no. 20)

To take the next steps that draw us further into the meaning of work, Albert allows himself to be guided by Paul: "In this matter you have both the teaching and example of the blessed apostle Paul." Through the words "in this matter," Albert connects to his main theme: the doing of some work. Now, however, rather than pressing home the apotropaic and demonological meaning of work and its impact on the psychosomatic level, he wants to focus on the social value of work. Albert invests Paul with great authority: he is holy, he is an apostle. Christ speaks through his mouth as if he were a prophet (see 2 Cor 13:3) appointed by God himself to be a preacher and teacher of the nations (1 Tm 2:7; see also 2 Tm 1:11). He is grounded in faith and truth. The usually succinct Albert cannot seem to find enough words to express Paul's authority. He hammers this home, as it were, with a steady double blow: teaching and example, appointed and given, preacher and teacher, and faith and truth. The conclusion must be clear: if you follow him, you cannot go astray.

On two points, Albert brings to the fore Paul's guidance: Paul is a teacher who gives sound teaching about work, and at the same time, he provides a good model of living. In a good spirituality both of these themes belong together. Both are also clothed with the 2 Thessalonians from which Albert quotes at a later point in number 20: "We wanted to give ourselves to you as a model so that you might imitate us" and "when we were with you we instructed you to this effect" (2 Thes 3:9–10).

Here, Albert turns around Paul's word order: he begins with Paul as a model and then focuses on Paul's teaching.

> "Laboring and weary we lived among you," he says,
>
> "working night and day
>
> so as not to be a burden to any of you.
>
> Not because we did not have the authority to do otherwise,
>
> but because we wanted to give ourselves to you
>
> as a model for you to imitate." (Carmelite Rule no. 20)

We have already seen how Albert addresses the Carmelites using "you"—"some work must be done *by you*"—giving it a community dimension. The Carmelite works to share the work of the community, which implicitly or explicitly legitimizes the type of work, the impact of it, and the extent of its regulation. Now, in the example of Paul, the social meaning of work presents itself clearly for discussion. What does this example look like?

## Laboring . . . Working Night and Day

With regard to Paul's form of life, it would seem that he has a double daily routine. We can deduce this in the Acts of the Apostles. On the one hand, Luke characterizes Paul as a tentmaker. When he is evangelizing in Corinth, he resides with Aquila and Priscilla: "Because he was of the same trade he stayed with them and they worked together, as by trade they were tent makers [*skenopoios; scenefactoria*]" (Acts 18:3). On the other hand, during the evening hours, for the Jews on the Sabbath and for the Christians on the Lord's Day, Paul devoted himself to proclaiming the Gospel. People can rightly say that Paul labored vigorously, working night and day, earning his living by making tents and proclaiming the Gospel. In this way he was in complete solidarity with his community—"among you" (*inter vos*)—working the same as everyone and supporting himself and, at the same time, working as a dedicated evangelist in his community with you (*apud vos*).

## So as Not to Be a Burden to Any of You

Why did Paul fulfill this double task? Why did he work night and day? In the presence of the Corinthians he gives as his motivation his desire to emphasize the grace-filled character of the Gospel. Thus, the community at Corinth was not required to fill a need in his daily life (see 1 Cor 9). In the presence of the Thessalonians his argument is, "So as not to be a burden to any of you." This is the motivation that Albert assumes in the Rule: in an exemplary way, Paul's life demonstrates to the lay hermits the community dimension of work. When someone is not working, he or she is a burden to the community (and therefore not really among us); and when a person works well, he or she builds up the community.

For centuries, this Pauline model has been held up as an example to all cenobitic forms of living. In this respect, Abba Pinufius was exemplary: "He performed secretly at night, certain necessary *duties* which were shunned and avoided by others, so that in the morning the whole *community* marvelled that this useful *work* had been *done*, though no one knew who had *done* it."[17] Very influential was Augustine's *Concerning the Work of the Monks*: physical work must be performed by everyone with an eye to the spirit and well-being of the community.[18] Also the new religious movements at the time of the founding of Carmel, including the early Franciscans who pursued total poverty, gave priority to working for their living. Insofar as it was necessary, they begged as a form of evangelization. Not until later did they travel around making work of their begging.

The eremitical meaning of work concentrates particularly around two points. First, it considers work to be something that guides, gives rhythm to, supports, and keeps in balance the life of prayer,[19] the *ora et labora* (prayer and work) of the monastic tradition. Second, work provides a living. Thus Abba Serapion cautioned a young monk: "Especially because he was young and strong, not to be idle or free and easy, floating around in a dream world; instead he should remain in his cell, and in accordance with the Rule of the Elders, live from his own *work* rather than from another man's generosity."[20]

The Carmelite Rule stresses the perspective of the community. Not working—but nevertheless still eating!—has direct implications for the others who will become burdened because of this. After all, everyone is a member of the community and invited to care for and maintain it. When all are not contributing to the community through their work, then is it difficult for each to receive "what he needs from the hand of the prior," that is, to receive what he needs from the brother who is appointed to his task by the prior (no. 12). The community dimension of working is therefore strongly connected to the chapter on the community of goods; while the apotropaic soul dimension is connected to the earlier number (10) which concerns working in or near the cell.

The community dimension of doing some work is also strongly connected to the chapter on silence, which comes immediately after the one on work. Albert explicitly links together these two numbers: "The apostle recommends silence when he prescribes that work must be done in it" (no. 21). One of the reasons for this connection between work and silence is that silence has a community dimension to it. According to Albert, silence means that during one's daily work, speaking with the other is respectful and measured. He underpins this with the saying from Isaiah: "Silence is the cultivation of justice" (Is 32:17). Working is much more than just being accountable to each other. It is also the mutual building up of each other; it is the bringing about of a culture of justice. Therefore, one who does not contribute to the existence of the community burdens and wrongs the other. That is unjust.

## Not Because We Did Not Have the Authority to Do Otherwise

Through doing the work of an apostle, the proclamation of the Gospel, Paul has "the authority to eat and drink" (1 Cor 9:4), that is, he has the right to be maintained by the community. He proclaims, "Have we no authority [*potestas*; see 1 Cor 9:4, 5–6, 12, 18, etc.] to eat and to drink [without having to labor to support ourselves]? . . . Or is it only Barnabas and I who do not have the authority to refrain from working?" (1 Cor 9:4, 6). Here, Paul affirms that he certainly has the authority, but he voluntarily gives this up. What is he expecting from this? "What then is my reward? Just this: that in my proclamation I make the Gospel free of charge, so as not to make full use of my rights in the Gospel" (1 Cor 9:18). Thus, he deviates from the line "that those who proclaim the Gospel should get their living by the Gospel" (1 Cor 9:14), in a way that expresses the absolute gratuitousness of the Gospel. This is Paul's example; this is the form that he passes to his community for them to imitate.

## We Wanted to Give Ourselves to You as a Model for You to Imitate

By the example that Paul gives he offers a form of life that through inner appropriation brings a person into contact with the divine power. So, for example, he complains about those who certainly possess the formation of a particular piety but deny the power of it (2 Tm 3:5). Albert and his contemporaries believed that, in every life situation, one must interiorize one's form of life. In the twelfth century, we see the proliferation of a specifically spiritual use of such words as example (*exemplum*), form (*forma*), rule (*regula*), and form of life (*propositum*).[21] These words point to a form of piety[22] (reading Scripture, work, forms of prayer, meditation, etc.[23]) that must be practiced in a way that impacts so powerfully on a person that he or she lives life from the inside out.[24] Consequently, the focus is not on a uniform adaptation to something external[25] but on an interiorization, which I (in the first person singular) can give form to and live out in my daily life. For this reason it is necessary that the form as such is practiced and at the same time let go, because only then does it meet the purpose for which it is intended: transformation in God.

Let us review the two steps that draw us into the meaning of work. The first step moved on a psychosomatic level; was demonologically apotropaic in nature; was strengthened by, and found its basis for working in, the ego (the I); and was adequately completed through the performing self. In contrast, the second step moves us on to the social communitarian level, which is directed to the divine-human transformation in justice (silence) and, in order to become fruitful, must be personally appropriated. The space of the community dimension must be personally explored and developed through a creative process of interiorization. Alongside an apotropaic aspect—"not to be a burden to any of you"—it has a positive orientation: the community is built up through mutual help and respect. In imitating Paul, this means not by a relationship of exchange but expressly through the cultivation of justice and the gratuitous character of an evangelical community.

## The Mystical Dimension of Work

After the apotropaic and social dimensions of work have been explored, the third step is to the mystical. This dimension of work is anchored in two sides of the Rule. On one side, in the number on silence, work must be done in silence, that is, in an atmosphere of mutual respect through which a culture of justice is called into being (no. 21). On the other side, as a consequence of the above, work is also anchored in the preceding chapter on the armor of God; work is the breastplate of justice, which is formed through the three-in-one love (the love of God, the love of neighbor, and the love of self) that is at the heart of life in Christian community (no. 19).

> For when we were with you,
>
> we impressed this on you:
>
> If someone is unwilling to work,
>
> let him not eat.
>
> Now we have heard,
>
> that among you are those who restlessly go around doing no work.
>
> We urge people of this kind and implore them in the Lord Jesus Christ,
>
> that they earn their bread, working in silence. (no. 20)

After Paul's example, his instruction (which is presented with some emphasis) follows: "For when we were with you, *we urge* you: . . . *We urge* people of this kind and *implore* them in the Lord Jesus Christ." The Rule presents Paul speaking to the community with the authority of an apostle (*denuntiare*) and imploring them (*obsecrare*) with the authority of the one who sent him: *Dominus Jhesus Christus*. His commanding stance toward them—"with you (*apud vos*)"— is grounded in what he brought to their attention: There are some Thessalonians who restlessly go around doing no work (*ambulantes inquiete nichil operantes*). What does "to restlessly go around" mean? And in connection with this, what is the significance of "doing no work"? Is the phrase "if someone is unwilling to work, let him not eat" more than simply a moral exhortation? And why is it necessary to mention this instruction? We can pose the same questions in relation to the command "that they earn their bread, working in silence." In relation to silence, what does this mean? And what is the relationship between working and eating? We shall see that the answers to these questions draw us gradually into the mystical dimension of work because, via Paul's teaching, that is what Albert is seeking to do.

## Restlessly Go Around Doing No Work

In 2 Thessalonians 3:11, from which Albert explicitly quotes, what does "to restlessly go around" (*inquiete ambulare*) mean? As presented in the Vulgate translation, Paul gives the phrase something of an enlightened explanation: "Disorderly going around and not according to the tradition that you have received from us" (2 Thes 3:6). Restlessly (*inquiete*) and disorderly (*inordinate*) are both translations of the same Greek word, *ataktoos* (2 Thes 3:6, 7, 11), which points to the violation of the divine order. To which order is Paul alluding? For an answer to this we turn again to 1 Corinthians 9, where he claims the authority to be able to eat from his work as an evangelist. In his argument he points to the basic rule of the Torah: "You shall not muzzle an ox" (1 Cor 9:9; see Dt 25:4), that is, the one who works has the right to eat. The same rule also applies to the order of the temple: "Do you not know that those who serve in the temple get their food from the temple?" (1 Cor 9:13). Indeed, it is the same order that we see in the everyday world of human beings: "Who does military service and pays their own expenses? Who plants a vineyard and does not eat any of its fruit? Or who tends a flock and does not get any of its milk?" (1 Cor 9:7). These examples bring forth the insight that from the time of the law of Moses (1 Cor 9:9) there is an unbreakable bond between working and eating, between sowing and reaping (1 Cor 9:11), and between effort and enjoying. In this basic rule of mutuality, the believing Israelites taste the working of God (see Psalm 128). Some in Thessalonica broke this basic rule. They argued that the end times had come and that this basic rule therefore no longer applies, thus one who does not work *may* eat. With this, their going around (*halacha*) is completely out of balance: they restlessly go on without working but continue to eat well.[26]

Paul's instruction—and Albert's—is therefore not concerned simply with working, with eating, or with restlessness but with the fundamental (and therefore rest-giving) mutuality between working and eating: the one who works will eat; whoever does not work should not eat. The one who disturbs this order, in which the law of God itself is revealed, no longer remains in the peace of God. When those who work cannot eat and those who don't work do eat, they are living in a disordered (*ataktoos*) way. This disorder is not part of God's reality or part of the final reality of God, in which the same law will be shown to apply. Only when God's order is respected will what came to birth in the work of creation be liberated and completed in God. Creation and redemption mutually reach out to each other.

## That They Earn Their Bread, Working in Silence

Between working and earning one's bread, what does silence mean? In order to find an answer to this question, we return once again to 1 Corinthians. Speaking about the unbreakable bond between work and eating, Paul says, "Whoever ploughs should plough in hope [*in spe*] and the thresher must thresh in the hope [*in spe*] of receiving his share" (1 Cor 9:10). Here, "in hope" is mentioned twice. Why? The bond between working and eating is not characterized simply by natural necessity, coercive causes, or fate. Time after time, working is seen to be characterized by hope. The threshing ox must hope that it will receive its just reward.

This is precisely the meaning of the silence that Paul (and Albert) calls for. Here, silence means restful anticipation. In the silence of its praxis, work itself looks forward, full of anticipation to its completion: the enjoyment of the harvest. The restful anticipation that glows in the work (Ps 39:5–7) finds no other support than the tranquility and stillness of working itself. Ultimately, it is only in God himself that the silence finds its footing: "In you alone is my hope" (Ps 39:8). Restful waiting is in itself the only basis of the hope of salvation: "In silence I wait on him who will be my salvation" (Lam 3:26).

This is the mystical layer into which (via Paul) we are drawn through the Carmelite Rule: working silently and peacefully, I entrust myself to God who shall bring my work to completion, as he desires it. This is the still hope about which the chapter on silence speaks: "In quietness and hope will be your strength" (Is 30:15). My work (no. 21) breathes quietly in God's still presence. But this restful waiting is not only anchored in the chapter on silence. This restful waiting is also secured by the armor of God: "On your head is to be put the helmet of salvation so that you may hope for salvation from the only Savior who saves his people from their sins" (no. 19).

By working to earn our bread, inwardly connected with silence, we practice the primal rhythm of action and contemplation and we are drawn into the secret of God's creation and liberation: "We know that the whole creation has been groaning in labor pains until now" (Rom 8:22). Here also is the hope, which mediates between the steady work of evolution and the final fulfillment: "For in hope [*in spe*] we are saved. Now hope that is seen is not hope. For who hopes for what is seen? But if we hope for what we do not see, we wait for it with patience" (Rom 8:24–25). Here, the contemplative heart of Carmel is beating: "In silence and hope will be your strength" (no. 21). This waiting in the night (see no. 10) is marked by human weakness. But "the Spirit comes to help us in our weakness; for we do not know how to pray as we ought, but the Spirit itself pleads for us with sighs too deep for words" (Rom 8:26).

Recapitulation: The Way of Work

This is the way, holy and good:

Go this way.

Albert concludes number 20, on work, with three biblical references: the holy way (*via sancta*) from Isaiah 35:8; the good way (*via bona*) from Wisdom spirituality; and this is the way: go this way (*haec est via, ambulate in ea*) from Isaiah 30:21. These three biblical references reflect the three steps (apotropaic, social, and mystical) by which Albert draws us into the meaning of work. Meanwhile, it is important that Albert calls work a "way." In doing so he uses a word that is characteristic of all spiritualities. Jewish spirituality signifies itself with terms such as *torah* (instruction in the way of life) and *halacha* (following the way). Christians are considered to be those of the way (Acts 9:22; see also 19:9, 23; 22:4; 24:14, 22). Buddhist spirituality views itself as a vehicle (*yana*) on the road to Enlightenment. Taoism revolves around the *tao*, which means way. Islam has the mystical paths (*tariqas*).[27]

## The Holy Way

When the exiles return from their exile through the desert, then a "highway shall be there and it shall be called the Holy Way" (Is 35:8). The exiles shall not suffer as they make the desert journey (Is 35:3–7). The holy way protects them: "No lion shall be there, you shall come across no ravenous beast" (Is 35:9). The desert is preeminently life threatening. The holy way, coming out of the sanctuary, already welcomes the pilgrims from afar, reaching out to rescue them from the claws of the desert (Is 35:4). The parallel with the apotropaic-demonological character of doing "some work" is not too difficult to discern: work protects the Carmel dwellers and rescues them from the claws of the devil (apotropaic), just as the holy way rescues the pilgrims from the grip of the desert. This apotropaic function is anchored in the armor of God, particularly in the belt of chastity and the tunic of holy ponderings (no. 19), the holy way that, in turn, closely connects with fasting (no. 16) and abstinence (no. 17). Looking forward, we see the same apotropaic function in the chapter on silence in which Albert speaks about the silence during the daytime that protects against violation and destruction, against the incurable falling into harm that lies in too much talking: "Who uses too many words, injures his soul" (no. 21).

## The Good Way

Wisdom spirituality comes clearly to expression in the book of Proverbs. Forty percent of these proverbs are concerned with work: building a house, caring for the land and livestock, safeguarding the city, administering justice, and so forth. Work builds up the community, while idleness or working too much breaks it down. Working with respect is good (Ps 34:9–15) and attracts the good that is wholesome and full of joy: "So shall you walk in the way of the good and follow the paths of the just" (Prv 2:20). This way draws us into the life, which is God himself, the soul and molder of all good. Whoever works within the community is in a creative partnership with God.

This is the community dimension of work into which Albert draws us. Working within the community is good and wholesome, because through it the other is not burdened by our idleness and because it builds up the community that, in its turn, cares for the underlying harmony and regulation. As we have seen, Albert anchors this good way of working in two sides of the Rule. What emerges from the number on silence is how an underlying respect percolates through the communal working and calls into being a culture of justice (no. 21). Via this culture of justice Albert also anchors the good way in the breastplate of justice that finds its heart in the three-in-one love: the love of God, the love of neighbor, and the love of self (no. 19), as well as in the community of goods, which is a sublime expression of this justice in love (no. 12).

## This Is the Way: Walk in It

The third reference is taken from Isaiah 30:21, the same chapter from which Albert draws the phrase about waiting in silence: "In silence and hope is your strength" (Is 30:15). Decisive for Israel is whether it can wait, in trust and continued silence, for God to reveal his plans (Is 30:1–7). But even where Israel goes its own way, God as its teacher will still support it from behind (Is 30:18–20). "And when you turn to the right or when you turn to the left, your ears shall hear a word behind you, saying, 'This is the way; walk in it'" (Is 30:21).

The link with work is clear. To be silently at work is, in all rest and simplicity, to be co-creating with God. God glides silently ahead of us; God is behind us. From behind, you hear the voice of the teacher who says, "Go this way: it is the way." One walks in blind trust, which finds no other support than the quiet attentiveness to one's work, a trust that remains hopeful that ultimately all shall be well. The number on silence boasts of this, as if to say that the Carmelite has no other compass than yearning in mystical stillness for the one who, from beyond all our horizons, is coming to meet us. Our power lies only in quiet expectation (cf. no. 21). That, then, is also the helmet of salvation which must be set on the head, "so that you may hope for salvation from the only Savior" (no. 19). In turn, this hope is anchored in the shield of faith (trust; no. 19), because "faith is the ground from which we hope" (Heb 11:1).

Thus, the collage of biblical references sums up in a nutshell the entire chapter about work (no. 20), which, in turn, appears to be anchored in two sides of the Rule: in the armor of God (nos. 18–19) and in silence (no. 21). This is why, when seeking to understand Carmelite spirituality, I am inclined to ascribe a central place to the chapter on work, which describes participating in God's work in silent expectation. Work, from the perspective of the virtues of the armor, as well as of the silence, looks forward in trust and provides the sense of concreteness and reality that are so characteristic of Carmel. Working is at the same time both ordinary and meaningful. It liberates us from speculation and draws us to the space of God's praxis in which we as laity all participate. Work holds in balance creation and salvation and makes us co-creators with the Spirit, who groans in us with ineffable sighs. Work immerses us in the praying church, the broad place of divine Wisdom that both steers us from behind and beckons us forward beyond our earthly future.

## Notes

1. Different versions and editions of the Carmelite Rule reference chapter and number in various ways. Since the Rule has numbered sections but no "chapters" that also include numbers, in this essay we consistently refer exclusively to "numbers." We follow the division of the Rule's text into twenty-four numbered sections, as established in 1998 by the Order of Carmel (O.Carm.) and the Discalced Carmelites (O.C.D.). In this text, this numbering of the sections of the Rule supercedes all other numberings, of which there are several.

2. For an individual description of each number and the underlying way in which they together form a coherent whole, see Kees Waaijman, *The Mystical Space of Carmel: A Commentary on the Carmelite Rule*, trans. John Vriend (Leuven, Belgium: Peters, 1999).

3. The idea and the formulation are not original. Already, in his letter to the monk Rusticus, St. Jerome says, "Do also some work (*Fac et aliquid operis*)" (Jerome, *Epistolae* [Paris, 1845; Migne, PL 22], 1078). Something similar was also in the Rule of the Canons Regular of the Holy Cross of Mortara, which Albert himself followed: "Some work must always be done (*Aliquid operis semper faciendum est*)" (chap. 57). See Vincenzo Mosca, *Alberto Patriarca di Gerusalemme. Tiempo, Vita, Opera* (Rome: Edizioni Carmelitane, 1996), 592.

4. This strange combination (*aliquid* in singular asyndetic connection with the plural *opera*) we find in the bull *Quae honorem* of Innocent III of 1247 and in the Rule's text of *Decem libri* of Ribot in the Arsenal manuscript (see Paul Chandler, *The Rule of Saint Albert* (Melbourne, Australia: Carmelite Communications, 2015). This text, which as *lectio difficilor* has the preference, in reception was changed to *aliquid operis*, the formulation we already encountered in the letter of Jerome and in the Rule which Albert himself followed, and that, in conclusion, we find in the accepted copy of the Rule and in the edition of *Decem libri* of 1680.

5. See Patrick Mullins, *St. Albert of Jerusalem and the Roots of Carmelite Spirituality* (Rome: Edizioni Carmelitane, 2012), 226.

6. Nicolaus Gallus, *Ignea Sagitta* (1270), VIII.

7. In 1993 the Carmelite General (O.Carm.) estimated that a total of 52,000 friars and nuns had made vows in his order since its inception. That figure does not include members of the Order of Discalced Carmelites (O.C.D.), or the thousands of lay members (secular Carmelites) of both branches.

8. Gerrit Achterberg, *Verzamelde gedichten* (Amsterdam: Singel, 1967), 607.

9. At this point, the text of the Rule no longer concerns itself with the second person singular, about which the source text speaks (*Fac et aliquid operis*), but is expressly concerned with the second person plural (*vobis*). Albert has an eye for community.

10. See Mullins, *St. Albert of Jerusalem*, 232–33.

11. "Démon," in *Dictionnaire de Spiritualité*, III (Paris, G. Beauchesne, 1957), 114–238.

12. Ibid., 189–223.

13. Ibid., 217–18.

14. See Mullins, *St. Albert of Jerusalem*, 226–27.

15. For a summary, see Kees Waaijman, *Spirituality: Forms, Foundations, Methods* (Leuven, Belgium: Peeters, 2002), 435–46.

16. "A skin for a skin" is an expression derived from trading in animal skins. At the conclusion of the negotiations there must be

an agreement about a similar value of exchange: a skin for a skin (*Hebräisches und Aramäisches Lexikon zum Alten Testament* [Leiden, Netherlands: Brill, 1983], 759).

17. John Cassian, *Collationes* 20.1.

18. Augustine, *De opere monachorum* (Paris, 1841; Migne, PL 40), 547–82.

19. See John Cassian, *Institutiones* 1.10.7–8.

20. John Cassian, *Collationes* 18.1.

21. Carolyn Bynum, *Docere verbo et exemplo: An Aspect of Twelfth-Century Spirituality* (Missoula, Mont.: Scholars Press, 1979), 82–109.

22. William of St-Thierry, *Epistola ad fratres de Monte Dei*, in *Opera didactica et spiritualia*, Stanislaus Ceglar and Paul Verdeyen, eds (Turnhout, Belgium: Brepols, 2003) 1; 24; 31.

23. William of St-Thierry, *Tractatus de contemplando Deo*, in Ibid., 12; *Epistola*, in Ibid., 113: *Meditativae Orationes*, in Jacques Hourlier, ed. (Paris, Cerf, 1985), 4, 2; 5, 1.

24. William of St-Thierry, *Expositio super cantico canticorum*, Paul Verdeyen et al., eds. (Turnhout, Belgium: Brepols, 1997), 193.

25. William of St-Thierry, *Epistola* 39.

26. In respect to this eschatological unrest, see M. J. J. Menken, "Paradise Regained or Still Lost? Eschatology and Disorderly Behavior in 2 Thessalonians," *New Testament Studies* 38 (1992): 271–89.

27. For a description of the different spiritual ways, see Waaijman, *Spirituality*, 123–37.

# PART II

---

*Wisdom and Prophetic Hope
in John of the Cross*

# St. John of the Cross:
## *A Spirituality of Wisdom*

### DANIEL CHOWNING, O.C.D.

UNTIL I RESEARCHED THE TOPIC for this essay, I didn't realize the immensity and depth of the theme of wisdom, the breadth of its evolution in Scripture, and the questions it raises. Since ancient times, so many human beings have been captivated by the search for this mysterious "wisdom." Our late Carmelite brother and renowned scholar of biblical Wisdom literature Father Roland Murphy wrote, "Wisdom has many faces."[1] This is definitely true in the writings of St. John of the Cross.

The introductory part of my essay provides a brief overview of the theme of wisdom in John's works, as well as his biblical sources for the theme. In no way will this be exhaustive. While wisdom is not the most all-encompassing theme in John's works, its presence is nonetheless extensive and profound. In the second and longest part of the essay, I will enter into the theme of wisdom through John's presentation of Jesus Christ as the incarnate and pure wisdom of God. John offers many avenues and approaches to this in his works, but this is the one I have found most fruitful for reflection. Finally, the concluding pages of the essay will explore how these insights can change our own ways of praying and living.

## Wisdom in John's Works

The word "wisdom" appears 207 times in John's writings. If one adds to this number the references in his first redaction of *The Spiritual Canticle* and *The Living Flame of Love*, it rises to 286.[2] Scriptural quotations from the Wisdom books—that is, Job, Proverbs, Ecclesiastes, the Wisdom of Solomon, Sirach, and the Psalms—abound in his explanations of the journey to union with God through love. John uses a rich variety of descriptive adjectives and attributes to describe wisdom: "the abyss of wisdom" (N 2.17.6); "loving light and wisdom" (N 2.12.2); "God's wisdom" (N 2.12.2); "divine wisdom" (N 2.17.3); "secret wisdom" (N 2.12.2); "hidden wisdom"; "obscure wisdom" (N 2.16.10); "interior wisdom" (N 2.17.3); "wondrous wisdom" (N 2.17.3); wisdom as a "secret ladder" (N 2.18.2); and wisdom as "a science of love" (N 2.18.5).[3]

John's understanding of wisdom has a strongly scriptural character. The wisdom that he knows and experiences transcends limited human knowledge with its worldly rhetoric, intellectual reasoning, and earth-bound criteria for discernment. God is Wisdom, a God who reaches out to us in love, creating, re-creating, drawing, and inviting us to God's self, which is our divine Source of true love and meaning. In *The Dark Night*, it is Wisdom who purifies us and unifies us. In *The Living Flame of Love*, this is the work of the Holy Spirit, the Spirit of the Bridegroom.

Early on in *The Ascent of Mount Carmel*, we meet Sophia, "Lady Wisdom,"[4] inviting the poor who are enslaved by their disordered relationships with the riches of this world to find in her lasting riches (A 1.8). Sophia reappears indirectly in *The Spiritual Canticle* where God, like a mother, "offers the soul the breast of his love in which he teaches her wisdom" (C 27.3).

Divine Wisdom is also evidenced in God's manner of communicating spiritual goods to us. In chapter 17 of book two of *The Ascent of Mount Carmel*, John explains how God, "who is all wise," takes us as we are. With order, gentleness, and according to our human mode of receiving spiritual goods, God begins by communicating spiritual good through the senses and then gradually brings us to the spiritual wisdom that is of the Spirit and incomprehensible to the senses. John asserts that he bases his insight on the *Book of Wisdom*: "This comes from the Holy Spirit in the Book of Wisdom: the Wisdom of God, though she touches from one end to the other, disposes all things gently" (A 2.17.2).

In *The Spiritual Canticle* John uses the Genesis story of creation and fall to describe how wisdom is also seen in God's knowledge of how to draw good out of evil. Human nature was corrupted in our first parents under the tree, but under the tree of the cross humanity was restored and brought to life. John concludes, "In such a way God manifests the degrees of his wisdom: he knows how to draw good out of evil so wisely and beautifully, and to ordain to a greater good what was the cause of evil" (C 23.5).

## Biblical Sources

We cannot be certain whether John did special studies on biblical Wisdom literature, but we do know that the Bible permeated the atmosphere of John's time. In the University of Salamanca, where he studied theology, the question of Scripture and its interpretation was a major concern. It appears that John attended Scripture classes for only a year.[5] Yet his writings give evidence that the Scriptures impregnated his mind and heart, for quotations and allusions flow abundantly from his pen on every page.

John immersed himself in the Word of God from many sources. The constant and repetitive reading of the Scriptures in the liturgy, and in particular the Divine Office, saturated him with the Psalms as well as with biblical commentaries by St. Bernard, Pope St. Gregory the Great, and St. Thomas Aquinas. Scripture was also read daily during meals in the refectory. The almost daily recitation of the office of the Blessed Virgin Mary exposed him to The Song of Songs. Another major source was a German Dominican, Helwic Teutónico de Erfurt, who compiled three short works with extensive biblical, philosophical, patristic, and theological references. Among the various authors Helwic quoted were writings from St. Bernard, St. Augustine, and St. Thomas Aquinas.[6] The "Moralia" of St. Gregory the Great (his "Commentaries on the Book of Job") had an especially strong impact on John.[7]

Several sources testify to John's assiduous reading of the Bible and how it influenced his writings. John's companion Friar Juan Evangelista asserted, "But among all of these books and of the many other things he wrote, and of his conferences, never did I see him open a book, nor did he have one in his cell except for the Bible and the *Flos Sanctorum*."[8] Another companion recalls how John read his Bible during his long journeys. "When the journeys were long, he traveled on his mule with its saddle and ordinarily he was seated reading his Bible."[9] There is also an often-quoted incident in Lisbon when the friars went to visit a nun renowned for bearing the wounds of Christ, but John preferred to stay on the beach reading his Bible.[10]

These testimonies give evidence of John's love for Scripture. "Meditating on the Law of the Lord day and night," as the Rule of St. Albert asked of him, opened him to riches of divine wisdom.

## Jesus, the Wisdom of God

Wisdom is a divine gift. It is God's self-communication—reaching out to us in love; drawing and inviting us; re-creating, purifying, and healing us; and gradually transforming us into Wisdom's Beauty, Jesus Christ the Wisdom of God. Its most resplendent face is Jesus Christ, the Son of God, incarnate Wisdom whom John names "Pure Wisdom" (A 2.15.4). For John, the incarnation of the Word of God and all that this profound and incomprehensible mystery tells us about God and its impact on human beings and creation are the doorway to the wisdom of God. It is by contemplating Jesus the Christ, who is God's self-revelation and the "Gift" par excellence, that we enter most deeply into John's wisdom spirituality. All the expressions of God's wisdom are mirrored in the face of Christ.

John explicitly identifies Wisdom with the Son of God, the second person of the Blessed Trinity, in several places in his works. If we wish to know God's truths and wisdom, John directs us to fasten our eyes on Christ. "If you desire me to declare some secret truths or events to you, fix your eyes only on him and you will discern hidden in him the most secret mysteries and wisdom and wonders of God, as my Apostle proclaims, 'In the Son of God are hidden all treasures of the wisdom and knowledge of God'" (A 2.22.6). Indeed, Christ, Wisdom of God, is the soul's end and goal: "If these souls would eliminate these impediments and veils, and live in pure nakedness and poverty of spirit, their soul in its simplicity and purity would be immediately transformed into simple and pure Wisdom, the Son of God" (A 2.15.4).

Knowing that the God of love created all that exists, the lovesick soul in *The Spiritual Canticle* turns to nature in her search for a sign of her Beloved's presence. She cries out, "O woods and thickets, planted by the hand of my Beloved! O green meadow, coated bright with flowers, tell me, has he passed by you?" Nature replies,

> Pouring out a thousand graces,
>
> he passed these groves in haste;
>
> and having looked at them,
>
> clothed them in beauty. (C 4)

Creation's response signifies that just as the *ruach* (the breath of God) hovered over the waters of chaos and created everything out of nothing, God as overflowing love and beauty created everything that exists with "remarkable ease and brevity" and left a trace of who God is. In this "passing" by, God looked at everything God created and clothed it with beauty. God, says John, did all this "through his own Wisdom, the Word, his only begotten Son" (C 5.1).

Moreover, not only did God pass by and, by looking at all that exists, imprint it with the figure of God's Son, but also God poured God's self out in creation and even took on human nature. "The Word became flesh and dwelt among us" (Jn 1:14). When God took on human nature, God imparted the image of his Son to natural being, thus elevating it in the beauty of God (C 5.4). All creation, therefore, is sacramental and reflects the beauty and wisdom of God in Jesus Christ. In the incarnation and through the glory of the resurrection, which is the new creation redeemed and transformed in Jesus Christ, God clothed creation and human beings in beauty and dignity (C 5.4). This means that an image of Christ, the Beloved, is woven into the very molecular structure of nature and of human beings.

God becoming flesh in the person of Jesus Christ created an indelible imprint on human nature. By virtue of the incarnation and resurrection of Jesus the Christ, an irrevocable union has taken place between God and humankind. In Jesus, incarnate Wisdom, we contemplate God's self-communicating and outpouring love and our divine vocation to become divinized human beings. This is expressed poetically in John's "Romances." The "Romances" are a meditation on the incarnation, a theme that captivated his mind and heart. John writes in section 4,

Those higher ones possessed
the Bridegroom in gladness;
The lower in hope, founded
on the faith he infused in them,
telling them that one day
he would exalt them,
and that he would lift them
up from their lowness so that no one
could mock it anymore;
for he would make himself wholly like them,
and he would come to them and dwell with them;
and God would be man
and man would be God,
and he would walk with them
and eat and drink with them;
and he himself would be
with them continually
until the consummation of this world,
when, joined, they would rejoice in eternal song;
for he was the Head of this bride of his
to whom all the members of the just would be joined,
who form the body of the bride.
He would take her tenderly in his arms
and there give her his love;
and when they were thus one,

he would lift her to the Father
where God's very joy would be her joy.
for as the Father and the Son
and he who proceeds from them
live in one another,
so it would be with the bride;
for, taken wholly into God,
she will live the life of God.

John tells us that by the incarnation and resurrection of
Jesus the Christ we bear within us "a sketch of love which is
an image of the Beloved, the Son of God" (C 11.12). Our
divine vocation is to complete this sketch, that is, to grow
in the image and likeness of Christ, or to express it another
way, to grow in Christ consciousness.

## Ever-Deepening Union

In stanza 36 of *The Spiritual Canticle*, the soul sings of her
intimate loving union with the Beloved. After having passed
through many trials and temptations, she experiences freedom and surrenders to her Beloved. She addresses her prayer
to the Beloved:

Let us rejoice, Beloved,
and let us go forth to behold ourselves in your beauty
to the mountain and to the hill,
to where the pure water flows,
and further, deep into the thicket.

Among the petitions to the Beloved, she asks to enter deeper into "the thicket." The "thicket" signifies two things: (1) "the splendid works and profound judgments of God in which there is abundant wisdom" (C 36.9); and (2) the cross, which is the doorway to God's wisdom (C 36.13).

The loving soul longs to enter deeper into divine wisdom, and the highest and most "savory wisdom" is the mysteries of the incarnation. The soul desires to know the "sublime mysteries of God and human beings" revealed in the incarnation. "These mysteries are exalted in wisdom." When John writes of "the mysteries of the Incarnation," he means more than just the moment when Jesus took flesh in the womb of the Virgin Mary. The incarnation was realized in the whole life of Christ: his birth; his childhood when he grew in wisdom and grace; his hidden years in Nazareth in the loving care of Mary and Joseph; his work as a carpenter; his public ministry; his healings, exorcisms, and teachings; and his passion, death, and resurrection. The most decisive event was his death when he shared fully in the poverty, suffering, and death of the human existence.[11]

In stanza 37 of *The Spiritual Canticle*, the soul continues to express her deepest desires. She desires to go to the high caverns of the rock, for this rock is Christ. "The high caverns of this rock are the sublime, exalted, and deep mysteries of God's wisdom in Christ, in the hypostatic union of the human nature with the divine Word, and in the corresponding union of human beings with God, and the mystery of the harmony between God's justice and mercy with respect to the manifestations of his judgments in the salvation of the human race" (C 37.3).

Let us pause here for a moment and reflect on the sublime mysteries of these caverns into which the ardent soul desires to enter. Looking back at the "Romances," we see that for John, God's longing for all eternity was to give his Son a bride who would love the Son and share a communion of life with them. "My Son, I wish to give you a bride who will love you. Because of you she will deserve to share our company and eat at our table; the same bread I eat, that she may know the good I have in such a Son; and rejoice with me in your grace and fullness" (R 3).

The incarnation reveals to us God's love affair with humanity. In Jesus, we have Emmanuel, "God with us." In Jesus, God poured God's love into creation to dwell with us, walk with us, eat and drink with us, struggle and suffer with us, and even die with us; to rise for us and to be continually with us until the consummation of the world; finally, to take us tenderly in his arms and there to give us his love, and then to lift us to God where God's joy will be our joy. Incarnate Wisdom came to take us wholly into God and to live the life of God.

God's outpouring and holy love in Jesus has irrevocably changed human nature. All of life is charged with the divine presence, and every human being now possesses a beauty and dignity beyond compare because God has entered into a marriage with us. As we have seen, God entered this marriage not only with human beings but also with all creation. Again in the "Romances," the world is depicted as the palace where the wedding between Christ the Bridegroom and humans takes place. God entered into this weak and frail "flesh" (*sarx*) to reveal to us God's passionate love for us, to divinize us so we can share fully in the Trinitarian life of love. "For God so loved the world that he gave his only Son, so that everyone who believes in him may not perish but may have eternal life" (Jn 3:16).

The phrase "For God so loved the world" is especially striking. God loved *this* world, with all its beauty and ugliness, joys and sorrows, life and death, riches and poverty, goodness and evil. Therefore, God's wisdom expressed in the incarnation of Jesus Christ is God's love affair with humanity and our loving union with God through Jesus Christ. As St. Paul expresses it, "This is not a wisdom of this age. But we speak of God's wisdom, secret and hidden, which God decreed before the ages for our glory. None of the rulers of this age understood this: for if they had, they would not have crucified the Lord of glory. But, as it is written, 'What no eye has seen, nor ear heard, nor the human heart conceived, what God has prepared for those who love him'" (1 Cor 2:7–9).

John tells us that "these mysteries of Christ are deep in wisdom and contain many secrets concerning the children of the earth" (C 36.3). "There is much to fathom in Christ, for he is like an abundant mine with many recesses of treasures, so that however deep individuals may go they never reach the end or bottom, but rather in every recess find new veins and riches everywhere. On this account St. Paul said of Christ: '*In Christ dwell hidden all treasures and wisdom*' (Col. 2:3)" (C 36.3).

# The Thicket of the Cross

To fathom these deep mysteries of Christ and the divine wisdom they contain implies that we enter into a process of spiritual transformation and allow them to transform our lives. "The soul cannot enter these caverns or reach these treasures if, as we said, she does not first pass over to the divine wisdom through the straits of exterior and interior suffering. For one cannot reach in this life what is attainable of these mysteries of Christ without having suffered much and without having received numerous intellectual and sensible favors from God, and without having undergone much spiritual activity; for all these favors are interior to the wisdom of the mysteries of Christ in that they serve as preparations for the coming to this wisdom" (C 37.4). "The gate entering into these riches of his wisdom is the cross, which is narrow, and few desire to enter by it, but many desire the delights from entering there" (C 36.13). The gate leading to these mysteries is the "thicket of the cross."

A question arises: Why the cross? John answers that it is because in Jesus crucified we contemplate the radical self-giving love of God. As Pope Benedict XVI wrote in his encyclical *God Is Love*, "By contemplating the pierced side of Christ, we can understand: God is Love. It is there that truth can be contemplated."[12] The cross reveals the depth of God's love and the extent to which God entered into solidarity with our human condition. But the cross is not simply an event that took place at one moment in history or a theme for pious meditation to produce devotional sentiments. It is a mystery we live. We have to enter into the paschal mystery of Jesus Christ, which is a living, dynamic mystery that takes place in our own flesh and blood. St. Paul tells us that our life is in Christ. At our baptism we were plunged into the life, death, and resurrection of Jesus Christ and embarked upon a path of dying and rising with Christ, allowing his saving death and resurrection to transform our lives (Rom 6:3–4).

This becomes clear in chapter 7 of book two of *The Ascent*, where John places before us Jesus crucified, our "model and light" (A 2.7.9). John explains that Christ is the narrow gate to life and few desire to enter through it. To enter through this gate is to pattern our lives on Jesus crucified. The image of Jesus crucified is far from dolorous or the exaltation of suffering; rather, it is one of self-giving love, a love that empties itself completely so that others may live. Jesus crucified is an icon of God's compassionate love for humankind and the power of God at work in human weakness and poverty, bringing new life out of suffering and death. In his outpouring love on the cross, in supreme emptiness and poverty, Jesus performed the greatest work of salvation, the reconciliation of God with humanity. Jesus' entire life was one of transcending self-gratification and self-glorification for the sake of his mission of compassionate love and dedication to his Abba. His love literally emptied him of everything on both the sensitive and spiritual levels.

Herein lies a wisdom that is not of this world. "Jews demand signs and Greeks desire wisdom," Paul tells us, "but we proclaim Christ crucified, a stumbling block to Jews and foolishness to Gentiles. Christ the power and the wisdom of God. For God's foolishness is wiser than human wisdom, and God's weakness is stronger than human strength" (1 Cor 1:23–25). John tells us that we have to enter into the paschal mystery of Jesus Christ and undergo a process of divestment of our false securities, distorted way of seeing life, and disordered selfish desires and behavior in order to receive God's wisdom.

How, then, can we enter "the thicket of the cross" that is the gateway to wisdom? As noted earlier, wisdom is a divine gift. It is God's self-communicating love—purifying, re-creating, and healing us, and gradually transforming us into wisdom's beauty, Jesus Christ the Wisdom of God. Neither human effort nor reason alone can bring about the transformation required for divine wisdom's inflow. We are poor beggars who stand in need of God's loving wisdom. We must be like King Solomon who prayed for God's wisdom: "O God of my ancestors and Lord of mercy, give me wisdom that sits by your throne. With you is wisdom, she who knows your works and was present when you made the world; she understands what is pleasing in your sight. Send her forth from the holy heavens that she may labor at my side, and that I may learn what is pleasing to you" (Wis 9:1–18).

God's wisdom must dispel the darkness of our ignorance, tear away the superficial veils that prevent us from penetrating into the deeper meaning of life. Loving Wisdom must circumcise our heart, that is, remove the protective layers of insensitivity and selfishness that block the flow of love in our lives. We have to allow ourselves to be led into Sophia's darkness, by an unknown path, in order to grasp the light

of true wisdom. We have to open ourselves to God's loving
and secret wisdom bestowed through infused contemplation, and allow God to hollow out all that prevents us from
living the life of Christ. Fundamental to John's doctrine is
our absolute dependence on God's transforming grace in
our lives.

## The Purifying Fire of Wisdom

In *The Ascent of Mount Carmel* and *The Dark Night*, wisdom
is synonymous with infused contemplation. Infused contemplation is "secret and loving wisdom." (N 2.5.1). "It calls
this dark contemplation 'secret' since, as we mentioned, contemplation is mystical theology, which theologians call secret
wisdom and which St. Thomas says is communicated and
infused in the soul through love" (N 2.17.2). "The wisdom of
this contemplation is the language of God" (N 2.17.4).

John refers to contemplation as "secret wisdom" (N
2.18.1); "loving wisdom" (N 2.12.2); "interior wisdom" (N
2.17.3); "mystical wisdom" (N 2.17.6); and the "abyss of
wisdom" (N 2.17.6). Infused wisdom is a "secret ladder" (N
2.17.1). It is "secret" for two main reasons. First, it is beyond
what we can grasp by our senses or by any clear image or idea.
Second, it is an ineffable experience; it is difficult to give it
expression. It is a wisdom that is communicated directly to
the spirit. Divine Wisdom is a path of unknowing (N 2.17.2).

God's wisdom is "loving wisdom." John says that God's
wisdom leads us to "the heart of the science of love" (N
2.17.6). Wisdom and love are inseparable. Wisdom leads
to love, and love leads to the deepest wisdom. Because

this is loving wisdom, it ushers us into the crucible of love where we participate in the dying and rising of Jesus Christ by surrendering to the purifying flames of God's love who illumines, purges, cleanses, and heals our sinfulness, imperfections, and deeply rooted emotional and spiritual wounds. John says, "On this earth we are cleansed and illumined only by love" (N 2.12.1). He writes,

> Jeremiah shows clearly that the soul is purged by the illumination of this fire of loving wisdom (for God never bestows mystical wisdom without love, since love itself infuses it) where he says: He sent fire into my bones and instructed me [Lam. 1:13]. And David says that God's wisdom is silver tried in the fire [Ps 12:6], that is, in the purgative fire of love. This contemplation infuses both love and wisdom in each soul according to its capacity and necessity. It illumines the soul and purges it of its ignorance, as the Wise Man declares it did to him [Sir 51:25–27]. (N 2.12.2)

We surrender to the paschal mystery of Jesus Christ. We die to the "old self" in order to rise to new life in Christ.

> First we can understand that the very loving light and wisdom into which the soul will be transformed is what in the beginning purges and prepares it, just as fire that transforms the wood by incorporating it into itself is what first prepares it for transformation.
>
> Second, we discern that the experience of these sufferings does not derive from this wisdom—for as the Wise Man says: All good things come to the soul together with

her [Wis 7:11]—but from the soul's own weakness and imperfection. Without this purgation it cannot receive the divine light, sweetness, and delight of wisdom, just as the log of wood until prepared cannot be transformed by the fire that is applied to it. And this is why the soul suffers so intensely. *Ecclesiasticus* confirms our assertion by telling what he suffered in order to be united with wisdom and enjoy it: My soul wrestled for her, and my entrails were disturbed in acquiring her; therefore, shall I possess a good possession [Sir 51:25, 29]. (N 2.10.3–4)

Wisdom is a purifying and unifying fire. John's description of Wisdom's flame is identical to his description of passive purification in stanza 1 of *The Living Flame of Love* where the Holy Spirit disposes the soul for divine union and transformation in God through love by first wounding the soul, destroying and consuming its bad habits. Loving Wisdom is the wounding, purifying, healing, transforming, and glorifying fire of the Holy Spirit that comes to us in prayer and in the myriad events of daily life. Herein lies the challenge. We have to make a choice and take a plunge into our depths and allow loving Wisdom to do her purifying work within us.

The purifying flames of Wisdom are not reserved to periods of formal, private prayer. It is also active in the concreteness of human life. Wisdom meets us and purges us in the combat of daily life: the delights, pains, and stresses of relationships, illnesses, financial setbacks, failures, struggles with depression or some other emotional wound. Suffering, trials, and temptations can be the source of deep wisdom if we are open to learn from what happens to us and embrace our suffering in faith, hope, and love—as best we can. It is like the old saying, "If you've never been tempted, what do you really know?"

Not only is wisdom "secret," but also it is a ladder of love. Mystical wisdom infused in contemplation purifies, heals, enlarges, and transforms our capacity to love. In chapters 19 and 20 of book two of *The Dark Night*, John outlines the ten steps of this ladder of love that he identifies as a science of love. Wisdom enlightens us to our selfishness and radical need for God's intervention, sets us on fire with a love that purifies and transforms our capacity to love. Step by step, little by little, the purification and healing brought about by the Living Flame of God's Spirit transforms our selfish love into unselfish love. John tells us that this journey up the ladder of love is one of ascending and descending; in other words, it has its ups and downs, moments of light and darkness, growth and failure. There are times of prosperity followed by times of tempests and trials, moments of abundance and tranquility followed by misery and torment (N 2.18.3). These ascending and descending experiences are the fodder for knowledge of self and of God and the grist for the mill of wisdom. John insists that growth in love is impossible to us naturally. It is pure gift infused within us secretly. "God alone measures and weighs it" (N 2.18.5).

## Silence, Seedbed of Wisdom

What can we do concretely to dispose ourselves for the inflow of the loving wisdom of contemplation in our lives?

In *The Sayings of Light and Love* John tells us quite simply, Be still; be silent; surrender gently to the Spirit. "The Father spoke one Word, which was His Son, and this Word he speaks always in eternal silence, and in silence must it be heard by the soul" (SLL 100). Silence and stillness prepare the ground for the birth and development of wisdom. "Wisdom enters through love, silence and mortification" (SLL 109). "What we need most in order to make progress is to be silent before this great God with our appetite and tongue, for the language he hears best is silent love" (SLL 132).

For John, silence is not the mere absence of verbal communication or exterior noise. The silence John recommends to us is a tranquil listening of the heart, a loving attention to the Beloved, openness to the divine presence in the here and now, and a gentle and trusting surrender, letting God be God without trying to manage and control our spiritual growth. In *The Living Flame*, he encourages the passivity and stillness required for infused Wisdom.

> It is impossible for this highest wisdom and language of God, which is contemplation, to be received in anything less than a spirit that is silent and detached from discursive knowledge and gratification. Bring it to as complete a withdrawal and solitude as possible, for the more solitude it obtains and the nearer it approaches this idle tranquility the more abundantly will the spirit of divine wisdom be infused in its soul. This wisdom is loving, tranquil, solitary, peaceful, mild, and an inebriator of the spirit. The reason is that this wisdom is communicated without the soul's activity. (F 2.37–38)

Although this text refers to the passivity required of a person who is graced with the gift of infused contemplation, it is also a helpful and important teaching for all stages of prayer and life because it impresses upon us that growth in loving wisdom is ultimately God's work, not ours. It also teaches us that the seeds of wisdom already live within us. We must become like the farmer in the Gospel parable who planted seeds in his field, and day after day he went to bed and got up, and all the while the seeds were growing without his knowing how.

We come before God with empty hands, not laden with merits, actions, or penances, but with hands open and empty, as a chalice, to receive the love of God, the gratuitous gift of God's wisdom, who gives more than we can ever desire.

In chapter 15 of book two of *The Ascent of Mount Carmel*, John recommends practicing "pacification of the soul," that is, making our hearts and minds calm, peaceful, inactive, and empty of desire, especially when discursive meditation becomes difficult. If we can remain in God's presence with a loving attention and tranquil intellect, even though we seem to be idle, "little by little and very soon the divine calm and peace with a wondrous, sublime knowledge of God, enveloped in divine love," will be infused into our hearts (A 2.15.5). John assures us that pacification of the soul is no small accomplishment, especially during those moments when loving Wisdom shows us our woundedness and sinfulness, and when doubts, trials, and temptations overwhelm us. Interior silence requires grace and effort. Ultimately, silence is the fruit of God's grace, but there is an ascetical dimension that calls for a decision to enter into silence and to cultivate a quiet heart and mind. We do this when we make a commitment to carve out space for contemplative prayer in our daily lives.

The cultivation of a quiet and peaceful heart also extends to our relationships. "Keep spiritually tranquil in a loving attentiveness to God, and when it is necessary to speak, let it be with the same calm and peace" (SLL 82). "Ignoring the imperfections of others, preserving silence and a continual communion with God will eradicate great imperfections from the soul" (SLL 118).

## Seeking the Beloved in Faith, Hope, and Love

Disposing our hearts for the inflow of divine wisdom requires more than a passive stance before God. Entering into the paschal mystery of Jesus Christ has an active as well as passive dimension. On both the personal and collective level, we have to actively seek Christ by doing something. In stanza 3 of *The Spiritual Canticle*, John launches a Gospel challenge. He reminds us that for "the attainment of God it is not enough to pray with the heart and tongue or receive favors from others, but that together with this a person must through her or his own efforts do everything possible" (C 3.2). In other words, relationship with God requires more than devotional words and sensible spiritual consolations. As Jesus teaches us in the Gospel, "Not everyone who says to me, 'Lord, Lord,' will enter the kingdom of heaven, but only one who does the will of my Father in heaven" (Mt 7:21). John writes,

> Many desire that God cost them no more than words, and even these they say badly. They desire to do for him scarcely anything that would cost them something. Some would not even rise from a place of their liking if they were not to receive some delight from God in their mouth and heart. They will not even take one step to mortify themselves and lose some of their satisfactions, comforts, and useless desires. Yet, unless they go in search for God, they will not find him, no matter how much they cry out for him. (C 3.2)

To attain God we have to move out of our comfort zone, go out of ourselves and actively seek to love the Beloved by striving to live the theological virtues of faith, hope, and love. Our search for the Beloved is expressed by living the Gospel values of self-giving love and service in our homes, in the streets, and wherever there is human need. In this way we are emptied out in the give and take of daily concrete existence. By getting up and actively seeking Christ through these means we find Wisdom. "When the soul has departed from the house of her own will and the bed of her own satisfaction, outside she will find divine Wisdom, the Son of God, her Spouse" (C 3.3).

There are two texts from *The Spiritual Canticle* to which I find myself returning again and again. Both relate to how we enter the "thicket of the cross" by patterning our lives on Jesus crucified. The first comes from stanza 13 where John tells us that God does not place his grace and love in us except according to our desire and love. We need to nourish our longing and love for God. If we desire to truly love God, we must strive not to fail in this love, for by our love we will "induce" God to further love and find delight in us. John becomes quite specific in how we strive not to fail in God's love: "And to acquire this charity, one ought to practice what St. Paul taught: Charity is patient, is kind, is not envious, does no evil, does not become proud, is not ambitious, seeks not its own, does not become disturbed, thinks no evil, rejoices not in iniquity, but rejoices in the truth, suffers all things (that are to be suffered), believes all things (that must be believed), hopes all things, and endures all things (that are in accord with charity) [1 Cor 13:4–7]" (C 13.12). There is nothing esoteric in this teaching. Love is expressed concretely through our patience, kindness, striving to let go of envy and pride, seeking to do good to others, suffering, and bearing all things in faith, hope, and charity.

The second text comes from stanza 29 of *The Spiritual Canticle* and illustrates further what it means to pattern our lives on Jesus crucified. The stanza reads,

> If, then, I am no longer
> seen or found on the common,
> you will say that I am lost;
> that stricken by love,
> I lost myself and was found.

What does it mean to be lost for John of the Cross? His own explanation is clear:

Few spiritual persons reach such daring and determination in their works. Though some do act in this way, and are considered far advanced, they never lose themselves entirely in some matters, whether worldly or natural, and never execute works for Christ with perfection and nakedness of spirit; they think about what others will say or how their work will appear. Since these persons are not lost to themselves in their work, they cannot declare: "You will say that I am lost." They are still ashamed to confess Christ before others by their works. Because of their human respect they do not live entirely in Christ. (C 29.8)

"To be lost," therefore, is to be "stricken by love for Jesus Christ" and thus to have that daring and determination to confess Christ before others by our works, fearless in the face of rejection and misunderstanding. The key phrase is "to live entirely in Christ." We live in Christ by nourishing an intimate loving relationship with him and proclaiming God's love by our works of compassion, forgiveness, and concern for the marginalized and poor, and by standing up for the values of justice, peace, and reconciliation in whatever way we can. This may definitely lead us into "the thicket of the cross," where we experience misunderstanding and rejection. To proclaim Christ this way requires inner freedom to transcend our false securities and inordinate need for self-glorification and to live for Christ alone and the values of the kingdom of God.

The one who walks in love of God seeks neither gain nor reward, but seeks only to lose with the will all things and self for God; and this loss the lover judges to be a gain. Thus, it is, as St. Paul asserts: *Mori lucrum* [Phil 1:21], that is, my death for Christ is my gain, spiritually, and of all things and of myself. Consequently, the soul declares: I was found. The soul that does not know how to lose herself does not find herself but rather loses herself, as Our Lord teaches in the Gospel: *Those who desire to gain their soul shall lose it, and those who lose it for my sake shall gain it* [Mt 16:25]. (C 29.11)

It must be emphasized that, although we have our part to play in disposing ourselves for the gift of divine wisdom, there is no way we can grow in an intimate relationship with the Beloved or realize the interior freedom to confess Christ by our frail human efforts. In the midst of all our efforts to live the Gospel, we require the infusion of God's love that comes through contemplation. "A soul enkindled with love is a gentle, meek, humble and patient soul. A soul that is hard because of self-love grows harder. O good Jesus, if you do not soften it, it will ever continue in its natural hardness" (SLL 29–31).

# Conclusion: Transformed into the Beauty of Wisdom

I begin my conclusion with one of John's *Sayings of Light and Love*: "The Lord has always revealed to mortals the treasures of his wisdom and his spirit, but now that the face of evil bares itself more and more, so does the Lord bare his treasures more" (SLL 1).

What are the treasures of divine wisdom and spirit that God has always revealed to mortals and continues to bare? The treasures of God's wisdom and spirit are found in the Word made flesh, Jesus Christ, incarnate Wisdom, the pure Wisdom of God. "Fix your eyes on him," John writes, "and you will discern hidden in him the most secret mysteries, and wisdom, and wonders of God, as my Apostle proclaims, 'In the Son of God are hidden all the treasures of the wisdom and knowledge of God' [Col. 2:3]" (A 2.22.6)

The "most savory" of all God's mysteries is the incarnation of Jesus Christ. The wisdom of the incarnation is God's outpouring love for humanity revealed in the Word made flesh who took on our human nature and endowed it with dignity and beauty. The incarnation is the revelation of God's love affair with humanity, God's desire to bring about a communion of life between God and creation and every human person. "To comprehend with all the saints what is the breadth and length and height and depth, and to know the love of Christ that surpasses knowledge," is the greatest wisdom for which we can hope (Eph 3:18–19). It is into these caverns of mysteries that we are called. However, entering into these caverns of the mysteries of God's love revealed in Christ implies that we enter into a transformation process whereby divine wisdom gradually transforms us little by little into the beauty of divine Wisdom himself, Jesus Christ, the Son of God.

In stanza 36 of *The Spiritual Canticle*, the loving soul prays thus: "Let us go forth to behold ourselves in your beauty." The loving soul asks to be transformed into the beauty of divine wisdom and to resemble the beauty of the Son of God.

"Let us go forth to behold ourselves in your beauty." This means: Let us so act that by means of this loving activity we may attain to the vision of ourselves in your beauty in eternal life. That is: That I be so transformed in your beauty that we may be alike in beauty, and both behold ourselves in your beauty, possessing then your very beauty; this, in such a way that each looking at the other may see in the other their own beauty, since both are your beauty alone, I begin absorbed in your beauty, hence, I shall see you in your beauty, and you will see yourself in me in your beauty; that I may resemble you in your beauty, and you resemble me in your beauty, and my beauty be your beauty and your beauty my beauty; wherefore I shall be you in your beauty, and you will be me in your beauty, because your very beauty will be my beauty; and thus we shall behold each other in your beauty. (C 36.5)

In John's wisdom spirituality, then, the ultimate goal of all wisdom is to be transformed into the beauty of the Son of God: God's Beautiful Face of Love that has looked upon this world giving it dignity and beauty. Even in our human relations, we know that the loving way a person looks at us can bring out our beauty. The beauty of the other gives us the capacity to know our own beauty. By fixing our gaze on the beauty of God's love revealed in Jesus Christ, we are gradually transformed into God's beauty. His beauty is ours, and ours is his. What a marvelous exchange and mixture of beauty is this shared life of divine wisdom!

# Notes

1. Roland E. Murphy, *The Tree of Life: An Exploration of Biblical Wisdom Literature*, 3rd ed. (Grand Rapids, Mich.: Eerdmans, 2002), 145.

2. See *Concordancias de los escritos de San Juan de la Cruz* (Rome: Teresianum, 1990), 1614–19.

3. References to John's works come from the *Collected Works of St. John of the Cross*, translated by Kieran Kavanaugh, O.C.D., and Otilio Rodriguez, O.C.D. (Washington, D.C.: ICS Publications, 1991). For abbreviation key, see Translations and Abbreviations in the front of this book.

4. Murphy, *The Tree of Life*, 133.

5. Gabriel Castro, "Escritura Sagrada," in *Diccionario de San Juan de la Cruz* (Burgos, Spain: Editorial Monte Carmelo, 2000), 528.

6. Miguel A. Díez González, *Lecturas Medievales de San Juan de la Cruz* (Burgos, Spain: Editorial Monte Carmelo, 1999), 13–33.

7. Lawrence Sullivan, "The 'Moralia' of Pope St. Gregory the Great and Its Influence on St. John of the Cross," *Ephemeredes Carmeliticae* 27 (1976): 453–88.

8. *Biblioteca Mística Carmelitana* 10 (Burgos, Spain: Editorial Monte Carmelo), 341.

9. *Biblioteca Mística Carmelitana* 23 (Burgos, Spain: Editorial Monte Carmelo), 59.

10. *Biblioteca Mística Carmelitana* 24 (Burgos, Spain: Editorial Monte Carmelo), 342, 381.

11. Federico Ruiz, *Maestro y místico San Juan de la Cruz* (Madrid: Editorial de Espiritualidad, 2006), 177.

12. Pope Benedict XVI, God Is Love (*Deus caritas est*) (Rome: Libreria Editrice Vaticana, 2005), 35–36.

# Carmelite Mysticism as Theology:

## John of the Cross's Mystical Theology of the Human Person

### VILMA SEELAUS, O.C.D.

EACH OF THE GREAT Carmelite mystics would have something unique to offer in the exploration of my topic, "Carmelite Mysticism as Theology." In this essay I limit myself to the writings of John of the Cross. I hope to show that through a theology of presence and a theology of silence, John constructs a mystical theology of the human person that unfolds to reveal deep meaning to the biblical understanding of the human person as created in the divine image and likeness.

John's writings take one ever deeper into the God of mystery. In the process, they mirror the mystery that is the human person in its relationship to God. As John unveils the soul's mystical journey into the thicket of God (C 36), into Holy Wisdom, significant theological understandings of the human person emerge.

John's experience of God—as is true of all the Carmelite mystics—is that of God's intimate presence to human life. In symbolic language, John's poetry reflects to us our own reality—that of God reaching out to each person in self-giving love made visible in Christ. Flowing from his mystical experience, John's writings give voice to a profound mystical anthropology with God as the center of the human person. Through a theology of presence, John skillfully guides the soul to the full realization of its innate potential, the sacred within.

## The Sacred at the Foundation of Our Beings

The mystical life is not something extrinsic to the framework of our being. The religious historian Mircea Eliade began his three-volume *History of Religious Ideas* with the assertion that from evidence in earliest-known cave drawings, the *sacred* is an element in the structure of consciousness and not a stage in the history of consciousness.[1] More recent work in such fields as evolutionary epistemology and paleoanthropology suggests the same, although not without controversy.[2] John of the Cross is among those who testify that mysticism is the full flowering of the innate sense of the sacred that is the common human heritage.

Early Christian writers grounded their theology in this profound sense of the sacred. The transforming knowledge of God, the fruit of their experience of God in prayer, was the foundation for their theological reflection. John's definition of mystical theology as "the secret or hidden knowledge of God" (C 39.12) is in keeping with this.[3]

Through centuries of development in religious thought, prayer and the mystical life became increasingly divorced from theological reflection.[4] While spirituality was considered a facet of ascetical theology, the relationship between theology and spirituality gradually diminished in the early burgeoning universities of Europe. Fortunately, through the efforts of many contemporary theologians such as Sandra Schneiders, Catherine Mowry La Cugna, William Johnston, Bernard McGinn, Mark McIntosh, Harvey Egan, William Thompson, and many others, the mystics are again finding their voice in theological discourse.[5]

John Paul II, in his many addresses on the theology of the body, images with mystical insight the biblical foundation of the human person. Using contemporary methods of phenomenology, John Paul mines the first three chapters of Genesis to unearth deep levels of meaning for human self-understanding. God's activity as creator mirrors what it is to be Godlike to the pristine, at first undifferentiated human being. Since this solitary human is unable to find a similar helpmate in all of creation, God places it into a deep sleep (Gn 2:21). From the silence of eternity, the once solitary human issues forth, re-created as man and woman with the ecstatic realization that God's eternal self-bestowal in love is now a human potential.[6]

John of the Cross's mystical writings stir the innate desires of the heart to personally know and to respond in love to this creating God of love made known in Christ as intimately present. Created in the divine image and likeness, we humans come to the full knowledge of ourselves and of how to act in a truly human way through our life in Christ. In revealing the face of God, Christ's intimate presence reveals us to ourselves. Through a *theology of presence,*

John skillfully guides the soul to the full realization of its innate potential, the sacred within. Finally, from a profound awareness of God's abiding presence, a *theology of silence* emerges in John's writings.

## Theological Insights: John's Theology of Presence

God's intimate, loving presence in all the varied situations in John's own life enabled him, through his writings, to develop a theological anthropology with God as the center and heart of the human person. God, who is love, ceaselessly beckons the heart to return love for love until, through love's enkindling, the words of John's poem "The Living Flame" pray themselves in the heart:

> O living flame of love,
>
> that tenderly wounds my soul
>
> in its deepest center! Since
>
> now you are not oppressive,
>
> now consummate! If it be your will:
>
> tear through the veil of this sweet encounter! (F 1)

This ultimate in divine transformation is grounded in what John first describes as God's essential presence to humankind.[7] The reality of God, always present to human life, in fact to all creation, is at the core of John's theology. Reflecting on stanza 11 of *The Spiritual Canticle*, beginning "Reveal your presence," John explains that God's presence can be of three kinds.

The first is God's presence by essence. In this way God is present not only in the holiest souls but also in sinners and all other creatures. With this presence God gives them life and being. Should this presence be lacking to them, they would be annihilated. Thus this presence is never wanting to the soul.

The second is God's presence by grace, in which God abides in the soul, pleased and satisfied with it. Not all have this presence of God; those who fall into mortal sin lose it. The soul cannot know naturally if it has this presence.

The third is God's presence by spiritual affection, for God usually grants God's spiritual presence to devout souls in many ways by which God refreshes, delights and gladdens them. (C 11.3)

Integral, then, to John's theological anthropology is how the presence of God to human life manifests itself. John places the human person within the wider horizon of openness to God whose divine, indwelling presence unceasingly draws the soul to itself. According to John of the Cross, all human knowing has the transcendent capacity for transformation into divine wisdom, and all human loving can be so divinely inflamed as to love with God's own love. Love as a human reality is only possible because it already exists in God. God's self-bestowal in love is what stirs the human heart with desire for God. How the heart can open itself to the lavishness of God's love so that love is reciprocal is the focus of John's writings, and this theme undergirds his teachings especially in *The Ascent of Mount Carmel* and

*The Dark Night.* With inspired pedagogy, the mystic John guides the soul step by step on the spiritual journey, so that once God has enlarged the heart for God, the heart of God and the human heart beat in unison. In the process, John enriches the church with a mystical theology of human/ divine interrelatedness.

## The Pedagogy of John the Mystic

Book two of *The Ascent of Mount Carmel* is about God preparing the soul for divine encounter and how the soul is to respond in order for God to open it to love. Borrowing from the sixth chapter of Isaiah, John introduces his essential message: the exercise of faith, hope, and charity must void the faculties initially in the night of sense and more profoundly in the night of spirit as preparation for ultimate transformation in God. Exposing the multilayered structure of human knowing by which a thing may be known and not known at the same time, John insists that "nothing in this life that could be imagined or received and understood by the intellect can be a proximate means of union with God." (A 2.8.4) Giving symbolic meaning to Isaiah's vision of the seraph with six wings (Is 6:2), John writes, "With two wings they covered their feet, which signified the blinding and quenching of the affections of the will for God; with two they covered their faces, which signified the darkness of the intellect in God's presence; and with the two remaining wings they flew, so as to indicate the flight of hope toward things that are not possessed, an elevation above everything outside of God that can be possessed, earthly or heavenly" (A 2.6.5).

The presence of God initially blinds the intellect to prepare it for deeper knowing through faith. Faith negates lesser knowledge because it is through faith that God's self-communication is experienced (A 2.8.5).[8] This happens in prayer, especially in the transition from meditation to contemplation. John advises, "When a spiritual person cannot meditate, they should learn to remain in God's presence with a loving attention and tranquil intellect, even though they seem to themselves to be idle" (A 2.16.5). Mary Magdalene in her desolation at the sepulcher failed to recognize Jesus until, as John writes, "by the warmth of his presence, Christ could finish instructing her in the belief she was lacking" (A 3.31.8). The heart of the matter for John is transformation in love, but faith is the means and is integral to love's realization. According to John, faith is our human mode of experiencing God's presence. It is not a thing, for faith mysteriously contains the divine Other and is the door of entry to the deeper regions of the heart where Love's presence is recognized and consummated in the embrace of love.[9]

In *The Dark Night* John teaches the important theological reality that, since contraries cannot coexist in the same subject, the great splendor of God's presence is like a ray of darkness to the intellect (N 2.5.3–4). He emphasizes the point again in *The Spiritual Canticle* when he writes, "No matter how elevated God's communications and the experiences of God's presence are, and however sublime a person's knowledge of God may be, these are not God essentially, nor are they comparable to God because, indeed, God is still hidden to the soul" (C 1.6).

In order to find God within, John would have the soul leave all things through affection and will. This is John's great message of detachment, and a significant theological insight. For a person truly to find God within, there can be no strings attached! In *The Spiritual Canticle*, as the bride persistently seeks her beloved, John reminds us that the search for the Beloved involves a long journey in which love only gradually matures (C 2.3–4). God's transforming presence "extinguishes our miseries . . . he extinguishes them by his presence and refreshes her [the soul] as cool water soothes a person exhausted from the heat" (C 10.5–6; C 2.3–4). In time the "favor of God's presence in the soul" gives the soul the perspective by which it understands that "in the excess of the lofty wisdom of God, the lowly wisdom of humans is ignorance" (C 26.13).[10]

As the divine indwelling presence along with the experience of seeming absence both purify and heal the soul, God begins to caress it like a mother who ministers to her child and nurses it at her own breasts (C 27.1). He brings it to a place where, in this mutual act of surrender, the soul's every act is love (C 29.7). In his *Degrees of Perfection*, John shares his wisdom about how this process can reach maturity. He encourages and exhorts, "Endeavor to remain always in the presence of God, either real, imaginative, or unitive, insofar as is permitted by your works."[11] With the soul's infinite capacity for God, the divine presence transforms the soul so that "she performs no work without God." She does this "united with Christ and in Christ" (C 37.6).

## Stanza 12 of *The Spiritual Canticle*

The twelfth stanza of *The Spiritual Canticle* is a key text for understanding John's spiritual theology of human/divine transformation. This stanza places the human person within the mystery of the incarnation—God's abiding presence to human life as presence in Christ. *The Spiritual Canticle* is like an icon of the desire for God that sparks the soul's innate longings. The bride, anxiously seeking her beloved, voices her desire that he reveal his presence. Passing a flowing steam she cries out,

> O spring like crystal!
> If only, on your silvered-over faces,
> You would suddenly form
> The eyes I have desired,
> Which I bear sketched deep within my heart.

In his commentary leading into this verse, John writes, "The soul experiences within herself a certain sketch of love, which is the sickness she mentions, and she desires the completion of the sketch *of this image, the image of her Bridegroom, the Word, the Son of God*, who as St. Paul says, is the splendor of his glory and image of his substance (Heb. 1.3) for this is the image referred to in this and into which the soul desires to be transformed through love" (C 11.12). As John begins his commentary on stanza 12, he writes, "At that period the soul feels that she is rushing toward God as rapidly as a falling stone when nearing its center. She also feels that she is like wax in which an impression, though being made, is not yet complete. She knows too, *that she is like a sketch or the first draft of a drawing* and calls out to the one who did this sketch to finish the painting and image" (C 12.1). Notice that not only is the sketch in process of completion the sketch of the soul's Bridegroom, the Word, the Son of God, but also the soul itself is like a sketch or first draft of a drawing. In our own prayer, like the bride in the Canticle, we too may feel impelled to call out to the one who did this sketch to finish the painting and image. The sketch—which is of both Christ and the soul—is our center and deepest identity.[12] The transformative process, the dynamism of the nights of sense and spirit, is toward the completion of the sketch. As the soul finds strength to embody God, the heart resonates with the words spoken to Christ at his baptism, "You are my beloved, upon you my favor rests" (Mk 1:11). John's mystical theology of the incarnation in his poem "Romances" has the Father say to the Son,

> Whoever resembles you most
>
> satisfies me most,
>
> and whoever is like you in nothing
>
> will find nothing in me.

From this we can see that an innate, mystical dimension characterizes the human person through its intersubjective identity with God. John's theology of the Trinity and incarnation reflects the mystery of the self. What John writes of the Trinity mirrors to the soul its own deepest mystery. In its transformed state, the dynamic of the soul is one movement with the dynamic energies of God's trinitarian life. John expresses this awesome reality in *The Spiritual Canticle* where he writes, "By His divine breath-like spiration, the Holy Spirit elevates the soul sublimely and informs her and makes her capable of breathing in God the same spiration of love that the Father breathes in the Son and the Son in the Father" (C 39.3).[13]

## The Problem of Sin and the Mystery of Redemption

From his mystical experience, John turns to poetry to describe otherwise indescribable, inner realities. In doing so, he makes a significant contribution toward a theological understanding of the mystery of incarnation and redemption in Christ as having its meaning in love rather than in appeasement. John provides a corrective to the theological message of appeasement, which derives from a problematic interpretation of Anselm's theology of the redemption. This interpretation asserts that Jesus, the eternal Son, intentionally became incarnate and took upon himself the burden of all the sins that would ever be committed down through the ages. He therefore incurred the wrath of God, which only the extremes of a divine retribution, the violent suffering and death of God's own Son, could appease. Even now, I can remember as a young person still in grammar school sitting in my parish church and, on hearing such a sermon during a parish mission, saying to myself, "That's not the God I know. God isn't like that." John of the Cross would agree, as is evident from the way he poetically weaves the story of creation, incarnation, and redemption.

In his poem "Romances," John's theological imagination ingeniously constructs a scene in which the Father and the Son confer among themselves. Expressing words of love, one for the other, the Father determines that the Son must have a bride who will resemble him. To fulfill this, the Father creates humankind to be the bride of his Son. Such a bride needs a palace, so *God creates the universe as the palace for the bride.* The universe, then, is our palace home where Christ, through his abiding presence, invites each one of us into marital intimacy. As the poem creatively constructs the stories of the entrance of sin into the world, of God becoming one of us in Christ, and of Christ's redemptive death, the underlying theme is always that of Christ wooing the bride, humankind, back to himself.

Imaging the Trinity as interactive self-giving in love, the divine persons communicating love one to the other, John writes in "Romances" 1,

> As the lover in the beloved
> each lived in the other,
> and the Love that unites them
> is one with them,
> their equal, excellent as
> the One and the Other;
> Three Persons, and one Beloved,
> among all three.
> One love in them all
> makes of them one Lover

and the Lover is the Beloved

in whom each one lives.

It is from such love that the Father wishes to give the Son a
bride who will love him—as the poem says, one "who will
share our company and eat at our table." The Son replies in
gratitude, "I will hold her in my arms and she will burn with
your love." And so, by these words, the world was created, a
luxurious palace for the bride. God also creates the angels,
and although these creatures are higher in form than humans,
God's care does not focus on them. Rather, in order to lift
humankind from its lowliness, as "Romances" 4 says,

God would make himself

wholly like them,

and he would come to them

and dwell with them;

and God would be man

and man would be God,

and he would walk with them

and eat and drink with them;

and he himself would be

with them continually

until the consummation of the world.

John's theology of incarnation/redemption, then, is not
about making satisfaction for sin but about the divine heart
of God allowing itself to be wounded with love for humankind, for each person.

Further, in a poem entitled "Stanzas Applied Spiritually to Christ and the Soul," John pictures the redemptive mystery:

A lone shepherd boy, . . .
His thoughts fixed on a shepherd girl, . . .
Bows to brutal handling in a foreign land,
His heart an open wound with love . . .
And after a long time, he climbed a tree,
And spread his shining arms
And hung by them, and died
His heart an open wound with love.

Christ, his arms wide open, his heart an open wound, sends energies of divine love into the heart of all people, stirring desire in them to return love for love. The purpose of the dark nights, the arduous ascent of Mount Carmel, is toward preparing the soul to receive this inflow of Christ's transforming love. The spiritual journey according to John is that of the soul "being freed from the house of the senses," since "all natural ability is insufficient to produce the supernatural goods God alone infuses into the soul passively, secretly and in silence" (N 2.14.3; N 2.14.1).

## A Theology of Silence

John summarizes his theology of presence in saying 142 of the *Sayings of Light and Love*: "Strive always to keep God present and to preserve within yourself the purity God teaches you." To teach us how to live it out, John develops what might be called a theology of silence. For us to arrive at the new self—the completion of the sketch within that is both Christ and the self—Christ must draw the soul into "the thicket of God's wisdom" so that it can "know its wisdom *from further within*." As John writes, "One of the reasons urging the soul most to enter this thicket of wisdom and to know its beauty from further within is her wish to unite her intellect with God in the knowledge of the mysteries of the incarnation in which is contained the highest and most savory wisdom of all God's works" (C 37.2). According to John, "The treasures of Christ are like an abundant mine with many recesses of treasures so that however deep individuals may go they never reach the end or bottom, but rather in every recess, find new veins with new riches everywhere" (C 37.4).

In this experience, theological understanding comes to birth within the silence of the heart, beyond intellectual inquiry. For as John insists in *Sayings of Light and Love,* "The Father spoke one Word, which is his Son, and this Word God speaks always in eternal Silence, and in silence must it be heard by the soul" (SLL 100). For this reason John urges the soul "to be fond of silence and solitude" (121) and "to draw near to God in silence" (124). Again in Saying 132 John writes, "What we need most in order to make progress is to be silent before this great God with our appetite and with our tongue, for the language God best hears is silent love." In such silence, immersed in the thicket of divine wisdom, the soul is drawn into the mystery of God's self-disclosure in Christ.[14]

John's insistence on detaching the heart from inordinate desire for created things is so that the heart can be totally free for God. Inordinate desires clutter space that belongs to God. "Since God is inaccessible," writes John, "be careful not to concern yourself with all that your faculties can comprehend and your senses feel, so that you do not become satisfied with less and lose the lightness of soul suitable for going to God" (SLL 55). *Detachment clears the space for the silence of God to overflow into the soul.* This silence is the silence not of emptiness but of divine fullness filling the heart as it communicates the one Word spoken by God, God's eternal Word revealed to us in Christ.

This is not a silence of our own making. No technique for quieting the mind can bring us to such depth. It is not a place we arrive at but a place we are invited into. As John writes, "All natural ability is insufficient to produce the supernatural goods that God alone infuses in the soul passively, secretly, and in silence" (N 2.14.1).[15] Teresa experiences this place within as the inner wine cellar of the soul. As she notes, "His majesty must place us there and enter Himself into the center of our soul" (IC 5.1.12). According to John, the soul has many centers, and with one degree of love it is already in its center. However, "The more degrees of love it has the more deeply it enters into God and centers itself in God" (F 1.13). The soul's center is God. Here, in the thicket of Holy Wisdom, God communicates Godself in language that has no human compatibility. This breaking though of wisdom into contemplative consciousness gives birth to new understandings of the profound mystery that is God. The only appropriate language for the person receiving such favors of God's self-communication, writes John, is "silent love" (SLL 132).

Language and concepts break down in the presence of God as the mind is drawn to a new level of perception by the transforming energy of divine Love invading the soul's center. From this center, through "the thicket of Holy Wisdom," the person experiences the complete inadequacy of all human concepts of God, of all human names for God. As the spirit becomes absorbed in the God of silence, God's one Word is heard speaking intimately to the heart giving mystical understandings too deep for words. The infinity of God disclosing the divine self within human finitude inevitably creates darkness in the intellect. Enveloped in deep silence, the only adequate descriptive name for God is "dark silence."

The Sacred within, this human capability for self-transcendence, can only be fully realized if the person allow herself or himself  to be drawn beyond attachment to the provisional existence of the life of the senses. Karl Rahner calls this movement "the echo of God's eternal self-disclosure in Christ."[16] As the soul moves from intellectual knowledge into Holy Wisdom, the truth of the self—the sketch of Christ within—opens the eyes of the soul to see the self as it truly is: caught up in the interpersonal Trinitarian life of God. What John calls God's essential presence, the presence that sustains us in existence, is in fact that which constitutes us in the very image and likeness of God. From the first moment of our existence, the Living Flame of God's love, the interpersonal Trinitarian life of God, shapes our being and calls us into loving interaction with others as a human expression of the Trinitarian God-life within.

As the individual increasingly lives from his or her center, with all energies directed toward love's service, the soul's deepest *within* becomes the root of all human activity. God *within* overflows into life's everydayness. The soul, having been purified, enlarged, and made capable of being at peace in the silence of God, is no longer a slave to impulsive reactions. At last those dimensions that John calls the "higher" and "lower" parts of the soul operate together in total harmony.[17]

## Conclusion

Through a theology of presence and a theology of silence, John constructs a mystical theology of the human person. As it unfolds, it reveals the deep meaning of the biblical understanding of the human as created in the divine image and likeness. Human and divine activity become one as "the soul comes to know creatures through God and not God through creatures." In *The Living Flame*, John calls this "essential knowledge" (F 4.5) and adds, "The soul also loves God, not through itself but through God" (F 3.82). God's essential presence, God's presence by grace and presence by spiritual affection, is experienced by the soul as one reality (F 4.7).

Toward the end of *The Living Flame*, John introduces a somber note as he reflects on chapter 15 of the book of Esther where Esther appeals to the king for her people who are about to be exterminated. Upon seeing the glory of the king clothed in royal garments, Esther faints, but she loses her fear in the king's embrace (Est 15:9–17). John weaves the story of Esther into a final exhortation to the soul to respond to God who dwells in its heart in secret (F 4.14), for as John writes, "When glory does not glorify, it weighs heavily on the one who beholds it" (F 4.11). Allison Peers has an even stronger translation: "For glory oppresses him that looks upon it if it glorifies him not."[18]

Perhaps this is the oppressive burden of our postmodern way of being: we behold the glory, but we do not allow glory to transform us into the truth of itself. Think what it would be like for our violent, war-torn world if the divine image and likeness shone forth in human behavior: respect for human life and for all of God's creatures; care for the earth as the palace created for the bride, humankind; concern for the poor and needy—for all are the beloved of God. This would be a world where the energies of God's transforming presence would make for lasting peace and harmony among all the diverse ways in which the divine image and likeness reflects itself, not only in human existence, but also in all the multiple forms of life on our beautiful planet Earth. The palace was created for the bride—who is each and every one of us.

## Notes

1. Mircea Eliade, *A History of Religious Ideas*, vol. 1, *From the Stone Age to the Eleusinian Mysteries*, trans. Willard R. Trask (Chicago: University of Chicago Press, 1978), xiii.
2. See chapter 5, "Human Uniqueness and Symbolization," in J. Wentzel van Huyssteen, *Alone in the World? Human Uniqueness in Science and Theology* (Grand Rapids, Mich.: Eerdmans, 2006), for a review of various contemporary approaches to this question.

3. All citations from John of the Cross and Teresa of Ávila are from *Collected Works* (Washington, D.C.: ICS Publications), trans. Kieran Kavanaugh, O.C.D., and Otilio Rodriguez, O.C.D., unless otherwise noted.

4. See Mark A. McIntosh, *Mystical Theology: The Integrity of Spirituality and Theology* (Hoboken, N.J.: Blackwell, 1998), 8.

5. To cite but a few examples, see Sandra M. Schneiders, in "Theology and Spirituality: Strangers, Rivals or Partners," *Horizons* 13, no. 2 (1986): 253–74, and "Spirituality in the Academy," *Theological Studies* 50, no. 4 (1989): 676–97, which develop the historical relationship between theology and spirituality along with the important observation that spirituality for Christians is *Christian*, and therefore theological considerations are relevant at every point. Harvey Egan, "Theology and Spirituality," in *The Cambridge Companion to Karl Rahner*, ed. Declan Marmion and Mary E. Hines (Cambridge: Cambridge University Press, 2005), esp. 19. Catherine Mowry La Cugna makes the doctrine of the Trinity accessible to Christian living as theology and spirituality intersect with each other in *God for Us: The Trinity and Christian Life* (San Francisco: Harper, 1991). In *The Foundations of Mysticism: The Presence of God*, vol. 1 (New York: Crossroad, 1999), Bernard McGinn has a section entitled "Theological Approaches to Mysticism," 266 ff., where he develops the various theological approaches to mysticism. In *Mystical Theology: The Science of Love* (Maryknoll, N.Y.: Orbis, 2000), William Johnston places theology within the context of desire for the living God. See also William M. Thompson, *Fire and Light: The Saints and Theology* (Mahwah, N.J.: Paulist, 1987).

6. See Richard M. Hogan, *The Theology of the Body in John Paul II: What It Means, Why It Matters* (Frederick, Md.: Word among Us, 2007), 48–62.

7. In the fourth century, years before the birth of John of the Cross, Augustine, who became bishop of Hippo, in book one of his *Confessions*, pondered at length the profound reality of God's abiding presence with words such as these: "Since nothing that exists would exist without you, does it not follow that whatever exists does in some way contain you? But if this is so, how can I who

am one of these existing things ask you to come into me when I would not exist at all unless you were already in me? . . . No, my God, I would not exist, I would not be at all, were you not in me. Or should I say, rather, that I should not exist if I were not in you, from whom are all things, through whom are all things, in whom are all things?" *The Confessions*, trans. Maria Boulding, ed. John E. Rotelle (Hyde Park, N.Y.: New City Press, 1997), 40.

8.  In an essay on the theology of Karl Rahner titled "Revelation and Faith," Daniel Donovan offers Rahner's understanding of the different levels of knowing they represent. "Our ordinary knowledge is categorical knowledge. It is the kind of knowledge that comes to us through the senses and that even as intellectual is known in relation to the data they present. Transcendental knowledge, or transcendental experience as it is also called, is non-categorical. It is not a knowing of something as an object but rather the awareness we have of ourselves in our categorical knowing and willing as reaching out to the mystery that surrounds and permeates and grounds our life. It is a knowledge that accompanies categorical knowing, a knowledge on which we can reflect and of which we can try to get some understanding but which even as we do so, tries to elude us." *The Cambridge Companion to Karl Rahner*, ed. Declan Marmion and Mary E. Hines (Cambridge: Cambridge University Press, 2005), 87.

9.  "Faith is the *realization* of things hoped for and *evidence* of things not seen" (Heb 11:1–2).

10. It is reported that as he approached death, St. Thomas Aquinas, after an overwhelming experience of God, exclaimed, "I cannot go on. . . . All that I have written seems to me like so much straw compared to what I have seen and what has been revealed to me."

11. John of the Cross, "Degrees of Perfection" 2, in *The Collected Works*.

12. Rahner writes, "This unity—experience of self, experience of God—consists far more in the fact that the original and ultimate experience of God constitutes the enabling condition of, and an intrinsic element in, the experience of self in such a way that without this experience of God no experience of self is possible." Karl Rahner, "Experience of Self and Experience of God," *Theological*

*Investigations*, vol. 5, *Later Writings* (London: Darton, Longman and Todd, 1966), 125.

13. Von Balthasar writes, "This is why Christians are given the Holy Spirit, not only as a treasure but even more crucially as a fiduciary trust: Christians do not just possess but must also exhale the Spirit." *Explorations in Theology*, vol. 4, *Spirit and Institutions*, trans. Edward T. Oakes (San Francisco: Ignatius Press, 1981), 443.

14. In a letter to the Discalced Carmelites nuns in Beas written December 7, 1587, from Granada, John gives more practical implications and helps toward being "enveloped in silence."

15. While there is a depth of silence that is not of our doing, there are practices that still the mind and lead it to inner silence. Martin Laird, in *Into the Silent Land: A Guide to the Christian Practice of Contemplation* (Oxford: Oxford University Press, 2006), guides us through the ancient Christian practice of attention to the breath for inner stillness in God.

16. Quoted in Ann Denham and Gert Wilkinson, eds., *Cloister of the Heart: Association of Contemplative Sisters* (Bloomington, Ind.: Xlibris, 2009), 105.

17. As Teresa puts it in the seventh dwelling places of her *Interior Castle*, "Martha and Mary must join together in serving the Lord" (IC 5.11.4.12). The two sisters are symbolic of the *higher and lower part in harmony*. Terrence W. Tilley, in *The Disciple's Jesus: Christology as Reconciling Practice* (Maryknoll, N.Y.: Orbis, 2008), 96–107, in a context of confessing Jesus as *ho Christos*, also develops the roles of Martha and Mary as interactive.

18. *The Complete Works of St. John of the Cross*, trans. and ed. Allison Peers, vol. 3 (London: Burns Oates & Washbourne, 1935), 212.

# The Wisdom of Emptiness

KEVIN CULLIGAN, O.C.D.

*Marvelous existence is true emptiness.*
—ZEN KOAN[1]

TURN THE KOAN AROUND and you have, "True emptiness is marvelous existence." Either way, this saying, like a true koan, challenges the assumptions of our American way of life, which state that a marvelous way to live is to have more of everything—money, beauty, reputation, power, pleasure, religious experience. Emptiness sounds like the existence of those on the fringes of our society—no home, no security, no influence, no sanity, no say—nothing. What could be so marvelous about that?

I first heard this koan on a Christian Zen retreat. You do not analyze a koan. You just receive it and let it sink deeper into your consciousness, and eventually its meaning for you will manifest itself. Several months after the retreat was over, as I was making my bed one Saturday morning, the lesson of the koan for me emerged clearly in my mind: *Of course, that's right! Emptiness, total nonattachment, clinging to nothing finally leaves you free to follow Jesus Christ. Is there a better way to live?* A Buddhist might similarly awaken one Saturday morning to the meaning of the koan in his or her life. Nonattachment to anything—external objects, interior ways of thinking and feeling—eventually leads to enlightenment, to an immediate grasp of the transitoriness of life, the inevitability of suffering, and the inherent limitation of everything. To live continually in this chaotic world with this wise awareness is indeed marvelous existence.

## Christian Emptiness

Buddhists are not alone in extolling the marvels of emptiness. St. Paul encouraged the Philippians to think like Christ Jesus who for our sake emptied himself of his divine prerogatives, even to death on a cross, and was consequently exalted by God the Father (Phil 2:5–11). Many Christians, too, have proclaimed its benefits, perhaps under other headings such as poverty of spirit or simplicity of life. St. John of the Cross, for example, uses the word *emptiness*, both in its noun and verb forms, over 180 times (*vacío* 142 and *vaciar* 40). It appears in each of his major writings, as well as in several of his sixteen surviving letters of spiritual guidance (Lt 6, 7, 13, 15, and 19).[2] Here I examine St. John's use of the word *emptiness* to discover its meaning for him, and how he thinks it leads to wisdom.

John never precisely defines *emptiness*, but his meaning becomes very clear when we review the way he uses the word in his treatises. He states, for example, that emptiness is necessary for union with God: "The soul [*el alma*] must *empty* itself of all that is not God in order to go to God" (A 3.7.2; see also A 1.5.2, 11.2; A 2.4.2, 9.1; Lt 7:13). The reason, he states further, is simple: "God does not fit in an occupied heart" (F 3.48). God does not share the riches of divine life with those who have no interest in God's gifts, or who fill their hearts and minds with other things. Counseling a Carmelite nun about the emptiness needed for union with God, John writes, "The more God wants to give, the more God makes us desire—even to the point of leaving us *empty* in order to fill us with goods. . . . The immense blessings of God can only enter and fit into an *empty* and solitary heart" (Lt 15 to Leonor de San Gabriel; see also Lt 7, 13). Were that all he said about emptiness, John's teaching on this important subject might be overlooked or misunderstood. Fortunately, in his major writings he has much more to say that helps to give a clear picture of his meaning.

## The Ascent of Mount Carmel

John wrote *The Ascent of Mount Carmel* as a spiritual commentary on his poem "The Dark Night," asserting that its theme is to "describe the way that leads to . . . that high state of perfection we here call union of the soul with God." Among other demands, journeying on this road to divine union requires that the spiritual traveler not be attached to any created thing, whether that be an object of the exterior senses (another human being, enchanting music, delicious food, a comfortable home—in short, whatever can delight our five senses) or the product of our own mind (our thoughts, images, memories, and emotions). This nonattachment to created objects simply allows a place in our lives for their Creator. The reason for nonattachment to sensory objects is easy enough to understand, although extremely

hard to practice. If we seek only to satisfy our sensory appetites, there is little room left in our lives for God. The desire
for things rather than the desire for God controls our minds
and hearts. Thus, if we want our desires to be centered in
God and not in the pleasures provided by sensory objects,
John counsels us,

> Have a habitual desire to imitate Christ in all your deeds
> by bringing your life into conformity with his. . . . To
> be successful in this imitation, renounce and remain *empty*
> of any sensory satisfaction that is not purely for the honor
> and glory of God. Do this out of love for Jesus Christ. In
> his life he had no other gratification, nor desired any other,
> than the fulfillment of his Father's will, which he called
> his meat and food (Jn 4:34). For example, . . . when
> you have an opportunity for the gratification of looking
> upon objects that will not help you love God more, do not
> desire this gratification or sight. . . . And so on with all
> the senses insofar as you can duly avoid such satisfaction.
> If you cannot escape the experience of this satisfaction, it
> will be sufficient to have no desire for it. By this method
> you should endeavor, then, to leave the senses as though in
> darkness, mortified, and *empty* of that satisfaction. With
> such vigilance you will gain a great deal in a short time. (A
> 1.13.3–4)

Note carefully what John says: it is not the absence of the
experience of sensory satisfaction that creates the necessary
interior emptiness but the lack of desire for this satisfaction.
The emptiness we seek is not created by the lack of objects
but by not desiring these objects. John makes this crucial

point earlier in book one of *The Ascent* when he writes, "We are not discussing the mere lack of things; this lack will not divest the soul if it craves for . . . objects. We are dealing with the stripping of the soul's appetites and gratifications. This is what leaves it free and *empty* of all things, even though it possesses them. Since the things of the world cannot enter the soul, they are not in themselves an encumbrance or harm to it; rather, it is the will and appetite dwelling within that cause the damage when set on these things" (A 1.3.4).

Colin Thompson, a modern commentator on John's works, observes that his teaching is "directed toward understanding the mechanisms which govern desire and its pleasure, in order to subordinate them to the will of God, in which the soul's true fulfillment is to be found. . . . It is the nature of human desire and attachment which is at issue, not the nature of the objects they seek to possess. The creatures are not in themselves valueless or worthless, because they are all God's good creation."[3] All created things are good and worthy of our desires, provided we desire them in the fulfillment of God's will. The emptiness that is marvelous existence is primarily the absence of disordered desire, leaving us free to center our lives solely in God. Thus, according to John, "perfect virtue . . . lies in keeping the soul *empty*, naked, and purified of every appetite" (A 1.5.6), or in other words, empty of every disordered desire.[4]

More difficult to comprehend, perhaps, is John's insistence that we be empty not only of disordered desires for pleasurable objects but also of attachment to thoughts, images, memories, and emotions, especially those that concern God (A 2.4.2). His reason is simple: God is beyond all that we can think, imagine, remember, or feel. These human experiences in themselves cannot be the means of union with a "God who is incomprehensible and transcendent" (A 2.24.9). "God does not fit in an occupied heart" (F 3.48), John insists. If our consciousness is filled with *our* thoughts about God, about *our* past and future, about *our* religious experience, there remains little room for us to receive what God wishes to communicate to us. And, ultimately, it is God's self-communication to us—not our religious thoughts, memories, images, and emotions—that purifies our disordered lives, transforms our consciousness, and unites us with God. John puts it this way: "Since this transformation and union is something that does not fall within the reach of the senses and of human capability, the soul must perfectly and voluntarily *empty* itself—I mean in its affection and will—of all the earthly and heavenly things it can grasp. It must do this insofar as it can. As for God, who will stop God from accomplishing his desires in [such a] soul?" (A 2.4.2). He thus maintains that "spiritual nakedness, poverty of spirit, and *emptiness* in faith . . . are the requisites for union with God" (A 2.24.9).

John was aware, of course, that through thoughts, images, memories, and emotions we come to know about God. We learn God's self-revelation through the mental processes involved in Christian education, meditation on Scripture, and liturgical celebration. But John's primary concern in *The Ascent of Mount Carmel* is to guide us not to knowledge *about* God but to union *with* God and transformation *in* God. This union exists, he says, "when God's will and the soul's are in conformity, so that nothing in the one is repugnant to the other" (A 2.5.3). "In the state of divine union a person's will is so completely transformed into God's will that it excludes everything contrary to God's will, and in all and through all is motivated by the will of God" (A 1.11.2). John will claim later in *The Living Flame of Love* that in this union and transformation we actually become "God through participation in God." Our thoughts are God's thoughts, we love only what God loves, our memory is the memory of God, our delight is God's delight, all our movements, operations, and inclinations are "changed into divine movements, and alive to God. For the soul, like a true daughter of God, is moved in all by the Spirit of God" (F 2.34).

This union and transformation of our lives in God is not solely our achievement, the result of a determined will alone. It is primarily God's gift to us, the work of God's grace in our lives. But we can dispose ourselves for this grace by emptying our hearts and minds, our sense and spirit of disordered attachment to any particular thing—temporal, natural, sensory, physical, supernatural, spiritual—that would impede God's transforming work within us. "To come to possess all," John advises his reader in *The Ascent of Mount Carmel*, "desire the possession of nothing" (A 1.13.11), a counsel he repeats in a letter of individual spiritual guidance to Magdalene of the Holy Spirit, a Carmelite nun in Córdoba: "To possess God in everything, you should possess nothing in everything" (Lt 17).[5]

John was particularly concerned about our inordinate attachments to thoughts about God and memories of our past experiences of God. As profound as they may be, our attachment to them can only be an obstacle to union with God. John speaks of the "apprehensions" of both the intellect and memory. In English this word often expresses foreboding or fear of a future evil, although etymologically it means to seize. The latter is how John uses the word. An apprehension is a distinct idea, concept, or image that has been seized or grasped by the intellect or memory. When these "apprehensions" concern God, they are always inadequate, because the transcendent God cannot be fully captured by the human intellect or memory. Thus attachment to these apprehensions may indeed block a fuller understanding of God that God wishes to reveal to a person, especially in contemplation. Throughout *The Ascent of Mount Carmel*, John cautions us to avoid clinging too tenaciously to our ideas and memories of God; rather, we should *empty* our intellects and memories of distinct apprehensions of God so that we are open to receive more of what God chooses to reveal of himself to us.

John also speaks of the "apprehensions" of the will—things or objects we take hold of and won't let go although they have no real relationship to "the service of God and the procurement of God's honor and glory in all things" (A 3.20.3) but serve only our selfish needs and interests. Our three faculties then—intellect, memory, and will—must all be emptied of their "apprehensions" or the specific objects they cling to so that faith, hope, and love can grow in our lives. These virtues—not the possession of thoughts, memories, images, and experiences of God—unite us with God. As we empty our faculties of their apprehensions, these virtues grow in us, and their growth in turn empties our faculties and prepares them to receive God's self-communication. John writes, "The soul is not united with God in this life through understanding, or through enjoyment, or through imagination, or through any other sense; but only faith, hope, and charity (according to the intellect, memory, and will) can unite the soul with God in this life" (A 2.6.1). John uses the risen Lord's appearance to the apostles in the upper room to reinforce his point:

> The soul should remain closed . . . without cares or afflictions, for he who entered the room of his disciples bodily while the doors were closed and gave them peace, without their knowing how this was possible [Jn 20:19–20], will enter the soul spiritually without its knowing how or using any effort of its own, once it has closed the doors of its intellect, memory, and will to all apprehensions. And he will fill them with peace, *descending on them*, as the prophet says, *like a river of peace* [Is 66:12]. In this peace he will remove all the misgivings, suspicions, disturbances, and darknesses that made the soul fear it had gone astray. The soul should persevere in prayer and should hope in the midst of nakedness and *emptiness*, for its blessings will not be long in coming. (A 3.3.6)

In another place, John writes similarly: The "pacification of the soul (making it calm, peaceful, without any labor or desire) is no small accomplishment. This, indeed, is what our Lord asks of us through David: *Vacate et videte quoniam ego sum Deus* [Ps 46:11]. This would be like saying: Learn to be *empty* of all things—interiorly and exteriorly—and you will behold that I am God" (A 2.15.5). Learn to be empty, John teaches us in *The Ascent of Mount Carmel*. This is what we can do on our own to prepare ourselves for union with God and the transformation of our lives in love. Learn and practice sensory and spiritual nonattachment. But this still is not enough. We cannot completely empty ourselves in sense and spirit by our own efforts alone. God must complete this work in us. How God does this is the subject of John's treatise *The Dark Night*.

## The Dark Night

John maintains in *The Dark Night* that God alone can completely empty us for divine union and transformation. God does this through the gift of contemplation, which John describes as "nothing else than a secret and peaceful and loving inflow of God, which, if not hampered, fires the soul in the spirit of love" (N 1.10.6, 12.4; N 2.5.1; C 13.10; F 49). This "infused" contemplation is really "the love of God poured into our hearts by the Holy Spirit who has been given to us" that St. Paul describes in Romans 5:5. Contemplation is "the loving wisdom of God"—mystical theology—that purges us of our habitual ignorances and all our imperfections, teaches us secretly, and instructs us in the perfection of love without our doing anything or understanding how this happens, and thus prepares us for "union with God through love" (N 2.5.1).

John's description of infused contemplation is admittedly attractive, but note carefully what he says. Contemplation both illumines and purifies us at the same time. In the process of uniting us with God, contemplation also empties us of our disordered attachments so that we may be filled with God's own life. This emptying is never pleasant, but it is God preparing us for the divine treasures God desires to share with us. God's ways of emptying us far surpasses our own limited attempt at self-emptying (N 2.9.2), although our efforts are indispensable to express our willingness for God to purify us for divine union and transformation.

We can better understand the purifying and emptying dimension of contemplation when we see it as God's self-communication to us. God is *always* communicating with us—through nature, through divine revelation, and most intimately, in contemplation when God communicates with us directly, God's spirit to our spirit, without the intermediaries of concepts, images, memories, or emotions (N 2.17.4; C 7.6–7, 19.4). God's self-communication in secret contemplation transforms our consciousness so that we know as God knows, love as God loves, and act as God acts, enabling us to be "perfect as our heavenly father is perfect" (Mt 5:48). In the process, God's self-communication empties us of our attachment to our own self. In what John calls the dark night of sense, contemplation works through dryness to purify us of our attachments to the sensory pleasure we derive from prayer and good works (N 1.9.6, 11.2, 12.4–7), so that our motive for serving God becomes God alone rather than the personal satisfaction we find in religious practices.

As our spiritual journey continues, God's self-communication reaches further beyond the senses into the very depths of our spirit. In what John calls the dark night of spirit, God empties us of inadequate images we have of both God and ourselves. God's self-communication purifies our hidden and deeply rooted attachments to our own self. God allows us to see with ever-deepening insight both the utter goodness of God and our own radical nothingness apart from God. In this awareness we gradually let go of our disordered attachment to our self and center our life completely in God. We are emptied of the inadequate images of both God and self that impede union with God. How long does this transformation process last? John observes that it lasts as long as it takes—perhaps years, perhaps a lifetime—for our spirit to be "humbled, softened, and purified until it becomes so delicate, simple, and refined that it can be one with the Spirit of God, according to the degree of union of love that, God, in his mercy, desires to grant" (A 2.7.3).

In *The Dark Night*, then, John describes how God, through infused contemplation or God's own self-communication to us, purifies our "creature affections and apprehensions" (N 2.8.2) and empties us of disordered attachments of sense and spirit that may still hinder union with God and transformation in love, attachments that we could not remove entirely by ourselves alone. Delineating the purgative and illuminative effects of this dark contemplation, John writes, "Even though this happy night darkens the spirit, it does so only to impart light concerning all things; and even though it humbles individuals and reveals their miseries, it does so only to exalt them; and even though it impoverishes and *empties* them of all possessions and natural affection, it does so only that they may reach out divinely to the enjoyment of all earthly and heavenly things, with a general freedom of spirit in them all" (N 2.9.1).

Thus, the journey to union with God and the transformation of our lives in love as John presents it in his treatises *The Ascent of Mount Carmel* and *The Dark Night* is a collaborative process between ourselves and God. *The Ascent of Mount Carmel* describes how we empty ourselves through nonattachment to material and spiritual objects to remove the barriers to the inflow of God into our lives, and *The Dark Night* shows how God completes our transformation through infused contemplation that finally empties us of all our apprehensions—natural and supernatural—and makes us one with God. John briefly summarizes this cooperative enterprise when he states, "God . . . by means of this dark and dry night of contemplation, supernaturally instructs in his divine wisdom the soul that is *empty* and unhindered (which is the requirement for God's divine inpouring)" (N 1.12.4).

## The Spiritual Canticle

In his poem and commentary entitled *The Spiritual Canticle*, John continues the divine/human collaboration theme but now in the context of a love story that he entitles "the exchange of love between the soul and Christ, its Bridegroom." Although he focuses on the relationship between the human person and God, John is careful to point out that true love follows the same general principles whether it is divine love or human love. He observes, for example, that "anyone truly in love will let all other things go in order to come closer to the loved one" (C 29.10; see also C 3.8). This "letting go," however, causes emptiness in lovers.

> Lovers are said to have their heart stolen or seized by the object of their love, for the heart will go out from self and become fixed on the loved object. Thus their heart or love is not for themselves but for what they love. . . . The heart cannot have peace and rest while not possessing, and when it is truly attracted it no longer has possession of self or of any other thing. And if it does not possess completely what it loves, it cannot help being weary, in proportion to its loss, until it possesses the loved object and is satisfied. Until this possession the soul is like *an empty vessel waiting to be filled.* (C 9.5–6)

Emptiness is simply one of the "wages of love," a price one pays in hopes of being repaid with the love of the beloved (C 9.7).

In relation to God, "the soul that loves God must not desire or hope for any other reward for her services than the perfect love of God" (C 9.7). This longing for God alone creates an interior emptiness as one voluntarily lets go of disordered sensory and spiritual attachments because of desire for God. "All the senses and faculties, interior and exterior, should be unoccupied, idle and *empty* of their own operations and objects" (C 16.11). In effect, this demands that "no image of any object belonging to any of these faculties or senses . . . appear before the soul and [Christ] the Bridegroom. This is like saying: Let there be no particular knowledge or affection or other consideration in any of the spiritual faculties (intellect, memory, and will); and let there be no other digressions, forms, images, or figures of objects, or other natural operations in any of the bodily senses and faculties, either interior or exterior (the imaginative power and phantasy, and so on, sight and hearing, and so on)" (C 16.10). Such emptiness caused by the soul's longing for God alone is intensely painful, yet just as the soul empties herself for God, God in turn, like a flowing river that fills an empty riverbed (C 14, 15.9), gradually fills the empty soul. The soul recognizes God's life, love, and grace growing within her. John describes this awareness in one who is spiritually betrothed with "the Word, the Son of God. . . . She tastes there a splendid spiritual sweetness and gratification, discovers true quiet and divine light, and tastes sublimely the wisdom of God, reflected in the harmony of his creatures and works. She has the feeling of being filled with blessings and being empty of evils and far removed from them. And, above all, she understand and enjoys inestimable refreshment of love, which confirms her in love" (C 14, 15.2, 15.4).

This love transforms a person in God. One's soul is changed "according to her operations and appetites into God, into a new kind of life in which she is undone and annihilated before all the old things she formerly made use of. . . . Not only is all her old knowing annihilated, seeming to her to be nothing, but her old life and imperfections are annihilated, and she is renewed in the new self [Col 3:10]" (C 26.17). In this transformation, God alone guides the soul. In the inner solitude created by the soul's self-emptying and God's self-communication,

the soul is alone with God and God guides, moves, and raises her to divine things. That is: God elevates her intellect to divine understanding, because it is alone and divested of other contrary and alien knowledge; God moves her will freely to the love of God, because it is alone and freed from other affections; and God fills her memory with divine knowledge, because it is now alone and *empty* of other images and phantasies. Once the soul disencumbers these faculties and *empties* them of everything inferior and of possessiveness in regard to superior things, leaving them alone without these things, God engages them in the invisible and divine. It is God who guides her in this solitude, as St. Paul declares of the perfect . . . they are moved by the Spirit of God [Rom 8:14]. (C 35.5)

Thus, explaining how God, the Beloved, is both "silent music" and "sounding solitude" for the transformed soul, John reiterates in *The Spiritual Canticle* the basic teaching of *The Ascent/Dark Night* when he states, "When [a person's] spiritual faculties are alone and *empty* of all natural forms and apprehensions, they can receive in a most sonorous way the spiritual sound of the excellence of God, in himself and in his creatures" (C 14, 15.26).

## The Living Flame of Love

In the commentary on his poem *The Living Flame of Love*, John again stresses the need for emptiness in the spiritual journey to union with God when he describes the true nature of the human person. John views every human being as a created infinite capacity for God, especially for God's own knowledge and love. This infinite capacity abides primarily in one's spiritual faculties of intellect, memory, and will. These are our natural abilities or capacities to know, to remember, and to love, which John poetically pictures as our "deep caverns of feeling" (F 3). He writes, "These caverns are the soul's faculties: memory, intellect, and will. They are as deep as the profound goods of which they are capable since anything less that the infinite fails to fill them. . . . The capacity of these caverns is deep because the object of this capacity, namely God, is profound and infinite" (F 3.18, 22). Drawing on St. Thomas Aquinas's theory of the active and passive intellect, John explains that although we are limited in our natural ability to conceive and love God as God truly is, we are virtually unlimited or infinite in our capacity to receive God, especially God's own loving knowledge (A 2.8.4, 10.2; C 14, 15.14, 39.12).

A particular concept that we form of God is not God. The image we have of God is less than God. Our emotional experience of God is not God. These are only our own concepts, images, and emotional experiences. "But," as John reminds us, "in the contemplation we are discussing (by which God infuses himself into the soul), particular knowledge as well as acts made by the soul are unnecessary. The reason for this is that God in one act is communicating light and love together, which is loving supernatural knowledge. We can assert that this knowledge is like light that transmits heat, for that light also enkindles love. This knowledge is general and dark to the intellect because it is contemplative knowing, which is a ray of darkness for the intellect, as St. Dionysus teaches" (F 3.49). For this reason, John constantly counsels nonattachment to our limited, particular thoughts, images, and experiences of God, so that we may be open and free to receive God's own general loving knowledge in contemplation that both purifies and unites us with God. He advises us to "not be tied to any particular knowledge, earthly or heavenly, or to any covetousness for some satisfaction or pleasure, or to any other apprehension; . . . in such a way [we] may be *empty* through the pure spiritual negation of every creature, and placed in spiritual poverty. This is what the soul must do of itself, as the Son of God counsels: *Whoever does not renounce all possessions cannot be my disciple* [Lk 14:33]." John continues,

> This counsel refers not only to the renunciation according to the will of all corporeal and temporal things, but also to the dispossession of spiritual things, which includes spiritual poverty, to which the Son of God ascribes beatitude [Mt 5:3]. When the soul frees itself of all things and attains to *emptiness* and dispossession concerning them, which is equivalent to what it can do of itself, it is impossible that God fail to do his part by communicating himself to it, at least silently and secretly. It is more impossible than it would be for the sun not to shine on clear and uncluttered ground. As the sun rises in the morning and shines on your house so that its light may enter if you open the shutters, so God, who in watching over Israel does not doze [Ps 121:4] or, still less, sleep, will enter the soul that is *empty*, and fill it with divine goods. (F 3.46; see also A 3.2.13)

Reading *The Living Flame of Love*, one can almost feel John's sadness that many persons never come to understand their human nature or their infinite capacity for God. He notes that God "highly values his [own] work of having introduced persons into this solitude and *emptiness* regarding their faculties and activity so that he might speak to their hearts, which is what God always desires" (F 3.54). But regretfully, many never allow God to fulfill his desires in them. Because their lives—especially their minds and hearts, their "deep caverns of feelings"—are so filled with attachments to material and spiritual things and to particular understandings, images, and affection, they never discover who they truly are or what they have been created for. They never realize that God desires to give them so much more, to fill their lives with God's own life, especially divine loving knowledge.

On the other hand, many who do understand God's desire to transform their lives in divine love and knowledge resist God because of the pain involved in the self-emptying that is a condition for receiving the inflow of God into their lives. John observes, "From what persons suffer when [the deep caverns of feeling and the spiritual faculties of intellect, memory, and will] are *empty*, we can gain some knowledge of their enjoyment and delight when they are filled with God, since one contrary sheds light on the other" (F 3.18). In other words, the pain we feel in the self-emptying process is not necessarily a sign that something has gone wrong in our spiritual journey; rather, it is a vivid reminder of our infinite capacity for God. God alone relieves this pain by his own presence, always to a limited degree in this present life of faith, but completely when the future life of vision after death removes the veil separating the two.

Reading *The Living Flame*, one can also feel John's anger at those spiritual guides (F 3.43) who, because they do not understand our infinite capacity to receive God's loving knowledge that transforms our lives in love—"these directors do not know what spirit is," John says (F 3.54)—attempt to lead persons to union with God by ways of particular theories of spirituality, inspiring images, and intense religious experiences. For such spiritual masters, John gives this reminder: "God, like the sun, stands above souls ready to communicate himself. Let directors be content with disposing them for this according to evangelical perfection, which lies in nakedness and *emptiness* of sense and spirit; and let them not desire to go any further than this in building, since that function belongs only to the Father of Lights from whom descends every good and perfect gift (Jas 1:7). *If the Lord,* as David says, *does not build the house, in vain do its builders labor* [Ps 127:1]" (F 3.47).

## Letters of Spiritual Guidance

It should come as no surprise that John follows his own advice in his letters of spiritual guidance. For several years after he first arrived in Andalusia following his escape from prison in Toledo, John was the spiritual guide for the community of Carmelite nuns in Beas de Segura. Seven years later, in November 1586, he wrote these words to his "daughters in Christ":

> [The] waters of inward delights do not spring from the earth. One must open toward heaven the mouth of desire, *empty* of all other fullness, that thus it may not be reduced or restricted by some mouthful of another pleasure, but *empty* and open toward Him who says [in the book of

Psalms]: *open your mouth wide and I will fill it* [Ps 81:11].
Accordingly, those who seek satisfaction in something no
longer keep themselves *empty* that God might fill them
with his ineffable delight. And thus just as they go to God
so do they return, for their hands are encumbered and cannot receive what God is giving. May God deliver us from
these evil obstacles that hinder such sweet and delightful
freedom. (Lt 7)

To one of his fellow Carmelite friars who asked his counsel
on how to occupy the "will in the Lord alone by loving him
above all things," John replied at some length:

None of [the] particular things in which [the will] can
rejoice is God. In order to be united with God, the will
must consequently be *emptied of* and detached from all
disordered appetite and satisfaction with respect to every
particular thing in which it can rejoice, whether earthly
or heavenly, temporal or spiritual, so that purged and
cleansed of all inordinate satisfaction, joys, and appetites
it might be wholly occupied in loving God with its affections. . . . It is impossible for the will to reach the sweetness and delight of divine union and receive and feel the
sweet and loving embraces of God without the nakedness
and *emptiness* of its appetite with respect to every particular satisfaction, earthly and heavenly. This is what David
meant [in Psalm 81:11] when he said: *open your mouth and
I will fill it.* . . . That the soul have success in journeying
to God and being joined to him, it must have the mouth
of its will opened only to God, *empty* and dispossessed of
every morsel of appetite, so God may fill it with his love

and sweetness; and it must remain with this hunger and thirst for God alone, without desiring to be satisfied by any other thing, since here below it cannot enjoy God as he is in himself And what is enjoyable—if there is a desire for it, as I say—impedes this union. (Lt 13)

In 1589, Doña Juana de Pedraza, a young single woman in Granada for whom John was a spiritual guide, had written to him asking for help with her spiritual dryness. He replied,

Since you walk in these darknesses and *emptiness* of spiritual poverty, you think that everyone and everything is failing you. It is no wonder that in this [dryness] it also seems God is failing you. But nothing is failing you. . . . Those who desire nothing else than God walk not in darkness, however poor and dark they are in their own sight. . . . You are making good progress. Do not worry, but be glad! . . . You were never better off than now because you were never so humble or so submissive, or considered yourself and all worldly things to be so small; nor did you know that you were so evil or God was so good, nor did you serve God so purely and so disinterestedly as now, nor do you follow after the imperfections of your own will and interests as perhaps you were accustomed to do. . . . What do you think serving God involves other than avoiding evil, keeping his commandments, and being occupied with the things of God as best we can? . . . God does one a great favor when he darkens the faculties and impoverishes the soul in such a way that one cannot err with these. And if one does not err in this, what need is there in order to be right other than

to walk along the level road of the law of God and of the
Church, and live only in dark and true faith and certain
hope and complete charity, expecting all our blessings in
heaven, living here below like the pilgrims, the poor, the
exiled, orphans, the thirsty, without a road and without
anything, hoping for everything in heaven?

Rejoice and trust in God, for he has given you signs
that you can very well do so, and in fact you must do
so. . . . Commend . . . me to God, my daughter in
the Lord. (Lt 19)

## Synonyms

Throughout John's writings the word *emptiness* appears
in conjunction with other concepts such as spiritual poverty, dryness, solitude, negation, mortification, nakedness of spirit, purification, and dispossession. These are
all synonyms for the evangelical self-denial required for
the journey to union with God. *Emptiness* is perhaps
most closely associated in meaning with *darkness* since
both words imply the voluntary deprivation of sensory
and spiritual gratification that is a prerequisite for transformation in God through love (A 1.3.1–2). The metaphor of darkness, especially in John's classic poem *Noche
Oscura* (*The Dark Night*), best reveals the place of emptiness in Christian life.

One dark night,
fired with love's urgent longing
—ah, the sheer grace!—

I went out unseen,

my house being now all stilled.

Emptiness places our souls at rest through mortification of disordered desires.

O guiding night!

O night more lovely than the dawn!

O night that has united

the Lover with his beloved,

transforming the beloved in her Lover.

Emptiness transforms us in our beloved, Jesus Christ, the incarnate Wisdom of God.

I abandoned and forgot myself,

laying my face on my Beloved;

all things ceased; I went out from myself,

leaving my cares

forgotten among the lilies.

In emptiness, we rely on God alone and created things no longer have power over us.

## Summary and Conclusion

In summary and conclusion, emptiness in the writings of St. John of the Cross means nonattachment to objects—material and spiritual, natural and supernatural. The Christian spiritual journey demands such nonattachment: "Souls will be unable to reach perfection who do not strive to be content with having nothing, in such fashion that their natural and spiritual desire is satisfied with *emptiness*; for this is necessary in order to reach the highest tranquility and peace of spirit. In this way, God's love is almost always active in pure and simple souls" (SLL 54). This nonattachment enables us to become truly loving persons and to realize our deepest human longings. Above all, nonattachment disposes us to receive God's loving knowledge that transforms us into "simple and pure Wisdom, the Son of God" (A 2.15.4). Nonattachment is, indeed, a wise way to live, or, as our Zen koan states, "True emptiness is marvelous existence."

## Notes

1. From Hsueh-Tou-Chih-Chin, *The Record of Transmitting the Light* (Somerville, Mass.: Wisdom Publications, 1996). Displayed in a calligraphy by Roshi Robert E. Kennedy, S.J. Original painting by Amy Yee (Morning Star Zendo, 2008).

2. J. L. Astigarraga, A. Borrell, and F. J. Martín de Lucas, eds., *Concordancias de los Escritos de San Juan de la Cruz* (Rome: Teresianum, 1990), 1869–72. Quotations from St. John of the Cross in this essay are taken from Kieran Kavanaugh and Otilio Rodriguez, trans., *The Collected Works of Saint John of the Cross*, rev. ed. (Washington, D.C.: ICS Publications, 1991). Citations are in parentheses following the quotations in the text. For abbreviation key, see Translations and Abbreviations in the front of the present volume.

3. Colin Thompson, *St. John of the Cross: Songs in the Night* (Washington, D.C.: Catholic University of America Press, 2003), 188–89.

4. Appetites are "generally: inordinate affective desires in which the will participates; that is, willful desires not ordered to a moral or spiritual good. Thus the term is generally used in a more restricted

way than might be expected" (A 1.11.1–3). "Especially when habitual, they both impede union with God and weary, torment, darken, defile, and weaken the soul" (A 1.6.1, 11.3, 12.2–6). From "Glossary of Terms," in Kavanaugh and Rodriguez, *Collected Works*, 767.

5. Translation from Thompson, *St. John of the Cross*, 128.

# "O Guiding Night!"

## The Psychology of Hope
## in John of the Cross's Dark Night

### EDWARD HOWELLS

JOHN OF THE CROSS IS BEST known today for his association with "the dark night of the soul." What he meant by the phrase is less well known, but the term itself is widely used. All the uses of the phrase seem to have in common some kind of inner experience of profound imprisonment and desolation.[1] This retains something of what John of the Cross was talking about, but a vital part of John's context is missing. A National Gallery exhibition in London in 2009, *The Sacred Made Real*, gave a nice impression of the intensely religious culture of the Spain of John's day.[2] It showed that in the sixteenth and seventeenth centuries there was a rapid improvement in the techniques for creating realistic pictures and statues of Christ and the saints, with an emphasis on the viewer's emotive response, in particular their suffering. The tears of Mary, the mother of Jesus, and the wounds and blood of Christ were represented with extraordinary realism. The "dark nights" of John of the Cross are the psychological equivalent of these images. They paint a psychological outline for the viewer or reader who seeks to join Christ inwardly in Christ's suffering. The dark night of the soul is, therefore, primarily a religious suffering, suffered first by Christ. The symptoms of the suffering, though of considerable interest to John, are less important than what they achieve, which is to enable the viewer or reader to join Christ in the inner depths of his suffering. One can perhaps see a parallel between the improved skills of the artist in this period and the new psychological detail of John's descriptions of the dark nights.

I would like to focus on just one aspect of John of the Cross's psychology, which is his treatment of hope. I have chosen hope because it was central in the sixteenth-century context of John's thought and also has resonance today. John is interested in hope because it is a theological virtue that points to God and the beatific vision. That context is largely missing in the modern or contemporary world, but like those sixteenth- and seventeenth-century artists, John is also interested in giving psychological color to hope as an inner response to suffering, and this view of hope remains of interest in a wider context today. How is it possible to hope when all the evidence is to the contrary? *How* does one hope when there is nothing in the present to give one hope but rather the opposite? What goes on inside a person who can hope even in the midst of suffering? These are psychological questions on which John can contribute.

The dilemma arises for John in the context of one who is seeking to join Christ in Christ's suffering. The difficulty that John pinpoints is that suffering on the model of Christ actually obscures the faith, hope, and love by which one first seeks to relate to Christ. To suffer with Christ is to find that one cannot maintain a grasp on one's secure ways of relating to God through faith, hope, and love. John asks what it would mean to join Christ in his cry of dereliction, "My God, my God, why have you forsaken me?" (Mt 27:46). At this moment of "extreme abandonment," John says, Christ was "annihilated in his soul, without any consolation and relief."[3] When we join Christ in abandonment, our faith, hope, and love become dark and empty, John says (A 2.6.2), as we pass through Christ's death with Christ, on the way to resurrection.

He understands this inner emptying and darkening in terms of an Augustinian psychology, where faith, hope, and charity belong to intellect, memory, and will respectively. Charity is of the will, faith is of the intellect, and hope is of the memory. John uses these correlations to structure the middle part of his journey through the dark nights, in *The Ascent of Mount Carmel*, books two and three (A 2.12–A 3.45). The reason that faith becomes dark is that when we seek God in an intimate and direct relation, as is the case when we enter with love into Christ's suffering on the cross, our intellects are unable to contain God's nature. God is a "general, pure act (*acto general y puro*)" in contrast to the particular forms of created things that we know (A 2.12.6, pp. 325/139). We are accustomed to knowing by grasping the particular forms of things, but in relation to God, we are faced with an uncategorizable divine otherness, which is therefore dark (faith/intellect is treated in A 2.12–32). Theological love or charity is darkened too, because we cannot unite with God with our wills in the way that we relate to the created things that we know. Again, there is no particular form of God to relate to, so we feel only that we lack God (A 3.16.2; love/will is treated in A 3.16–45).[4] Hope is also darkened, because our power to reach out to God is found to be empty of anything we can grasp. John relates this darkness of hope to the memory, for reasons I shall come to in a moment (hope/memory is treated in A 3.1–15). John's concern in *The Ascent of Mount Carmel* and *The Dark Night* is specifically for those who "feel lost" in the midst of these darknesses, and the inner conflict that they feel when they experience an abandonment like Christ's death on the cross. He wants to tell them how to recognize the psychological symptoms of this suffering and how to respond, so they can ultimately find light in the darkness. To return to their former spiritual exercises is not the answer; rather, a new intensity of engagement with God is to be discerned in the midst of the suffering (A Prol 4–6).

For John, hope focuses on the paradoxical possession of what we do not yet have. He quotes three biblical verses as his starting place. The first is from the book of Hebrews: "Faith is the substance of things to be hoped for, the evidence of things not seen" (Heb 11:1, Vulgate; A 2.6.3, A 3.7.2). The second and third are from Romans: "We ourselves who have the first fruits of the spirit moan within ourselves, hoping for the adoption of sons" (Rom 8:23, Vulgate; C 1.14); and "hope that is seen is not hope, for how does a man hope for what he sees" (Rom 8:24, Vulgate)— that is, John adds, how does one hope for what one possesses (A 2.6.3)?[5] Hope, when it is directed to God in pure love, rather than to creaturely projections of God, is felt initially as darkness and pain. Hope is a "moan" (*gemido*)

arising from the "wound of love" (*herida de amor*) in relation to Christ, John says—the moan of longing for God
who feels absent when one enters in love into the place of
Christ's abandonment (C 1.14, p. 747/422). It is an inward
flight toward things that are not possessed (A 2.6.5). In the
background is John's view that complete inward and outward dispossession lies at the heart of the Gospel. Christ's
command is to renounce all possessions, and he gives this
an interior interpretation, regarding it primarily in terms of
inner dispositions. Yet, since Christ too is the one who fully
dispossesses himself in the suffering of the cross, paradoxically it can be asserted that God is indeed to be found most
immediately in this place of dispossession. John says, "Every
possession is against hope; as St. Paul says, hope is for that
which is not possessed [Heb 11:1]. In the measure that the
memory becomes dispossessed of things, in that measure it
will have hope. . . . When, precisely, it is more dispossessed of things, it hopes more; and when it has reached
perfect dispossession, it will remain with the perfect possession of God in divine union. . . . For whoever does not
renounce all his possessions cannot be Christ's disciple [Lk
14:33]."[6] The paradox of hope thus centers on the complete
dispossession of all that we thought we were hoping for, in
preference for the possession of God, which is yet incon-
ceivable and ungraspable—strictly unpossessable. What we
possess in hope is had by means of complete inward dispossession, just as Christ, by dispossession, is the presence of
God for us on earth (in *kenosis*).

   John seeks a psychological analysis of this paradox, in
terms of the faculty of memory. Why does he relate hope to

memory, when it is more obviously a matter of the will and the intellect? To hope for something is to know it in some sense and to go out to it with the will. John has a particular view of memory that he takes from Augustine (probably not directly; the transmission from Augustine is complex).[7] Following Augustine, John takes memory to be not merely a brain function for storing things, like a computer's memory, but the seat of human identity. In Augustine's *On the Trinity*, memory is said to be the means "by which the mind is available to itself (*sibi praesto*), ready to be understood by its thought about itself, and for both to be conjoined by its love of itself."[8] Memory supplies the self to the mind, making its acts of knowing and willing personal. This is a distinct faculty of the mind and not merely part of intellect and will. Memory is the mind's presentation of itself to itself within its mental acts. Thus, for John, memory is the manner in which I *possess myself*, both in relation to myself and to God. By linking hope to memory, John is focusing on the manner in which I possess myself in this act. Hope is an act of dispossession, while memory is the ground of self-possession, so they are related in a way that, initially at least, is antagonistic. The memory must give up its self-possession, in hope. When I go out to God in faith and love, I must let go not just of what I know about God in faith, and of any finite object of the will in charity, but also of my self-possession in memory. In hope, I go out to God by letting go of my possession of myself, in relation to my acts of loving and knowing.[9]

For John, the element of dispossession in hope must be complete. The way to possess God in hope is not to return to one's former means of possession. One can never possess God in the way that one formerly possessed oneself. But memory is, at this point, subjected to an internal differentiation by John. It is not an option for John, any more than for Augustine, to say that memory is simply removed. If memory is the seat of the identity, to remove it altogether—to say that it is eradicated by hope—would be to destroy the human person. One may *feel* that this is happening in the dark night. John says that one feels one is losing all sense of oneself, in a complete internal oblivion, caused by the loss of memory (A 3.2.5–6). One even feels one is without hope, paradoxically, because one loses any sense of orientation to the things one had formerly hoped for (N 2.9.9).[10] But the memory is not eradicated. In John's view, what is happening is that the *particular* memories that one has of who one is and "how it feels to be me" are being detached from the memory, while at a deeper level, the memory itself is emerging as an entity that is not constituted by these memories. The true essence of memory lies beyond, John suggests, in the sheer power of recall. Memory is not my individual memories of myself but the deeper level of identity in which I am present to myself by a sheer act of recall. One does not remember things *about* oneself at this level but relates to one's acts of willing and knowing purely as oneself.

André Bord has shown that John departs from Augustine's view of memory when he separates the recall and storage functions of memory.[11] John ascribes the storage function of memory, where particular memories are stored, to a separate interior sense of the soul, called the phantasy [hereafter fantasy]. When we use the memory in relation to things in the world, we draw on the fantasy, to recall the objects stored from previous acts of knowledge. Fantasy and memory work together, giving memory both recall and storage functions. But unlike Augustine, when the memory works in relation to God, John makes a distinction between storage and recall. Memory now works without fantasy, and without all particular memories. The significance of this is that here we see clearly how John develops Augustine's psychology in order to understand the psychology of Christ's suffering. The new distinction enables him to say that memory can be wholly dispossessed in the suffering of self-annihilation, in respect of particular memories, while at a deeper level, the power of recall is coming into its own in relation to God. At this deeper level, memory is a pure relationality, the purified image of God in the soul, orientated to God for God to possess. As an aside, John points out that there is nothing wrong with particular memories of created things; we of course need them to function in the world (A 3.15.1). The point is that they are not essential to the memory. In essence, the memory is a purely relational act. It can possess the created self, in relation to the fantasy, or it can possess the divine selfhood in relation to God, without the fantasy.[12] It is not limited by its link to creatures in the fantasy.

John is saying that the true psychology of the human person is in no sense to be identified with what a person knows, even of themselves. The soul's particular memories, and the storage function of memory in general, are peripheral to selfhood. The self is constituted rather by the power of recall, which brings the self to bear in knowing and loving, and this is a sheer relational dynamism. As a sheer relational dynamism, memory is unlimited by the finite objects of the created world. The memory seeks to be "free and disencumbered and unattached to any earthly or heavenly consideration."[13] It seeks the unlimited dynamism of possession by God. Thus, in hope, memory stretches out to the divine other, and at the same time, even while dispossessing itself in relation to creatures, comes into its own full possession of itself in relation to God.

What kind of possession is this? John says that the possession of memory here is by an act of recall that is both "formally within itself [*en sí . . . formalmente*]" and yet also beyond. Memory recalls not the images and forms preserved in the fantasy but what it has in itself "as an image in a mirror [*la imagen en el espejo*]" (A 3.13.7, p. 422/234).[14] That is, it is by reflecting what it is in relation to another, as a mirror does, that memory possesses itself truly. It is as a responsive, purely relational activity that memory possesses itself.

The structure of this relationality is understood by John on the pattern of his mystical interpretation of the Song of Songs. Memory, which no longer seeks to touch or take hold of God in the manner of things in the world, goes out to God in the manner of love toward a Spouse. It is content only with him. Hope enables the memory to identify solely with the love of the Spouse (N 2.21.6–8). The logic of dispossession and possession is thus fleshed out by the relationality of charity, as developed at length in his two later major works, *The Spiritual Canticle* and *The Living Flame of Love*. In love, what is possessed is possessed by mutual surrender.

The former painful emptiness of love, in the "wound of love," which took the soul out of itself in hope, is now met by an infinite love, also an act of surrender, which the intellect, transformed by faith, begins to recognize and know as the uncreated form of God.[15] The memory, in turn, is able to possess this uncreated form of God in the manner of love, by mutual dispossession, as sheer relationality. John quotes St. Paul's saying, that while having nothing, the soul is here possessing all things (*nihil habentes, et omnia possidentes* [2 Cor 6:10, Vulgate, cited N 2.8.5). The mutual dispossession of love becomes the soul's manner of possession, in the love relationship.

Still, it requires some more working out to say how memory can function in the context of the mutual dispossession of ecstatic love. John has three further suggestions. First, for the memory, dispossession of this kind is no longer debilitating and dark. In the love of union, going out to the other is met by the other's love with such simultaneity that dispossession becomes sheer gift. Hope in the memory is therefore "no longer heavy and constraining to the substance of my soul, but rather its glory and delight and amplitude."[16] Dispossession is no longer an obstacle but the unfettered activity of sheer relationality that is the essence of memory. Second, the memory is not only regained but enlarged by this transformation. John links memory closely to what he calls "the substance of the soul."[17] The substance of the soul is one of a number of terms that John uses for what is generally known as the *apex mentis* in the tradition, where the soul is most like God; other terms he uses are the "soul itself," the "innermost being," "depth," the "abyss," and the "center" of the soul.[18] The substance of the soul means for John not a static substance but the aspect of the soul that most closely resembles the divine substance, which is pure act. The pure act of God, which becomes incarnate in the complete dispossession of Christ, touches us in our own complete dispossession, which at its deepest point is the dispossession of memory in the substance of the soul. This expands memory from a narrow, limited faculty into the unlimited dynamism of shared life with God. Memory is not reduced but greatly enlarged and energized.

Third, John takes up a further correlation of memory, intellect, and will from the tradition of Augustine, this time the correlation with Father, Son, and Holy Spirit. He associates memory with the Father, intellect with the Son, and will with the Holy Spirit. In the case of memory, he uses the correlation to signal that, even within a wholly relational context, the memory has a distinct role, still as the means by which we possesses ourselves as selves. The memory, he says, "which by itself perceived only the figures and phantasms of creatures, is changed through this union so as to have in its mind the eternal years mentioned by David [Ps 76:6]."[19] He links the possession of eternity in the memory to the Father in the Trinity in the respect that the Father is the eternal, unsourced source of the Trinity. Though in pure relationality with the other persons, the Father is also the source of the Trinity. The memory, John suggests, is able to ground the selfhood of the soul in the same way, but now in the unlimited source of the eternal years. The "I" of the memory, the way in which the self is present in the soul's knowing and loving, is as a self extended by relationship with God, but still as a self. It is a self sourced in what John calls the "abyssal embrace of the Father's sweetness."[20]

What can be drawn from this treatment of hope and memory? The context of the dark nights, which is the intense suffering of Christ's inner abandonment as it is shared by us, situates hope at an extreme. John uses the theological structure of classical theism to deny that there is anything that a human being can grasp in hope, at the deepest level. Hope, while yet remaining true hope, can be had when there is nothing to hope for that we can grasp. In fact, in any conventional sense, there is no hope here, for what is hoped for is not known, even as a distant goal; it can only be desired negatively, as a sheer lack, and it is beyond all natural possession.

However, in spite of the uncompromising God-centered structure from which John begins, he also offers a rich human psychology of hope. His treatment of the memory suggests that the psychology of hope should be understood as pointing to a deep "doubleness" in human nature. To be human is to be hopeful, and it has to be asked why we remain hopeful even when we have nothing to hope for, when all the evidence is to the contrary, and even our inner powers of hoping are empty and dark. When all the things that we can hope for in the world—ordinary human happiness, health, security, and so on—are lost, why is it possible for humans to go on hoping? For John, it is because the manner in which we possess ourselves as humans is not in relation to those things but rather in an unlimited dynamism that is always going out beyond what it currently knows and rests in. We are constituted in relation not only to the particular things we hope for but also more deeply to what is beyond those things. Further, this dynamism is a personal relationality, which seeks selfhood through relationship with another. Of course, this other is the divine other for John and must be infinite, but in human terms he is making the suggestion simply that our deepest selfhood is not possessed by ourselves alone. We are not the limits of our own self-possession.

Humans are capable of remaining hopeful whatever they suffer, because as selves we seek self-constitution in sheer relationality, not in what is already possessed. Human hope springs from the fact that we are not basically autonomous but relational. Hope is possible because selfhood is a greater, more hidden thing than anything we can grasp, constituted most of all by that which is not itself, with which it seeks an ever-new, self-defining relationship. In this way, John of the Cross shows that precisely what we cannot *possess* of hope is our hope. It is the darkness of our inner unpossessability that gives us the hope, even when we can see nothing to hope for.

### Notes

1. The Carmelite writer Constance FitzGerald, seeking to situate the dark night in common human experience, describes it as an experience of "impasse," where one feels imprisoned by a "whole life situation" with no way out and nowhere to turn. Constance FitzGerald, "Impasse and Dark Night," in Joann Wolski Conn, ed. *Women's Spirituality: Resources for Christian Development*, 2nd ed. (New York: Paulist Press, 1996), 286–311 at 288.

2. Accompanied by the exhibition catalog *The Sacred Made Real: Spanish Painting and Culture, 1600–1700* (London: National Gallery Company/Yale University Press, 2009).

3. "El mayor desamparo"; "anihilado en el alma sin consuelo y alivio alguno" (A 2.7.11, p. 310/124). Editions and abbreviations of John's works are as follows. Spanish text: *Obras Completas de San Juan de la* Cruz, ed. Lucinio Ruano, 14th ed. (Madrid: Biblioteca de Autores Cristianos, 1994); English text: *The Collected Works of John of the Cross*, trans. Kieran Kavanaugh and Otilio Rodriguez (Washington D.C.: ICS Publications, 1979). Where words are quoted, page numbers are given first for the Spanish text, second for the English text.

4. In *The Spiritual Canticle*, John expands on this lack in the will, in commenting on this stanza of his poem: "Why, since you wounded / This heart, don't you heal it? / And why, since You stole it from me, / Do you leave it so, / And fail to carry off what you have stolen?"(stanza 9) He comments, "The soul is like an empty vessel waiting to be filled, or like a hungry man craving for food, or like a sick person moaning for health, or like one suspended in the air with nothing to lean on" (C 9.6, p. 771/444).

5. "Est autem fides sperandorum substantia rerum argumentum non parentum" (Heb 11:1); "Nosotros mismos, que tenemos las primicias del espíritu, dentro de nosotros mismos gemimos, esperando la adopcíon de hijos de Dios" (Rom 8:23, cited in Spanish by John); "Spes, quae videtur, non est spes; nam quod videt quis, quid sperat?" (Rom 8:24). For a recent discussion of the "possession" of hope in Hebrews 11:1, relevant to the discussion here, see Benedict XVI's encyclical letter *Spe Salvi* (November 30, 2007), para. 7–9, http://www.vatican.va.

6. "Toda posesión es contra esperanza, la cual, como dice san Pablo, *es de lo que no se posee* [Heb 11:1]. De donde, cuanto más la memoria se deposee tanto más tiene de esperanza . . . y entonces espera más cuande se desposee más, y cuando se hubiere desposeído perfectamente, quedará con las posesión de Dios en unión divina. . . . Porque *el que no renuncia a todo lo que posee no puede ser su discípulo* [Lk 14:33]" (A 3.7.2, p. 413/225). For further passages on this dispossession, particularly in hope/memory, see A 3.11.1–2; N 2.8.5, 2.6–11; and on the possession of God by means of dispossession, C 1.14, 12.7, 26.9; F 3.21, 79.

7. See Edward Howells, "John of the Cross (1542–91)," in *The Oxford Guide to the Historical Reception of Augustine* (Oxford: Oxford University Press, 2013). Whether John holds that there are two rational faculties (intellect and will), following Aquinas, or three (including memory), following Augustine, has been a long-running topic of debate in John of the Cross scholarship. I take the view that there are three, following, for example, André Bord, *Mémoire et espérance chez Jean de la Croix*, Bibliothèque de Spiritualité 8 (Paris: Beauchesne, 1971); for an opposing view, see Dominic Doyle, "From Triadic to Dyadic Soul: A Genetic Study of John of the Cross on the Anthropological Basis of Hope," *Studies in Spirituality* 21 (2011): 219–41.

8. Augustine, *The Trinity*, trans. Edmund Hill, ed. John E. Rotelle, in *The Works of St. Augustine*, part 1, vol. 5 (Hyde Park, N.Y.: New City Press, 1991), 14.14, 382.

9. John, like Augustine, does not regard memory, intellect, and will as capable of operating separately. Consequently, as he says, faith, hope, and love always grow together (C 26.8).

10. John regards hope for what is not God—for anything created— as a passion, as distinct from the theological virtue of hope. He names the passion of hope as one of four passions: joy, hope, sorrow, and fear (A 2.16.2; C 20, 21.4). One must become detached from the passion of hope in order to possess theological hope.

11. Bord, *Mémoire et espérance*, 69–97.

12. Note that there is a return to the created self in union with God, though now by means of dispossession (i.e., in a fully detached manner) that passes beyond the stark alternatives of creatures versus God set up in the dark nights. See Edward Howells, *John of the Cross and Teresa of Ávila: Mystical Knowing and Selfhood* (New York: Crossroad, 2002), esp. chaps. 2 and 3.

13. "Libre y desembarazada, no atándola a ninguna consideración de arriba ni de abajo" (A 3.2.14, p. 407/218).

14. Bord, *Mémoire et espérance*, 88–93. Bord notes that John uses the phrases "soul itself" and "substance of the soul" in close

association with the spiritual memory—practically as a synonym—as in this passage.

15. On the shape of this mutual dispossession/possession in love, see F 3.79; C 6.6, 12.7, 27.1, 33. On the way in which, by this means, God becomes knowable and known by the soul, see Howells, *John of the Cross*, chap. 3.

16. "Ya no eres pesadumbre y aprieto para la sustancia de mi alma, mas antes eres la gloria y deleites y anchura de ella" (F 1.26, p. 933/589).

17. For this term, in addition to the passage just cited, see A 2.24.4, 32.2; N 2.13.3; C 14, 15.2, 15.14; F 2.17, 21, 4.10; and connected passages, N 2.23.11; C 20, 21.13, 26.5, 26.11; F 3.69.

18. For a treatment of these terms, see Howells, *John of the Cross*, 47–59; also, on the relation of memory, intellect, and will to the substance/depth/center of the soul, 31–34.

19. "La memoria, que de suyo percibía solo las figuras y fantasmas de las criaturas, es trocada por medio de esta unión a *tener en la mente los años eternos* que David dice [Ps 76:6]" (F 2.34, p. 965/608).

20. "En el abrazo abisal de su dulzura" (F 1.15, p. 925/585).

# PART III

―――◆―――

*Prophetic Intimations
from Teresa of Ávila*

# The Jesus Mysticism of Teresa of Ávila:

## *Its Importance for Theology and Contemporary Spirituality*

### SANDRA M. SCHNEIDERS, I.H.M.

THIS STUDY ARISES FROM a convergence of several biblical, theological, and spirituality issues that I have been concerned about for several years. In no particular order, these concerns are the following: the nature of spiritual, and especially mystical, experience and its expression; revelation and its relation to Scripture, hermeneutics, and theopoetics; the bodily resurrection of Jesus and the role of the risen Jesus in the life of the believer; and, most recently, what strikes me as a highly questionable "drift" in the area of Christian spirituality, both academically and practically, toward substituting some, often quite vague, notion of the "cosmic Christ" for the real personal risen human being, Jesus. Jesus is deemed by some of our contemporaries to be too limited—in historical time and place, by ethnicity and gender, by personal life experience, in evolutionary location, and so on—to carry the soteriological "weight" traditionally assigned to him. Can a single Jewish male human being, they ask, who lived a short life in a particular time and place and who died a real human death, be realistically regarded by modern people as the unique and universal Savior of the world; as the subject and object of a personal relationship with the Christian believer in all times and places including our own; as the central focus and norm of Christian theology; in short, as the unique center of Christian faith and life with universal significance for humankind?

All of these issues converge, explicitly or implicitly, in the theological writings of Teresa of Ávila, a Carmelite nun who was born in 1515 in Ávila, Spain; died in 1582; was canonized by the Catholic Church in 1622; and was declared a Doctor of the Universal Church—the first woman to be so honored—in 1970. So, I want to interrogate her writing on these subjects, in particular her most highly developed theological work, *The Interior Castle*, completed in 1577, when Teresa was sixty-two years old—forty years into her life as a religious, seventeen years after her most important mystical experience upon which this book pivots, and five years from her death. I will be concerned especially with the sixth of the seven mansions of the interior life that Teresa describes in this classic work of mystical theology, and particularly with chapters 7–10 of the sixth mansions.

As a woman in sixteenth-century Spain, Teresa of Ávila had little formal education and no academic training in theology. There is evidence in her writings, however, of her assiduous reading of the Bible and of her hearing and reciting it in the Divine Office she prayed daily. She also read and heard passages from classical spiritual and theological texts that were readings in the Office. She studied the works of certain contemporary spiritual writers and some of the classics of spirituality, to which she refers. She listened avidly to the sermons preached in her convent or places where she traveled. And she consulted frequently with confessors, spiritual directors, and those she called "learned men," that is, theologians, as well as "persons of spiritual experience" living in or visiting the area around her convent in Ávila in that period of intense spiritual ferment and mystical controversy that was sixteenth-century Spain. And she clearly knew, whether from reading, preaching, or personal instruction by her advisors, something of the theology of such giants as Augustine and Thomas Aquinas.

But none of these, nor all of them together, can adequately account for the extraordinary theological content of Teresa's writing, especially her masterpiece, *The Interior Castle*. So the question is, where did she get the doctrine we find in her works, especially her teaching on the nature and experience of prayer from its beginnings through the highest stages of the mystical life? And how did she develop the remarkable literary forms through which she makes her doctrine available to her readers? These two questions bring us to the primary concerns of this essay, the *revelatory character* of Teresa's mystical experience and the *theopoetic character* of her writing.

Before getting into these questions, I want to address an important preliminary question: why, given the volume of learned writing on these topics by twenty centuries of professional theologians, should we listen to Teresa of Ávila, a sixteenth-century cloistered nun without formal theological credentials? There are at least two important reasons: first, she is a Doctor of the Universal Church; second, she was, and is, by biblical standards, a prophet in the church.

A Doctor of the Church—and there are only thirty-seven as compared with the countless canonized martyrs, confessors, and other categories of saints—is someone declared such on the basis of two criteria: outstanding holiness of life and eminent doctrine expressed in a significant body of writings. The person is declared a doctor by the authoritative (though not *de fide*) declaration by an ecumenical council or the pope. (In fact, all thirty-seven have been declared doctors by the pope, not by a council.) Though the conferring of the title "doctor" is not an assertion that there are no errors of any kind anywhere in the person's writings, there obviously are no significant or systemic *doctrinal* errors.[1] Thus, the teaching of a Doctor of the Church is proposed to the whole church, not simply to his or her compatriots or contemporaries, and not merely as interesting or edifying for those attracted to it, but as a powerful, original, singularly articulate presentation of the faith itself or some aspect of it.

The conferral of the title of Doctor of the Church on Teresa of Ávila was a formal declaration that her writings on Christian spirituality are regarded as a doctrinal gift meant for the whole church, and thus eminently worthy of our study. While there are many canonized saints and respected theologians in the church's history, Doctors of the Church are recognized for the singular conjunction of extraordinary holiness with extraordinary theological brilliance. So, in a certain sense, the Doctors of the Church could be considered the models for scholars of religion in every age.

The second reason for studying Teresa of Ávila, namely, the prophetic character of her ministry, is propounded by the Discalced Carmelite Kieran Kavanaugh, certainly one of the best Teresian scholars of the twentieth century, in his commentary on chapter 8 of the sixth mansions of *The Interior Castle.*[2] In this chapter (IC 6.8.1; also described in L 27), Teresa describes what she calls an "intellectual vision" of Christ that took place in 1560 when Teresa was forty-five years old. Kavanaugh claims, and I think he is from a biblical point of view quite correct, that this experience of the glorified Christ was, in Teresa's life, analogous to the theophany of Moses at the burning bush or the Christophany of Paul on the road to Damascus, that is, it was a divine vocation to prophetic ministry among the people of God. The great prophets of both testaments were called, commissioned, and sent to their people precisely as *prophets* by means of a revelatory inaugural experience, usually involving either or both "seeing" and "hearing" of some sort. Jesus, as is recounted in the Gospel narratives of his baptism in the Jordan (see Mt 3:13–17; Mk 1:9–11; Lk 3:21–22), is the primary example of this vocational phenomenon, and Jesus interprets his own prophetic call in the synagogue scene recounted in Luke 4:16–30 in which he assimilates himself to the prophet Isaiah (see Is 61:11–2) who proclaimed, "The Spirit of the Lord is upon me; he has anointed me . . . to proclaim good news to the poor."

Moses, Isaiah, Jeremiah, Ezekiel, Amos, Hosea, and others in the Old Testament and then Mary Magdalene, Paul, and others in the New Testament testify to their inaugural prophetic experience that is simultaneously vocation to and commissioning for public ministry of the Word and personal enlightenment about the content of the message entrusted to them. The inaugural vision/experience that creates the prophet's identity and launches his or her ministry is some kind of mystical experience described as seeing, hearing, or feeling. And we will spend some time reflecting on what such an experience involves. But the important thing here is to recognize the pattern of prophetic vocation in the life of Teresa as a warrant of the authority she claims, her later readers recognize, and the church acknowledges for her teaching on the spiritual life that, as Kavanaugh says, is in essence Christological.

Kavanaugh bases his claim that Teresa's mystical experience in 1560 was a genuine prophetic inaugural vision on his interpretation of the historical facts of her life. Prior to this event, he says, there "was still nothing of the prophet, or the doctor, or the foundress" (IC, p. 345[3]) in Teresa's life. She was certainly deeply immersed in her own spiritual life, in practicing and trying to understand her prayer and in increasing fidelity, both outer and inner, to her vocation to solitude and silence. But after the experiences of 1560, she became a ministerial dynamo. She produced her large body of spiritual writing[4] and made all of her seventeen foundations of the Carmelite Reform.[5] In other words, from 1560 on she begins to function prophetically in the public sphere as apostle and teacher. (A fascinating theme in Teresa's writing, which cannot be followed up in this essay, is her ongoing reflection on the classical trope of the relation between Mary and Martha as a biblical treatment of the relationship between contemplative prayer and prophetic ministry, which are progressively integrated in the mature Teresa as they so clearly are in the life of Jesus.)

This critical turning point in Teresa's life, beginning with her mystical experience in 1560, was expressed in her vow to "do always the more perfect thing," which in someone not moved and sustained by such a call, would have been a classic recipe for spiritual shipwreck in the churning waters of scrupulosity and pusillanimity, a vice Teresa particularly abhorred. Perhaps most beautifully symbolic of Teresa's complete possession by Christ as a prophet among the people of God was her changing of her name at this point from Teresa de Ahumada, drawing her dignity and worth from her human origins, to Teresa of Jesus, who was now the center and driving force of her identity, mission, and ministry.

So, to sum up, here is why we should listen to Teresa of Ávila on such important questions as the reality and nature of spiritual experience, revelation, the bodily resurrection of Jesus, and his real presence in the life of the believer and his universal salvific significance: first, because the church, by declaring Teresa a Doctor of the Church, authoritatively proposes her teaching to all believers as preeminently worth studying; and second, because the evident characteristics of the genuine prophetic vocation as it is presented in Scripture mark Teresa's life and teaching as "from God" and "intended for God's people."

In light of this, we turn to our major concern: Teresa's teaching as a resource for reflection on major theological and religious questions of our own day. I will discuss Teresa's mature synthesis on mystical experience under three rubrics:

first, the *nature* and *mode* of Teresa's experience of Jesus, which I will suggest is *objective revelation mediated primarily by visions and locutions*; second, the *content* of her revelatory experience, which is *Jesus, bodily risen, within the mystery of the Trinity*; third, the unique *expression* of these experiences in her writings, which I will suggest is best understood not as systematic or speculative theology but as *theopoiesis*. This synthetic treatment will, I hope, shed some light on the contemporary issues I have raised and others related to them.

## The Nature and Mode of Teresa's Mystical Experience of Jesus: Revelation Mediated by Visions and Locutions

Revelation, or God's self-manifestation to and engagement with rational creatures, is the source and the content of our faith. Thus revelation is the foundational category of all theology. Unless God makes Godself known to humans, we simply have no access to God. Unlike the created phenomena in our world, material or spiritual, God as ultimate mystery from and in which all created being exists, is not a being in the series of beings of which we are a part, and thus God is not subject to our investigations, no matter how sophisticated or subtle our methods. This is why we call faith, the ability to perceive and respond to God in some way, a "gift." Strictly speaking, it is God who is not only the giver but also the Gift as Jesus said to the Samaritan woman: "If you knew the gift of God and who it is who speaks to you" (see Jn 4:10). But we humans cannot make revelation "happen."

Teresa experienced God directly and desired to communicate that experience. However, she was very aware that humans are easily mistaken even in very ordinary and terrestrial matters and so much more likely to be deceived in regard to things completely beyond our ordinary sensible and intellectual capacities. And her culture, both secular and especially ecclesiastical, insisted vehemently that women, because of their intrinsically inferior nature, were especially prone to hysteria and self-deception, above all in the area of religion. Consequently, Teresa had an almost inordinate fear that, even though her spiritual experiences were powerfully self-authenticating, she could be mistaken. Although she did not assume that everything that passed through her head was divine revelation, and gave lip service to the cultural caveats about the "weaker sex" and its propensity for delusion, Teresa was actually quite discerning about this matter. In her writing she identifies three possible sources of what appear to be what she calls "spiritual experiences." Only one of these sources, Teresa believed, was to be trusted.

First, there is psychological pathology, conditions we would call hysteria, depression, and so on, and which she often attributes to (or even equates with) overactivity of the "imagination," by which she meant fantasy. Such *psychological imbalances* give rise to hallucinations, psychosomatic illnesses, melancholy, trances, and so on, to which she feared she, like most "weak women," could be particularly susceptible. Second, unusual religious experiences can be the work of the *devil*, who was patently real to Teresa in a way we moderns can find a bit disconcerting. Or third, spiritual experiences can come *from God* who can manifest Godself to the soul in very direct and sometimes extraordinary ways.

In her consultations with theologians and spiritually experienced persons, and by her own gradually developed gift of discernment under the influence of God's inner teaching, Teresa developed a whole system of criteria for discerning the authenticity and proper interpretation of spiritual experiences. She was quite astute in her ability to recognize psychological pathology and had some remarkably modern practical suggestions for superiors in the treatment of such: they should moderate the person's physical austerities especially in regard to food and sleep, provide deliberate distraction by assigning absorbing work or moderate relaxation, and generally not make the fuss hysterics, hypochondriacs, and narcissists crave over their supposed mystical experiences. Teresa herself was embarrassed and fearful when her spiritual experiences had physical reverberations that were publicly visible. However, she was adamant in her conviction that her mystical experience, while it sometimes *caused* psychological and physical symptoms such as deep fear, guilt, or anxiety—and we might guess a certain amount of psychosomatic illness, especially headaches, nausea, and such— as well as genuine ecstasies and raptures, was *not caused by* psychological imbalance. Her oft-repeated insistence that she had such a weak imagination that she could not even engage in ordinary discursive meditation, much less dream up visions, was perhaps, at least in part, self-defense against the notion that her religious experience was due to an overactive fantasy life.

Handling diabolical influence called for much greater subtlety. Teresa was a sixteenth-century woman living with one foot in the medieval three-tiered universe whose deepest tier, hell, was populated by legions of evil spirits under the command of God's archenemy, Satan. Her other foot was in the emerging modern world of experimental science and philosophical enlightenment, which gave Teresa an extraordinary avidity for and confidence in theologically sound teaching. But in any case, she had to learn to recognize the devil's fingerprints if she were not to live in constant crippling spiritual fear and incessant self-doubt.

As in relation to psychological illusions, Teresa developed a quite sophisticated system of criteria for discernment of diabolical influence. For example, anything that seemed to contradict Scripture or explicit church teaching was highly (though not apodictically) suspect. Anything that had negative moral effects, for example, that did not conduce to humility and charity or, worse, led to spiritual complacency or overconfidence; that produced distraction or led to dissipation; that decreased fear of and reverence toward God; or that produced tepidity, lack of generosity, overattachment to persons or objects, and so on, was definitely not to be trusted no matter how pious the causes might appear.

On the other hand, Teresa was convinced that the devil's ability to mimic God's action in her life was extremely limited. If what she experienced had good spiritual effects manifested in a deeper desire for prayer, greater generosity, deeper humility, or a more steady practice of virtue, she felt fairly certain that the devil could not be the cause. Not only could an evil cause not produce genuinely good effects, but also Teresa had enough respect for the devil to doubt that he was into self-defeating behavior. Even if he could, Satan would not lead her deeper into the love of God.

The third possible cause of spiritual experience is God's direct self-revelatory action in the life of the person. Difficult as this is for many moderns to process, Teresa maintained that she received her doctrine basically from her experience, that is, her immediate, personal encounter with Jesus within the mystery of the triune God. She usually speaks of the context of this revelatory encounter as "prayer," but it was actually not restricted to times of formal prayer. Rather, it suffused her active and community life as well, especially as her Jesus consciousness became more and more continuous and all embracing.

Teresa was often upset by these divine communications, concerned about how she could know whether they were real, were from God, meant what she thought they meant, and so on. She was almost driven by the need to confide, consult about, and appropriate her experience, both by conversation with people she felt knew (or at least should know) more than she about such matters, and in her extensive writings in which she struggles to articulate her experience. Teresa's extraordinary literary output, in a variety of forms, is as much self-exploration and self-appropriation as instruction for others.

All of the above works to the advantage of Teresa's readers. No one of any spiritual maturity, reading Teresa of Ávila, can conclude that she was a religious neurotic, or even a gullible or unstable "weak woman" with too much time on her hands. Reading her seriously leads to a very sober judgment that, whatever we are to make of it, what Teresa said she experienced she actually experienced. And what she was experiencing, when we examine it, as it were, "from the outside" through her texts, must in my judgment be called revelation in the strict theological sense of the term. In naming her a doctor, the church proposes that this revelation is meant not just for her but also for the whole church. But before examining the content of these experiences, we must ask what leads to the judgment that these experiences are in fact revelation, divine self-communication.

Teresa claims that by means of these experiences, which she describes often (but not always) in the sense language of sound, sight, and feeling, that is, visions, locutions, and touches, God himself revealed to her deep and completely certain knowledge of Godself as a Trinity of Persons in ineffable oneness of being, and of Jesus Christ in his humanity and divinity, as well as profound knowledge of herself, human nature, sin, the church, the meaning of Scripture, and more.

Several features of Teresa's witness allow us to judge that they express not personal reflection or piety, not constructive imagination much less pure fantasy, and not speculative theological knowledge derived from reading, hearing sermons, discussion with her confidants, or any other publicly available source but actual direct revelation of God to her spirit. There are several such features, but I will signal two complementary ones that may be the most important and that I think are adequate to establish the character of the experiences: from the "divine side," *objectivity*; from the subjective, that is, Teresa's side, *passivity*.

First, Teresa's mystical experience was characterized by its objectivity. Teresa knows she could not have anticipated or "thought up" what she is hearing, seeing, or feeling because of the startling originality of the content. (If Teresa were alive today she might find singularly apt the colloquial claim "I couldn't make this stuff up!") Revelatory experience, she insists, is not something she works herself up to or laboriously constructs. Indeed, she claims that such imaginative construction can be recognized by the fact that it leads to emotional fatigue and intellectual flatness which does not improve one's life or one's theology whereas genuine revelatory experience invigorates, inflames, enlivens, and emboldens the recipient. Very often Teresa's mystical experience came upon her when she was not even thinking about the subject in question or not in circumstances that allowed her to deal with it as she would have desired. In fact, she says she is so lacking in what she calls "imagination" that she cannot discursively create even the material for her meditations much less come up with the extraordinarily original content of the visions and locutions that she receives.

Revelation, as Scripture abundantly testifies, does not arise within a person's ordinary experience. It "happens to" the person, for example, to Moses at the burning bush, to the prophets in their inaugural visions, to Mary at the annunciation, to Jesus at the transfiguration, to Paul on the Damascus road, to Peter in his vision at Joppa. Teresa says she "heard," or "saw," or "felt" something that she was not previously thinking about, expecting or hoping for, meditating on, or even capable of understanding immediately. She does not describe her experiences in philosophical, theological, or devotional categories or language but in experiential ones, indeed, often in bodily ones.

It is helpful for moderns, in reading Teresa, to realize that she was relying, for her understanding and expression of her experience, on the faculty psychology and epistemology of her time. Basically, that theory proposed that if we can exercise a certain activity, such as seeing or hearing, we must have a faculty or power for such activity, for example, sight or audition, and these faculties are seated in physical organs, for instance, seeing in the eyes and hearing in the ears, which are attuned to particular objects, for example, color and sounds. Teresa was also familiar with the theory of "spiritual senses" that goes back to the fathers of the church.[6] According to this theory, we have interior senses, spiritual sight, spiritual hearing, and so on, that are analogous to our physical senses but by which we perceive spiritual realities, that is, revelation, not accessible to ordinary sensation.

Teresa describes her "auditory" mystical experiences, that is, *locutions*, as something akin to infused knowledge. God puts something into her mind that she did not know, that she could not have thought up, such as God's identity as absolute Truth, and she understands with a clarity and unshakable conviction that could not be derived from discursive reasoning. At other times, she "hears" a word that effects what it says, for example, Jesus saying to her, "Peace be with you," which instantly replaces her deep anxiety with profound, lasting calm and certitude that is immune to disturbance by external events of any kind (see, for example, IC 6.3).

But most interesting for our purposes are Teresa's visions. She says there are three kinds of visions: bodily or corporeal, imaginative, and intellectual. Teresa says she never experienced bodily visions. Even when her visions made her aware of Jesus' presence in his glorified bodily humanity and she was able to perceive him right next to her, at her side, she says she did not see anything with either her bodily or spiritual eyes.

Intellectual visions, such as her vision of the Trinity, are much like locutions in that they communicate interior knowledge; cause deep insight, unshakable certitude, and profound peace rooted in irrefutable truth; and are often accompanied by a sense of light, beauty, clarity, and so on.

Imaginative visions, which in my opinion are the most interesting in Teresa's accounts, are more closely related to the faculty of sight. They bear specifically on the corporeality, the bodiliness of what she is "seeing," sometimes the saints or other persons living or dead, but most remarkably Jesus himself in his divine humanity. Teresa believed these imaginative visions of Jesus were even superior in a way to intellectual visions because they enabled her to experience Jesus in his humanity by means of her humanity. As she says, they are more suited to our human condition. These visions led to her definitive repudiation of the arguments of some of the neoplatonic theologians of her day that as one progresses in the life of prayer one should leave behind all material things—including the humanity of Jesus—and ascend to the purely spiritual. Teresa maintained, largely on the basis of her imaginative visions, that Jesus never "drops" or abandons or supersedes his humanity. The divinity does not swallow up the humanity even when the glorified humanity shines, as it were, with the divinity of the Word, as it did in his transfiguration or his post-Easter appearances (see esp. IC 6.7).

Teresa compares her mystical experiences of Jesus to that of Saul on the road to Damascus when he had a revelatory experience of the risen Jesus that those with him did not fully share (see Acts 9:3–7 where Paul hears and sees but his companions only hear; Acts 22:6–9 where Paul sees the light and hears the voice but his companions see the light without understanding the voice) or to the Easter Christophanies in the resurrection narratives, such as Mary Magdalene's encounter with the risen Lord in the garden of the tomb or the recognition of Jesus in the "burning of their hearts" and the "breaking of the bread" by the disciples on the road to Emmaus. The recipients of these visions of the glorified Lord could only testify, "We have seen the Lord and this is what he said." We have seen and heard. Teresa's experiences, like these resurrection Christophanies, are not bizarre or fantastic, but they are totally original and unusual. Something had entered Teresa's experience, somewhat like Jesus' entrance into the locked upper room on Easter evening, and even as she assents to it she knows it did not come from her and she is not in control of it. Like Mary Magdalene in the garden, Teresa "recognizes" Jesus in his self-revelation to her but could not have anticipated his appearance, much less caused it. Nor is she able to say what he looks like. The vision is in no sense constructed but simply given. In other words, the experiences are self-authenticating, as when one sees a flash of lightning, hears a crashing noise, or feels something touch one's skin and knows that whatever it is *is real* and *there* but one cannot account for it, alter it, or refuse it.

The objectivity of the experiences corresponds, on the subjective side, to the passivity of the experiencer. Teresa says she could not resist the experiences even when, in obedience to her timorous confessors, she tried to (see IC 6.6, esp. 2). They come upon her and take over her perceptive capacity. She experiences what is given. Just as she cannot cause the experiences, so she cannot halt them, refuse them, or manipulate them.

Such language of objectivity-passivity—of something occurring like a thunderstorm out of a cloudless summer sky, over which one has no control but cannot not be affected by if one is in the midst of it—is the language of revelation. It is, as we have seen, the language of Moses, of Mary at the annunciation, of Mary Magdalene and the Emmaus disciples, and of Peter at Joppa. And Teresa testifies to the revelatory character of her experience repeatedly in her autobiographical writings such as her *Life*, *The Soliloquies*, and *The Spiritual Testimonies*, as she does in her more discursive and analytical descriptions and analyses in *The Interior Castle*.

Although she calls the seeing experiences "visions" and the hearing experiences "locutions," she cannot describe what she saw, heard, or felt in the ordinary vocabulary of physical sensation. In fact, she denied that she actually saw or heard anything when she felt that her interlocutor was using sense language in a physical sense. When her confessor at one point asked her what Jesus, whom she said she "saw," looked like, she replied that she did not know, that she did not see any face. She simply knew that it was the One who had previously spoken to her and that she was not imagining him (IC 6.8.3). She speaks of brightness, brilliance, extraordinary "whiteness," and especially of his overwhelming, unbelievable beauty. She recognizes Jesus as his own bodily self, as did the disciples in the upper room on Easter night who "rejoiced at seeing the Lord" (see Jn 20:20), and she knows he is present at her right side (see, e.g., IC 6.8.3), but she says she saw him neither with her bodily nor with her spiritual eyes.

Furthermore, Teresa speaks of "seeing" the three Persons of the Trinity in their distinctiveness and oneness and knowing which Person was speaking but immediately denies that these sights and sounds were perceived with either her physical or spiritual senses. And when she talks about locutions or auditory revelations, she gives signs of their authenticity that are not physically audible, such as that they could not have been thought up, are powerful and effect what they express, remain in the memory for a long time, and cannot be doubted. These locutions generate deep and invulnerable peace, certitude, and stability. But again she cannot describe the experience in terms of physicality. Jesus' voice is beautiful, powerful, effective, indubitable, unforgettable. But it is not describable in physical terms and, as in the case of Paul's companions on the road to Damascus, could not be heard by anyone present except the one to whom Jesus spoke. These reciprocal features of Teresa's mystical experience, objectivity, and passivity, combined of course with the subject matter or content of what she came to know through these experiences, which is our next topic, characterize her experience as truly revelatory.

## The Content of Teresa's Mystical Experience: The Risen Jesus in the Mystery of the Trinity

Teresa's mystical experience encompassed a wide range of subjects. But at the heart of her mystical life was her experience of the risen Jesus as the mediator of the trinitarian God in and to creation whose personal focus is the human race, and it is this content on which I now want to concentrate. If Teresa's experience can be accurately categorized as revelation, what is revealed?

In chapters 7 and 8 of the sixth mansions of *The Interior Castle*, Teresa provides what Kieran Kavanaugh calls a kind of Christological diptych that communicates to her reader the very heart and soul of her mystical experience. Teresa describes and analyzes what she calls her *intellectual vision* of the risen Jesus as the Word of God, the second Person of the Trinity incarnate. (Later, in the seventh mansions, she describes actually "seeing" the Trinity, the mystery of the Godhead, ineffably one in being and yet three personed, and that the second Person only is the divine human whom she recognizes as the risen Jesus.)

After the Christological diptych of chapters 7 and 8, she describes in chapter 9 her experience of Jesus himself in an *imaginative vision*, better suited, she claims, for communicating his humanity, in which she is able to "see" him and "hear" him in a way very comparable to the Damascus road Christophany to Paul.

Together these two experiences, the intellectual vision of the Trinity (see IC 7.1.2) in which the second Person is the Word Incarnate who is Jesus, and the intellectual and imaginative visions in which Jesus in his divine humanity mediates the mystery of the triune God to the human person, reveal to Teresa the mystery of mysteries that is at the heart of, indeed constitutes, the salvific reality of the Christian life, namely, the participation in the divine life that is communicated to the believer in and by Jesus.

I want, first, to concentrate on the content of Teresa's trinitarian and Christological experience. But we will turn shortly to the expression in theopoetic construction of this experience. At that point, and to relate the two aspects (mystical experience and theopoetic expression), I will evoke a comparison that I want to propose here by way of preparation.

Let us imagine a party, an evening soirée, going on in a mansion situated a short distance from the brow of a cliff overlooking the ocean. During the festivities one member of the group slips out to the cliff's edge and is caught up in a profound experience in which she "sees" the inner structure of the universe she is contemplating in the finite reality of the scene before her. In sky, ocean, stars, moon, darkness, roaring surf—all physically sensible—she actually "sees" the moving relationship among the seemingly stationary stars, "sees" gravity at work holding and ordering the whole, "sees" not just the waves crashing on the shore but also the mysterious tide itself that is moving the whole ocean and the powerful attraction of the moon creating that tide. She "hears," not just imagines but actually hears, the singing of the spheres, the music of the endless silence of space itself. She "sees" and "hears" the inner structure and functioning of the entire universe not as something separate from and other than the physical world before her—the sky and stars, the water and waves, the silence and sound, and the very vastness itself—but precisely as the inner being of all the phenomena we usually see when we look at the oceanscape. She comes back into the party and tries to communicate what she experienced, and the other guests go out to the brow of the cliff hoping to share her experience. What they see is a very beautiful scene. Some have some imaginative inkling, even a kind of intuition, of what she has described even though they do not really see or hear it. Most try to imagine it and actually seem to see something unusual about what is before them, something they have not seen before. But virtually no one sees what the seer saw and described even though they vaguely realize that she is bearing witness to something that is more "there" than ordinary experience reveals and that could well be true. If the seer at some point finds a somewhat adequate way to express what she experienced it will probably be a poem that could only be written by the one who experienced it and can give rise in some readers to something akin to the original revelation. She is most unlikely to write a scientific paper on the subject, try to photograph what she saw, or try to convince someone by argument that it really happened. But she will adamantly deny that she dreamed it up, fantasized it, or invented it.

The people to whom the seer bore witness will have to make judgments about two things. One is about the seer: is she delusional, a harmless romantic, an hysteric, an artist, or a genuine visionary of some kind bearing witness to reality beyond normal perception? The other judgment they have to make is about what she claims to have seen: was it a delusion or a psychologized version of what she has read about the cosmos as expanding universe and that she has projected onto an admittedly awe-inspiring natural vista? Was what she claimed to have seen not there at all? Was she hallucinating? Or has she indeed seen what is really there but not visible to most people?

These are the very questions that have echoed down through two thousand years about the Easter Christophanies upon which millions of people have based their Christian faith commitment. Millions of pages of scholarly ink has been spilled, and billions of words spoken, at biblical and theological conventions, while many people have decided that the whole idea of the bodily resurrection of Jesus is simply too good to be true. Teresa's Jesus mysticism, in other words, is very akin to the revelatory experiences of the risen Jesus that are the foundation of Christian faith.

Teresa, in her pivotal Christological visions, saw and heard (she speaks of visions and locutions) the inner being and life of God. That is why the Inquisition decided to examine her writings and why some of her staunchest theological supporters tried to tone down her text before the Inquisition saw it.[7] No one of her time with any theological training, or even minimal Christian catechesis, doubted that God exists, is triune, became incarnate in Jesus of Nazareth who rose from the dead, and so on, any more than the party guests in our example doubt that gravity controls the movement and relation of physical bodies, that the stars and planets are in motion, that the moon controls the tides, and so on. What the nonmystics in any age often doubt is that anyone can have seen the inner structure and functioning of these divine realities—Trinity, incarnation, creation, and so on—and be in a position to testify to what she or he has seen, especially if it does not match up, point for point, with what is thought to be known from more controllable sources such as science, philosophy, or theology.

Nonmystics have questions, in other words, about the seer and about the seen. When someone claims to have experienced what other people might believe exists but to which they have no direct access, those other people often become fearful. Some will simply brand the testimony unverifiable, thereby rendering the discussion moot. But some, especially religious authorities who are not themselves mystics, know that knowledge is power and if they do not know where the knowledge of another is coming from, they do not know the extent or character of that person's power and they have no control over it. What cannot be verified, tested, or controlled is always vaguely dangerous, unsettling, even frightening to those—especially those in authority—who have no personal access to such experience. Seers in any sphere, whether they are transported by artistic beauty, overwhelmed by the mysteries of the physical cosmos, engaging the depths of the unconscious through dreams, or participating in the inner life of God in prayer, are people apart. In every age they have been a threat to some of the authorities, especially religious ones. The Inquisition, which was especially active in Teresa's time and always fearful of what exceeded the reach of its control, was a source of continual threat during Teresa's lifetime and remained so right through to the time of her canonization in 1622.

But Teresa was bearing witness to what she had experienced, which upon examination, was in no way contradictory to what theology had more or less explicated using the philosophical categories of Plato, Aristotle, and the Neoplatonists. But Teresa's testimony went beyond even the best theological explications precisely in its experiential character. Teresa the writer, as we will see in a moment, was an artist in relation to the theologian as scientist. She was the one who "knows" by personal experience in relation to the one who knows by observation, experiment, or reasoning. Her writing does not contradict the "learned men" of the schools but complements, that is, augments or completes, them. And if Teresa completes them, it is clear that the theologians do not have the whole picture. Mundane society always wants to believe that artists are dispensable while scientists and technicians are necessary, that the beautiful is decorative while the logical is substantial. It may well be—and the mystics are prime examples of the possibility—the other way around.

This brings us to the all-important question: what did Teresa actually experience? She tells us that she saw God in God's triune being, each of the three Persons distinct in a oneness of being utterly beyond expression. And most importantly for us, she saw that Jesus was not simply a messenger, a human being sent by God who lived in a particular time and place, died, and left behind a moral message about how to live in such a way as to merit a share in God's life after death. She understood that in the Word, the second Person of the Trinity, God had created all things from all eternity (see Jn 1:1–5). As the Prologue of John's

Gospel says, in him, the Word, all things were made. And at a moment in time, that divine Word became human and took up his abode in his own creation. So, the Word-made-human is *in* all things, forever, as they are all in him. That human being, Jesus, because he was human, could and did die, but because he was the Word Incarnate he did not cease to be. The incarnation was never interrupted much less cancelled as Jesus passed through the ultimate human experience, through the portal of mortality, into eternal life. The Word Incarnate rose from the dead, and the risen Jesus, after assuring his disciples by visionary experience, by Christophany, that he was indeed alive, disappeared from their fleshly sight to take up his abode in God and in them. Teresa's language about her visions is redolent of the last discourses in John's Gospel where the mystery of the mutual indwelling of Jesus and his disciples is rooted in the mutual indwelling of the Father and the Son in and through the Spirit.

Most human beings do not experience directly, that is, by way of a Christophany, the bodily risen Jesus. They experience him in the signs of the community, Scripture, sacraments, prayer, ministry, and so on. As most people experience the universe through the manifestations of the laws of nature in the physical world and so do not doubt that there is a universe but do not see the inner structure and working of that universe, so most believers experience the real presence and action of God in Jesus in their life in the Christian community. And just as the scientists mediate, by means of their explanations, models, and diagrams, the inner structure and functioning of the universe so that it is rationally comprehensible to the nonscientists, so the theologians mediate the realities of God present and active in the risen Jesus in rationally comprehensible formulations to the nontheologians.

But just as there are some people—we call them artists—who have some kind of immediate experience of the inner reality of the universe not accessible either to ordinary people or to the scientists, so there are people—we call them mystics—who have some kind of immediate experience of the inner reality of God not accessible either to ordinary people or to the theologians. Teresa of Ávila, Julian of Norwich, Catherine of Siena, Francis of Assisi, back to the evangelist John and the apostle Paul who were the earliest mystics of the Christian tradition, and down to the contemporary mystics like Thomas Merton *are* these experiencers of Christian revelation embodied in the risen Christ.[8] They bear witness to their experience and through that experience to the reality of what most believers hold by faith and understand by theology.

The conclusion I want to draw from this exploration is that the mystics are not interesting oddities who are decorative and even fascinating, but nonessential to the Christian story, any more than are artists in a culture. Religious mystics are essential to the church's faith life and to its theological enterprise, just as artists are essential to humanity's historical life, both personal and political, because there is a dimension of our faith life, as there is a dimension of our cultural life, that cannot be accessed or made available by those powers and processes we control, such as syllogistic reasoning, experiment, argument, and so on. The mystics do not prove anything. They do not prove the existence of

God, the reality and salvific power of Jesus, or the ultimate triumph of good over evil. They do not explain anything, the meaning or value of suffering, or how a good God can allow such. They bear witness to the existential truth that underlies all experience and gives ultimate meaning to everything else.

The particular importance of Teresa of Ávila's mystical experience for our time is that the incarnation is the dimension of Christian faith and life that is most problematic, most "incredible" for many contemporary believers. What Teresa saw and heard, what she bears witness to in her writing, is that the incarnation is not a stage of human religious history or cosmic evolution that ended with Jesus' death. Jesus is not one savior figure in a pantheon of such figures. Nor is Christ a myth spun out of a first-century historical person named Jesus by the human architects of the Christian edifice. Teresa testifies, on the basis of her experience of him, that Jesus, in the full integrity of his transcendent and glorified humanity, including his pre-Easter historical career, his risen actuality, and his eucharistic presence, is real, alive, present, and active in the personal life of the believer in every age and in the cosmos in every time and place of human and extra-human existence. The incarnation is an ever-expanding reality, but it is never separated from, nor can it transcend or dispense with, that personal human being in which it ever and always "happens." As the remarkable Brazilian philosopher Rubem Alves put it, we do not ask if a Beethoven sonata "really happened." It happens every time it is played.[9] And so it is with Jesus.

Theology cannot reason to this even if it can help explain how it is possible and credible and what it means. The direct experience of the mystics is not a dispensable decoration in relation to the reasoning of the theologians. It is necessary to assure us that there is indeed something *for* theology *to* explain. If there is no Jesus, alive and present and active in the "now," there is no basis for Christianity as a living religion and no root of a cosmic Christ, however understood. Teresa says, "I saw Him; I heard Him; He is alive." And then she adds, if I may put words in her mouth, "I leave it to the theologians to explain this and will agree to whatever formulations they come up with or the church teaches. That is their job, to explain the 'how.' But Jesus himself has assured me of the 'that' and the 'what.' I cannot doubt what I have experienced and will not make 'the fig' (a dismissive gesture she was ordered by a confessor to make), literally or figuratively, no matter who commands it, toward any representation of the One who has revealed himself to me and whom my heart loves."

I want now, finally, to make the connection between what Teresa experienced and what she produced in her writing that mediates her experience to the church, that is, the connection between the mystic and the prophet.

# The Expression of Teresa's Mystical Experience of Jesus: Theopoiesis

Let me recall the example I evoked earlier, of the person who leaves the "party" of ordinary reality to contemplate the phenomenal world in its immensity and mystery and is suddenly transported by an ecstatic revelatory experience of the inner reality of the cosmos by a vision of what cannot be "seen" with the bodily eyes and the hearing of the music of the singing spheres that cannot be "heard" with the bodily ears. When the seer tries to communicate what she has experienced, what she now deeply and irrefutably knows not just with her rational mind but also with her whole being, she can only point toward the reality that, to the others at the party, remains largely if not completely opaque.

This is the experience of artists, of those people among us who are in some way sensitive to a dimension of reality that remains largely imperceptible to most people. The artists see and hear, in the mundane reality we all encounter, a glory, a beauty, a symmetry, a mystery, and indeed a truth that remains experientially inaccessible to most people. But the experience itself is insufficient to make them artists. It is the fact that they also have the talent, the capacity to express what they have experienced in an embodiment worthy, at least to some extent, of the magnificence they have perceived. That expression, whether in poetry, painting, dance, or architecture, which we call a "work of art," is what makes the seer an artist, the mystic a prophet. In other words, it is not just the heightened capacity for experiencing the transcendent in the ordinary but also the extraordinary capacity to shape the experience in aesthetic form so that the transcendent can be "seen"—as it were secondhand—by those who participate in the work of art. And the work of art is not simply a transcription or a mirroring of the seer's experience. Rather, the personality and sensibility of the artist shapes the experience just as the experience shapes the artist.

It is the experience that possesses the artist and drives her or him to paint, sing, compose, build, or dance. The symbiosis between the transcendent "given" in the experience and the aesthetic "expression" in creativity that produces the work of art can give rise, in the receptive perceivers, to the ever-new, ever-personal appreciation that creates the community between the artist and those who respond to her or his work, and among those who are formed by the work.

Often what the artist experiences cannot be brought forth in the grammar and syntax of the ordinary or the daily. The representational painter, the classical composer, the choreographer, or the realistic photographer is certainly a valuable shaper of cultural experience. But sometimes the artist must invent a whole new idiom to shape and express the experience. And then we have an abstract painter like Mark Rothko, the modern composer like Maurice Ravel, the choreographer like Paul Taylor, or a poet like Gerard Manley Hopkins in his sprung rhythm, artists who break out of the expressive boundaries of their times. In some cases artistic creation achieves sublimity precisely by its embodiment in the classical forms, and in other cases it is by going beyond the boundaries of such forms that the truth embodied in the artistic production beckons and lures the spirit beyond its familiar bounds.

The writings of many of the saints could be seen as transcendence within the established forms. Their writing illuminates, often in highly original ways, the truth and beauty in the tradition. One might say this of much of the writing of some of the best theologians in the history of the church. But the writing of some of the mystics transcends the boundaries of the known and leaves the reader struggling not with the superb presentation and explication of the familiar but with an unfamiliarity that shocks, confounds, or astounds. Someone like Julian of Norwich or the author of the *Cloud of Unknowing* or Meister Eckhart (and I think Teresa) might fall into this category. It is not surprising that so many of the greatest mystics in the Christian tradition ran afoul of the church's doctrinal authority. Just as the French "Impressionists" had a hard time explaining their work to the realists and romantics of their day, and Hopkins's sprung rhythm was incomprehensible to many, so Meister Eckhart was not able to successfully defend his mystical writings to the Inquisition, and some of Teresa's greatest admirers tried to "tone down" her writing before it was examined by the same body.

What I am suggesting in this article is that some of the writing of Teresa of Ávila, especially about her post-1560 experiences, falls into the category of the theopoetic rather than the theologic. In other words, she was not constructing philosophically based interpretations of the faith or using the devotional or even theological categories of her day; rather, she was using essentially aesthetic or theopoetic language to articulate what she had actually experienced of God. Like the dancer, the painter, the poet, or the playwright, she constructs, by her theopoetic creation, a space for the encounter with God rather than an argument for or explanation of God or God's communications. As theology is the product of vigorous intellectual activity; theopoiesis is the product primarily of imaginative activity. The poet is constructing a dwelling place for the beautiful, or even

better, a mediation of the beautiful. Wisdom is building her
house, setting her table, mixing her wine, and calling out to
those who pass by to come in, to sit down, and to delight in
the beauty that mediates truth as lovable (see Prv 9:1–11).

Theopoetics, which is what I believe is the proper category for Teresa's writing, is not anti-intellectual, but it is first
and foremost a work of the imagination in the strong sense
of that word. The philosopher Ray Hart says that imagination is the cognitive mode of the will.[10] Or we might say
imagination is the power by which we construct the world as
aesthetically, rather than logically, coherent. *The* theopoet of
God is Jesus, and it is not surprising, therefore, that he did
virtually all his teaching about God and the things of God,
not through the literal language his disciples so desired, but
through figurative language, through similes, allegories,
metaphors, and other forms of imaginative discourse that
are gathered together under the rubric of "parables."[11] His
disciples asked him why he always taught in parables rather
than speaking plainly, and Jesus said he did this so that those
who think they see will be confounded and those who know
they cannot see will be enlightened (see Mt 13:1–17 in light
of Ps 78:1–2).

Teresa often said she had a poor imagination. Even though
she knew from her reading and the instruction of the theologians of the day that the first stage of the life of prayer should
be discursive meditation by means of which the materials for
more advanced prayer are laid in, she says she was never able
to meditate because her imagination was unable to produce
the appropriate images. Actually, Teresa seems not to have
understood the ambiguity of the word "imagination," which

we use for both the *imaginary* (which Teresa really had no taste or ability for) and the *imaginative*, at which she excelled. Teresa could not do the kind of imagining that was characteristic of many of the schools of methodical prayer that developed in the time of the scientific revolution in which she lived. She could not create or call up imaginary scenes, develop imaginary narratives, or insert herself as an imaginary participant in such scenes or narratives, even those based on Scripture (see esp. IC 6.7).

But Teresa spontaneously developed extraordinary imaginative hermeneutical devices to evoke spiritual experience such as her elaborate and exquisite allegory of the soul's development from the fat, ugly silkworm who spins and enters the cocoon of the prayer of union only to emerge much later to risen life as the beautiful white butterfly. Her prolonged simile of the four waters of prayer by which she explained the inverse ratio between human effort and divine grace as a person advances in the spiritual life is a brilliant work of imagination. One of her most supple and sophisticated exercises of theopoetic imagination is her great work that we have been examining, *The Interior Castle*. And, as Kieran Kavanaugh remarks, she was well ahead of her time in her effortless imaginative "flip" of the castle image toward the end of the work. The interior castle was, originally, the soul of the individual with its many rooms, hallways, antechambers, stairways, passages, and dungeons and its plethora of creatures, helpful and noxious, with God hidden and waiting for his beloved in the innermost chamber of the soul. But quite suddenly in the tenth chapter of the sixth mansions (IC 6.10.6), she literally turns the image inside out and says the castle is God in whom all things, good and evil alike, live and move and have their being. The soul is among the inhabitants of the cosmic God-castle rather than the castle in which God dwells.

As Kavanaugh points out, Teresa here effortlessly anticipates, through imagination, the development beyond the impasse between theism (God and the world outside each other) and pantheism (world and God identified with each other) to panentheism, the mysterious mutual indwelling of God and the soul, which Jesus speaks of in the last discourses, especially John 14–17, and of the Creator in all creation evoked by the Johannine Prologue. Teresa thereby imaginatively handles the theological conundrum of the compatibility of an all-powerful God with the existence of real evil.

My personal favorite among Teresa's theopoetic constructions is her imaginative explanation of the difference between spiritual betrothal and the final stage of consummated love, the spiritual marriage. She says the betrothal is like two candles whose flames are brought together to become one flame. Yet the two can be re-separated, and each candle will burn with its own flame from its own wick. But spiritual marriage is like a drop of water falling into the sea. No future separation is even imaginable. The oneness is total. The drop has become the sea (see IC 7.2.4).

In short, far from having a theological or spiritual impediment in the form of a weak imagination, Teresa's theopoetic imagination is so dynamic and fertile that she simply has no use for the imaginary, however spiritually useful it is for most people.

## Conclusion

Let me briefly summarize this exploration of the contribution of Teresa of Ávila's Jesus mysticism to contemporary theology, both as content and as process. As I mentioned at the outset, there is a complex of contemporary theological issues that are mutually exacerbating and that are of supreme practical importance for Christian faith and life today: the nature and reality of spiritual experience; the possibility and reality of revelation; the bodily resurrection of Jesus; and the problem of the presence and role of Jesus in his humanity for the contemporary Christian in the context of planetary evolution toward the fullness of the cosmic Christ.

I have tried to address these questions, not individually and serially but globally, through an examination of Teresa of Ávila's contribution under three headings: the nature of her mystical experience as revelation proposed to the whole church by her recognition as a Doctor of the Church; the content and mode of her mystical experience, which is the risen Jesus in the mystery of the Trinity revealed in her visions and locutions, as essentially aesthetic-personal and objective rather than either purely rational or merely devotional; and the resulting theopoiesis or imaginative-aesthetic construction of her experience that she offers to her readers, especially in *The Interior Castle*, as an experiential hermeneutical dwelling place for unfolding their own spiritual lives.

When all is said and done, Teresa of Ávila appears in the church with the words of Paul of the Damascus road on her lips, inviting us to share her experience: "I live now not I but Christ lives in me" (Gal 2:20).

## Notes

1. The declaration, made by Pope Paul VI on September 27, 1970, is as follows: "Therefore, in complete certainty and after mature deliberation, with the fullness of the Apostolic authority, we proclaim Saint Teresa of Jesus, virgin from Ávila, Doctor of the Universal Church."

2. Unless otherwise noted, the English-language texts of Teresa's writings referred to in this essay are those translated by Kieran Kavanaugh and Otilio Rodriguez. Their translations, commentaries, and notes are available in multiple publications, but the ones to which I will refer will be Teresa of Ávila, *The Interior Castle*, trans. by Kieran Kavanaugh and Otilio Rodriguez (Washington, D.C.: ICS Publications, 2010); and *The Collected Works of St. Teresa of Ávila*, vol. 1, *The Book of Her Life; Spiritual Testimonies; Soliloquies*, trans. by Kieran Kavanaugh and Otilio Rodriguez, 2nd ed. (Washington, D.C.: ICS Publications, 1987).

3. References to Teresa's text itself are by mansion, chapter, and paragraph, and those to Kavanaugh's commentary, by page number in the volume.

4. Teresa's writings include her spiritual autobiography (*The Book of Her Life*); two treatises on the spiritual life (*The Way of Perfection* and *The Interior Castle*); the historical record of the foundations (*The Book of the Foundations*); four personal spiritual treatises (*Meditations on the Song of Songs, Spiritual Testimonies, Soliloquies*, and *Poems*); *Letters*; and *Guidelines for the Visitations of the Convents of the Reform*.

5. A new book specifically on Teresa's seventeen foundations of monasteries of the Reform was published in English during the year of her 500th anniversary (2015): *The Divine Adventure: St. Teresa of Ávila's Journeys and Foundations* by Tomás Álvarez and Fernando Domingo, with introduction by Kieran Kavanaugh and translation by Christopher O'Mahoney, with additional translation and adaptation by Patricia Lynn Morrison (Washington, D.C.: ICS Publications, 2015). The original was published in Spanish in 2012.

6. An excellent contemporary resource on the history and theology of the theory of the "spiritual sense" is *The Spiritual Senses: Perceiving God in Western Christianity*, ed. Paul L. Gavrilyuk and Sarah Coakley (Cambridge: Cambridge University Press, 2012). For a fine treatment of the functioning and significance of the spiritual senses in the life of the faithful, see Ormond Rush, *The Eyes of Faith: The Sense of the Faithful and the Church's Reception of Revelation* (Washington, D.C.: Catholic University of America Press, 2009).

7. See Kavanaugh, pp. 398–99, commenting on IC 7.1.

8. A remarkable contemporary exploration of the Christ mysticism of Thomas Merton is Christopher Pramuk, *Sophia: The Hidden Christ of Thomas Merton* (Collegeville, Minn.: Liturgical Press, 2009).

9. See Rubem A. Alves's Edward Cadbury Lectures published as *The Poet, The Warrior, The Prophet* (London: SCM Press, 1990).

10. See the remarkable study of the religious imagination in Ray L. Hart, *Unfinished Man and the Imagination: Toward an Ontology and a Rhetoric of Revelation* (New York: Seabury, 1979).

11. Probably no one in our era has explained this better than Amos Niven Wilder. See his two books on the subject: *Early Christian Rhetoric: The Language of the Gospel* (Cambridge, Mass.: Harvard University Press, 1964; reissued in 1976) and *Jesus' Parables and the War of Myths: Essays on Imagination in the Scripture*, edited, with a preface, by James Breech (Philadelphia: Fortress, 1982).

# How Love Transforms:

## Teresa and the Impact of Sanctity

MARY FROHLICH, R.S.C.J.

WE STILL CELEBRATE Teresa of Ávila five hundred years after her birth because of the remarkable impact she has had on millions of human beings. Her writings have been translated into dozens of languages and then have been anthologized, quoted, discussed, and analyzed by thousands of other commentators. On top of that we must add the oral proclamation of her life and teachings through innumerable retreats, courses, homilies, spiritual direction sessions, and personal conversations. How did it come about that one woman from a small town in Spain in the sixteenth century could have such a widespread and powerful impact?

We cannot understand Teresa's impact without tracing how it developed and flowed within the social networks of her time and since. In recent years scholars have done much excellent work identifying the social and political conditions within which Teresa negotiated her identity and discovered ways to claim spiritual authority during her lifetime, as well as how others took up her cause and promoted her sainthood after her death. Yet from a spiritual and theological perspective, sanctity cannot be reduced simply to a social construction. Theologically, sanctity is closeness to God such that God's own holiness is manifested in the holy person's life. In my view, we need to think of these inward and outward aspects as deeply implicated in one another, in a rhythm like the breathing in and out that constitutes the breath of life. I would contend that Teresa was not just someone identified as holy because she fulfilled certain social expectations of sanctity; rather, she was a woman whose real transformation in holiness was as much a social phenomenon as a personal one. In this essay, therefore, I aim to look at *both* the interior process by which Teresa became a saint—a holy person—through the transforming action of God in the depth of her being, *and* the social conditions that surrounded this process and have enabled it to reverberate so powerfully through the centuries.

The essay is developed in three parts. The first explores how Teresa's life and surrounding environment shaped the "inner drama of the self" that she conveys in her writings in such a compelling and engaging manner. The second examines how this inner story was profoundly reconfigured by a key moment of her spiritual transformation, namely, that described in the fifth dwelling places of her *Interior Castle*. The third and final part explores how her story interacted with social networks in ways that have enabled it to have global impact.

# Part One: Shaping the Inner Drama of the Self

It is the psychological construction of the self that mediates between individuals' inner spiritual transformation and their participation in social networks. Many psychologists today envision the life of the self primarily in terms of narrative—that is, an ongoing inner drama, in which the self is both author and hero of the developing story of a person's life. This drama of selfhood is always relational and social; it is by no means a story of a solitary soul but rather a story of a person creatively negotiating relationships and social networks in search of ways to build up and express an inner sense of aliveness, initiative, meaning, cohesiveness, and so on. The late Chicago psychoanalyst Heinz Kohut suggested that the motors of this process are our ambitions and our ideals. We ambitiously seek a story in which we will achieve great things and be recognized for them, and we idealistically seek a story in which we will be followers of idealized figures and participate in noble endeavors.[1]

One of the chief characteristics of a person who becomes a real leader, according to Kohut, is the ability to offer people a story of meaning that responds to their deepest ambitious and idealizing longings. The leader's own journey of narrative self-construction bears a deep empathic resonance with the characters, symbols, and story lines that will enable the people around them to feel more alive, joyful, and purposeful. In some cases the leader is even able to catalyze the formation of what Kohut calls a "group self" that shares a common story and aspires to common ambitions and ideals.[2] These concepts can help us to think about how Teresa has been able to have such a remarkable impact on so many individuals and communities over these five centuries. How did her story become one that is able to draw so many people to find their own soul story reflected in her vastly ambitious and vastly idealizing journey of transformation?

The drama of the self begins, of course, in the family. Teresa was born into a large family that consisted mostly of boys. Among eleven siblings, she had one sister who was about eight years older and another thirteen years younger. Teresa arrived right in the middle among nine boys. Teresa was a natural leader among her brothers, nearly all of whom grew up to become conquistadors in the New World of the Americas. As children in Golden Age Spain, their games played out the stories of adventure, conquest, and glory across the seas. Teresa's sickly mother enjoyed reading popular novels of chivalry and shared them with her daughter, thus inflaming Teresa's youthful imagination with these melodramatic, rather risqué stories of romance and heroism (L 2.1). The girls of Ávila were also taught to admire *la mujer fuerte* (strong woman) Jimena Blazquez who, in the eleventh century, had organized the town's women to defend the city when all the men were away fighting. Surrounded by such a brood of boys, Teresa was the darling of her father—and no doubt even more so when her mother died when Teresa was twelve years old. All these familial elements laid the foundations of the imaginative world that Teresa continued to elaborate in her adult life.[3]

Also important, however, were factors in the larger culture that surrounded the family. It was a culture permeated with anxiety about maintaining one's "honor," and in the early sixteenth century one of the chief aspects of this was proving that one carried the so-called pure blood of an "Old Christian"—meaning, one whose heritage was not "tainted" by Jewish or Muslim ancestry.[4] Scholars have located documentation showing that Teresa's father came from a family of Jews who were among those who chose to convert to Christianity (rather than to emigrate) during the persecutions of the fifteenth century.[5] Like other *conversos*, Teresa's family was seeking to gain a foothold in the ranks of the *hidalgos* or lower nobility. In order to achieve this economic and political advantage in a fiercely competitive environment, they had to scrupulously hide the truth about their ancestry.[6] This reality gives an edge of social critique to Teresa's sense of self, as she found herself in the situation of having to maintain the family secret while rejecting its premise that "pure blood" made one a more worthy person.

As far as we can tell, Teresa's parents were sincere and quite devout practitioners of Christianity. In a 2004 essay entitled "The Architectonics of Desire: Pageantry, Procession, and Protagonists in Teresa of Ávila's 'Interior Castle,'" Elizabeth Adams describes in some detail the milieu of popular devotion that permeated daily life in a late medieval Castilian town such as Ávila. She describes how frequently Teresa would have encountered exuberant, colorful, and dramatic devotional processions winding their way through the streets, stopping at various stations for public prayers as they made their way toward a shrine or church.[7] Adams discusses how this body memory of seeing and participating in the pageantry of religious processions played into Teresa's narrative of the soul on its way to the center of the "interior castle."

While still a teenager, Teresa was a boarder at an Augustinian convent school where she was immersed in the Liturgy of the Hours and perhaps was taught other prayer practices as well (L 2.6). But it was a few years later, when she was in her twenties and already a nun, that she was thoroughly initiated into the practices of recollection that were increasingly popular in Spain during the early decades of the sixteenth century. Teresa had fallen ill, and during a recuperation period in the countryside, her uncle Pedro encouraged her to ponder the *Third Spiritual Alphabet* of Francisco de Osuna (L 4.7). Osuna was the most prominent among several, mainly Franciscan authors who taught a practice of emptying and stilling the mind in order to become more available to God's work in the soul. At the time Teresa was learning this practice, a debate was raging between the *dejados* or "abandoned ones" who apparently advocated complete passivity and self-emptying, even to the point of refusing mental attention to the humanity of Christ, and the *recogidos* or "recollected ones" such as Osuna who taught a more balanced practice that recognized the need for elements of active attention and meditation on the human Christ. Despite Osuna's efforts at balance, later on Teresa would say that during this early stage she herself went too far in the direction of the *dejados*, believing for a time that meditation on the humanity of Christ would distract her from the self-emptying necessary for union with God (L 22). A hallmark of her mature approach to prayer, as we will see, will be active imaginative interaction with the human Christ as the royal road to union with God.

A key teacher of this practice of imaginatively entering into the events and feelings of Jesus was the *Vita Christi* of Ludolph the Carthusian. Originally composed in the fourteenth century, this devotional text was made available in the early sixteenth century in vernacular Spanish due to the efforts of the reforming Cardinal Francisco Cisneros. The book taught a practice of visualizing and making present the events of Christ's life, with the aim of stirring up the emotions and enkindling devotion in the heart. In an era when the Scriptures were not generally available in the vernacular, this book provided literate Christians with access to an imaginatively and affectively elaborated "biography" of Jesus.[8]

Tomás Alvarez notes that Teresa had all four volumes of the Spanish version of this work at her disposal and often took them with her when she retired to pray in one of the hermitages on the grounds of her monastery. In her *Constitutions*, Teresa included it as one of the indispensable books for the monasteries of her reform (C 8). Alvarez provides a review of the text's contents, asserting that it was Teresa's "real manual of Christological formation."[9] Like Teresa, Ignatius of Loyola spent long hours with this book and incorporated much of its structure, theology, and method into his *Exercises*.[10] Thus later on when Teresa had Jesuit spiritual directors, they found her already imbued with similar practices to those which they prescribed.

Elena Carrera, in her book *Teresa of Ávila's Autobiography: Authority, Power, and the Self in Mid-Sixteenth-Century Spain*, explores in depth what she calls the "affective hermeneutics" through which Teresa constructed her self in dialogue with books such as those of Osuna and Ludolph.[11] Following Paul Ricoeur, Carrera sees a mutual interpretation process going on between text and self. The text offers a world into which the self enters, thus reinterpreting both the text and the self. In the case of Ludolph's *Vita Christi*, Teresa was invited to place herself right in the midst of the drama and emotions of Jesus' human life. In doing so, she took that story and those imaginatively projected feelings into herself, thus giving a Christological shape to her own inner story while at the same time offering her hearers and readers a new, deeply engaging story about Jesus.

Carrera discusses in detail how this affective hermeneutics of the self in dialogue with devotional texts was typical of the prayer practices taught in Teresa's milieu. Even though she had little formal education, Teresa absorbed the love of reading from her mother. Beginning in youth with the stories of chivalry and their melodramas of adventure and love, and continuing throughout her adulthood with whatever religious and devotional texts she could get her hands on, Teresa continually strove to feed her mind and imagination. Through books, her own inner drama was placed in dynamic dialogue with stories, images, and conceptual frameworks far wider than those of her quite limited physical world. This is an essential dimension of her later ability to have an impact on worlds beyond her own.

Yet the affective hermeneutics of the self that Carrera describes did not take place only in relation to books. As we will see later, Teresa was also profoundly shaped by two key communities of discourse: first, the community of women who were her daily companions, colleagues, and disciples; and second, the painful yet formative dialogue with theologically educated male clerics who demanded that she discern and define her self-expression ever more carefully. Before examining these in greater depth, however, let us explore how Teresa's "drama of the self" was transformed from the inside out in her dialogue with God.

## Part Two: The Story Transformed

To sum up what we learned in Part One about what could be called the natural sources of Teresa's drama of the self, as a child growing up in Golden Age Spain, Teresa's imagination was imbued with colorful stories of romance, adventure, conquest, and heroism. Religious pageantry and devotional practices played out these same dramatic themes *a lo divino*, that is, in a spiritual mode.[12] As an adult she embraced prayer practices that explicitly encouraged placing herself in the feelings and events of Christ's life. All these factors shape the color, drama, and verve that so powerfully attract readers into her story. Teresa's global impact comes from the fact that she has been able to create this kind of effect not only among the people of her own time and place but also among people across a remarkable array of times and cultures. This, I would suggest, is because of the central transformation that Teresa describes and how it shifts the whole story into a different register—a register in which the "little woman"[13] from Ávila becomes a world-renowned giant of the spiritual world.

One might say that Teresa's entire life and work can be summed up as her attempt to welcome, understand, and teach about a particular type of radical, all-encompassing experience of being transformed by divine love. In his book *John of the Cross and Teresa of Ávila: Mystical Knowing and Selfhood*, Edward Howells traces out how Teresa's description and explanation of this experience changed as her mystical life matured.[14] When she wrote her *Life* at age forty-seven, she spoke of unitive experience as a kind of suspension of the soul that takes one outside of oneself and essentially paralyzes the ability to think or act until the experience passes (L 10.1; 20.18; etc.). She wrote, for example, that the soul "feels with the most marvelous and gentlest delight that everything is almost fading away through a kind of swoon in which breathing and all the bodily energies gradually fail. . . . All the external energy is lost, and that of the soul is increased so that it might better enjoy its glory" (L 18.10). A bit later she added, "This complete transformation of the soul in God lasts only a short time; but while it lasts no faculty is felt, nor does the soul know what is happening in this prayer" (L 20.18).

Fifteen more years passed before she wrote *The Interior Castle*, and by then both her experience and her ability to express it had matured considerably. It is in the fifth dwelling places of *The Interior Castle* that Teresa develops a series of extraordinary images that offer her most profound insight into "how love transforms." The transformation that she describes at this stage is really the pivot point of the journey described in *The Interior Castle*. As she puts it, all that has happened in the first four dwelling places is like the growth from egg to caterpillar; it is all preparatory to the momentous transformation when the caterpillar enters its cocoon, dies, and comes forth as a butterfly.

Teresa's development of the image of the caterpillar, cocoon, and butterfly is full of paradoxes and yet is masterful in its simple expression of the truth she wishes to communicate. The core of the paradox and the transformation is described in this key text as she writes about the little worm's entrance to the cocoon:

> Well once this silkworm is grown—in the beginning I dealt with its growth—it begins to spin the silk and build the house wherein it will die. I would like to point out here that the house is Christ. . . . His Majesty Himself, as He does in this prayer of union, becomes the dwelling place we build for ourselves. It seems I'm saying that we can build up God and take Him away since I say that He is the dwelling place and we ourselves can build it so as to place ourselves in it. And, indeed, we can! Not that we can take God away or build Him up, but we can take away from ourselves and build up, as do these little silkworms. (IC 5.2.4–5)

First, let us admire the simplicity of the image. Everyone has seen and been amazed by caterpillars becoming butterflies. Even her statement that the worm "takes away from itself" to build its cocoon corresponds to natural reality, since caterpillars do indeed spin their cocoons with excretions from their own bodies. A child or a very simple person can grasp the main point of the image: something lowly and earthbound builds itself a hidden place where it is wonderfully transformed into something beautiful and free to fly.

The complexity of the image emerges in its theological application. Teresa is not just describing a natural process of transformation; she is describing how God's love transforms. The paradoxes of an event of transformation that is at once active and passive, psychological and mystical, interior and corporeal, and human and divine are all woven into the texture of the image. To unpack it, let us walk through it slowly.

The soul that is imaged as a "fat and ugly" silkworm (IC 5.2.2) has been growing for a long time. It is not a beginner in the life of walking with God. Teresa says that this soul has been "going to confession, reading good books, and hearing sermons" (IC 5.2.3). It is no doubt long practiced in imaginatively placing itself into the stories and emotions of Jesus, as taught in the methods of Ludolph, Osuna, and others. Through these practices the soul has already learned a way of imaginatively "building up Christ" and entering into him. But one day something radically different begins to happen. The worm is not the one who chooses when it is time to become a butterfly; it is a movement that begins to ferment in its whole being, beyond its control. The worm must be active in that it must spin the cocoon, yet it is passive in that it is moved to do so by a process it has nothing to do with. Similarly, transformation by divine love takes place at the initiative and under the direction of God; the human person can only participate through surrender to the demands of the process.

As the soul "spins its cocoon," it withdraws deeper and deeper into a hidden place. The faculties begin to lose touch with their outward objects and become blind, as if lost in the thickest of fog. The deeper the soul goes into this inner womb, the more imaginative engagement with Christ transmutes into radical surrender of self into Christ. In her writings Teresa often describes the difference between simply imagining Christ and encountering the living person of Christ (for examples, see L 29.1 and IC 6.9). Of this encounter in the fifth dwelling places, she wrote, "Through the work of the senses and the faculties [the soul] couldn't in any way or in a thousand years understand what she understands here in the shortest time. . . . In this prayer nothing is seen that can be called seeing, nor is anything seen with the imagination" (IC 5.4.4; 6.1.1). The shift that happens as the cocoon is spun begins in active imagination but transmutes into awareness that the living God is moving in utmost intimacy throughout one's whole being, body and soul. Finally, as the cocoon is completed, the soul so completely surrenders into God that it loses awareness of anything else. Its senses, mind, and imagination are utterly blinded by the overwhelming light of God; it is as if dead yet also alive as never before. It is in union with God.

Perhaps the most complicated aspect of this simile is Teresa's effort to explain the relationship between the soul's activity of "building up" and that of God. She acknowledges that it is difficult to see how we—mere humans—can "build up" God. Let us listen to this part of her text:

> It seems I'm saying that we can build up God and take Him away since I say that He is the dwelling place and we ourselves can build it so as to place ourselves in it. And, indeed, we can! Not that we can take God away or build

Him up, but we can take away from ourselves and build
up, as do these little silkworms. For we will not have finished doing all that we can in this work when, to the little
we do, which is nothing, God will unite himself, with His
greatness, and give it such high value that the Lord Himself will become the reward of this work. Thus, since it was
He who paid the highest price, His Majesty wants to join
our little labors with the great ones He suffered so that all
the work may become one. (IC 5.2.5)

Whereas one begins by "building up" Christ actively by
imaginatively entering his story and his feelings and thus
making them one's own, the effect of unitive love is that
Christ himself moves to operate through all one's human
faculties and energies to build up his ongoing life and mission. Like a caterpillar that has become a butterfly, the
person is no longer only the small, culturally and psycholog-
ically limited being that she or he originally was but instead
has become in a profoundly new way a "member of the
body of Christ" who is freed to participate in the mission
of Christ within a vastly expanded range of space and relationships. Perhaps the best way to understand what Teresa is
expressing here is through the text of Galatians 2:20, where
St. Paul wrote, "It is no longer I who live, but Christ who
lives in me."

Articulating the process in more theological terms,
Mary Margaret Anderson describes it as the Christological
refounding of human subjectivity.[15] In Teresa's imagistic
language of the "inner drama of the self," what *The Interior Castle* portrays as following upon this transforming

encounter is a new story in which the self's ambitions and ideals crystallize around a drama of betrothal and marriage. Teresa follows in the long tradition of Jewish and Christian spiritual writers who have played upon the imagery of the Song of Songs to portray the relationship of God to human- ity as a drama of the romantic quest and union of bride and bridegroom.[16] Teresa meditated deeply on these themes as she wrote a commentary on the Song of Songs a few years before writing *The Interior Castle*.[17]

In view of our focus here on the key transforming event as a kind of breaking open of the self into a new dimension of participation in the communal Christ-self, it is notewor- thy that in Christian interpretation there has always been an ambiguity about whether the "bride" is the individual soul whom the divine bridegroom embraces in the intimacy of the marriage chamber, or is the communal church whom Christ publicly claims, celebrates, and brings to fulfillment. In Teresa's drama, the answer is that these two aspects are not separate from one another. The deeper the intimate embrace of the soul by the divine lover, the more all encom- passing becomes her public outpouring into Christ's mission of building up his ongoing community in history.[18] This is the import of Teresa's soul story as it shifts definitively into the drama of the bride and bridegroom.

# Part Three: The Impact of Sanctity

Part Two has offered an interpretation of Teresa's essentially theological view of the process of sanctification—that is, how a person becomes interiorly united with the work of

God in the world. My claim is that having been transformed by love, the person becomes in quite literal ways a historical ambassador of that love as the impact of sanctity radiates in wide circles far beyond the immediate time and place of the holy person. The present project is to try to understand how this actually worked in Teresa's case. Here I will focus on two aspects of her insertion into social networks that, I think, give special insight into her public impact. The first is her participation in the community of women, which is really at the center of her identity and her writing style. The second is her highly fraught lifelong dialogue with male guides and confessors, through which she learned to speak in a way that could be heard in circles of power. Since our topic is Teresa's public impact, it will be helpful to speak about the second aspect first.

Teresa's dialogue with her male confessors and spiritual guides was lifelong but was especially intense during the period described in her *Life*, when she was first beginning to have more unusual spiritual experiences. Her own anxiety to try to understand and articulate what was happening to her, along with the anxiety of the religious authority figures in her milieu about the possibility that she might be being deceived or deceiving others when she described these mystical encounters, led to lengthy conversations and even, we might say, interrogations by a series of male spiritual "experts." In this process, Teresa had to learn how to speak and write about her experiences in ways that conformed to what these men—nearly all of whom had far more formal theological education than she did—expected an authentic experience of God to sound like. This process was emotionally stressful because these men often doubted her, threatened her, or disciplined her when her descriptions failed to correspond to their expectations. At the same time, they educated her. Dialoguing with them, she learned how to incorporate into her self-expression the terminology and conceptual frameworks that enabled her to present her experiences in a manner that resonates deeply with the theological and spiritual wisdom enshrined in the texts of Christian tradition.

Of course, the formative aspect of this dialogue was not just one way. There is no doubt that Teresa also educated her confessors and guides, helping them to recognize and understand profound spiritual experiences that many of them had probably only read about. The contentious aspect of these dialogues sharpened Teresa's wits and forced her to think both deeply and strategically about theological issues as well as about the politics of her situation. Still, Teresa regarded many of these men as supporters and even as friends, so she generally strove to share her life drama honestly with them even when their probing was painful and humiliating. The end result is that as we are invited into these dialogues through Teresa's writings, we greatly enjoy the flying intellectual sparks while never losing touch with the underlying personal drama that situates them and gives them life.

Teresa's dialogues with men are crucial to understanding her ability to have a still-growing impact in the realms of theological and ecclesial thinking. Yet let us not forget that her daily life unfolded largely within communities of women. Moreover, even though she always had to write in a state of high alert to the sensitivities of the male authorities who monitored and censored her works, her main support group and the audience that she cared most about were the women she called her "sisters" and "daughters"—the women who formed her communities and who looked up to her as an authority and guide in spiritual matters. Alison Weber's 1990 book *Teresa of Ávila and the Rhetoric of Femininity* explores in exquisite detail how Teresa strategically exploited for her own purposes the surrounding cultural expectations for how *mujercillas*—"little women"—could and should communicate.[19] Caught in a double bind between controlling male authorities who denied the possibility of a woman having knowledge or authority and her emerging recognition as a female authority, Teresa masterfully deployed rhetorical strategies such as self-deprecation, irony, and obfuscation in order to appear submissive to the male authority structure while, in the same act, giving voice to her own feminine authority and inviting other women to do likewise.

Teresa's style of writing from within the contested solidarity of the community of women, then, is a central clue to her ongoing impact. As Weber puts it, "By exploiting features from the low-register, private discourse of subordinate groups in general, and women in particular, she created a discourse that is at once public and private, didactic and affiliative, authoritative and familiar."[20] Reading Teresa, one feels like both her best friend and her favored pupil; one is drawn into the intimacy of friendly, almost informal sharing, like that of a group of women sitting around and chatting, while at the same time one finds oneself instructed by the authoritative voice of the spiritual master. At a distance of 500 years, this is still an intoxicating brew for both female and male readers!

Yet for Teresa to have the impact that she did, it was not enough that her writings be compelling for individual readers. She had to be raised up by the social networks of the institutional church as a canonized saint. This was by no means a foregone conclusion. Teresa had enthusiastic supporters but also fierce opponents. The irony is that, as feminist interpreter Gillian Ahlgren has detailed, in some aspects her opponents understood her better than her supporters did.[21] The most vocal posthumous critic of her writings, the Dominican Alonso de la Fuente, repeatedly pointed out Teresa's boldness in speaking as a woman and to women. In his view, this was contrary to nature because women could not have authentic spiritual knowledge, let alone teach or write about it. De la Fuente saw through her rhetorical humility and recognized her insistent claim to spiritual authority based on her visionary experience. He correctly recognized that her teaching sought to liberate Christians, especially women, to go beyond the strictly controlled mediations of ecclesial authorities. In short, de la Fuente already understood what recent feminist interpreters have proclaimed as new discoveries, namely, Teresa's primary identification with the community of women, her wily exploitation for her own purposes of a womanly way of speaking, and her agenda of empowering others to follow her in a more autonomous approach to the spiritual life than ecclesial authorities preferred.

For Teresa to be officially recognized as a saint in the Counter-Reformation church, however, all this had to be downplayed, or at least reframed within acceptable categories. Some recent scholars have spoken of this as a co-optation of Teresa by the Counter-Reformation church as it sought what Ahlgren calls "strong Tridentine models for the laity, role models who respected the church hierarchy, adhered to the sacramental system, and, in short, epitomized what it meant to be a 'good Roman Catholic.'"[22] Above all, Teresa's liberating message to women had to be firmly redirected. Following an unfortunate but venerable tradition, supporters of her canonization argued that a woman who showed such "manly" qualities could not really be categorized as a woman but had instead become a kind of honorary man.[23] Her writings, they opined, came to her in ecstasies; thus they did not depend on the abilities of a mere woman but were of supernatural origin. Thus Teresa was presented as so exceptional that no other woman could possibly emulate her—except, of course, in the virtues of humility, obedience, and penitence that demonstrated her submission to church authority. As Antonio Pérez-Romero put it, the canonized Teresa was reframed as "a staunch supporter and promoter of traditionalism; this was accomplished through the ignoring or discarding of the core of her message—the important ideological aspects that challenged the established order."[24]

While this kind of rewriting of the saint's story may seem distasteful to us, in reality it is a common and probably necessary stage in the impact of sanctity. The radicalness of what really happens in a saint's story of transformation has to find a way of being received and sent forth within the more mundane networks of social, cultural, and political power that actually hold sway at the time. This pattern can be traced with any saint, beginning even with Jesus himself. Could his story have had its astonishing impact if it had not been taken up by the Constantinian networks of power? But the evidence of true sanctity is that the deeper transformed life, fruit of union with God, refuses to remain confined by such tactics. Like a butterfly, it will always fly free to awaken and astonish afresh with its power of truth.

## Conclusion

What we find in Teresa, then, is an extraordinary ability to draw the reader into a sense of intimate sharing in her compelling personal drama and sparkling intellectual content. We have seen how, on the natural level, these qualities of her writing have been shaped not only by her personal gifts and formation but also by the social networks that supported her, called her forth, and eventually canonized her. Yet identifying all these natural factors only gets us as far as describing the caterpillar, so to speak. Without the transformation that she imaged as entering the cocoon and coming forth as a butterfly, she would remain as simply one of the myriads of talented people whose names and activities are long lost to history. It was this transformation that catalyzed her gifts and circumstances from being simply those of a charming, creative, very smart woman to being those of a saint through whom the course of ecclesial history and theology—not to mention the spiritual lives of millions of people—has been profoundly changed.

Finally, what about us? While few of us can expect to have a public and global impact of the magnitude of

Teresa's, we know that we too are called to be transformed by love. Teresa's story models for us the depth of fidelity to the inward contemplative practice of "building up Christ" that is demanded of us if we are to be open to the call to go beyond being caterpillars. At the same time, her story graphically shows how that most inward of transformations is always dynamically situated within an expanding web of social relations that both support it and make it concretely fruitful for the mission of Christ. Like breathing in and breathing out, the contemplative movement inward is at one with being sent forth to make a difference in the world.

### Notes

1. Heinz Kohut, *The Analysis of the Self: A Systematic Approach to the Psychoanalytic Treatment of Narcissistic Personality Disorders* (Chicago: University of Chicago Press, 2009).

2. On leadership and the "group self," see essays in Heinz Kohut and Charles B. Strozier, *Self Psychology and the Humanities: Reflections on a New Psychoanalytic Approach* (New York: Norton, 1985).

3. Carole Slade, "'Este Gran Dios de Las Cavallerías' [This Great God of Chivalric Deeds]: St Teresa's Performances of the Novels of Chivalry," in *Vernacular Spirit: Essays on Medieval Religious Literature*, ed. Renate Blumenfeld-Kosinski (New York: Palgrave, 2002), 297–316.

4. Teófanes Egido López, "The Historical Setting of St. Teresa's Life," in *Spiritual Direction*, Carmelite Studies (Washington, D.C.: ICS Publications, 1980).

5. Teófanes Egido López, *El Linaje Judeoconverso de Santa Teresa: Pleito de Hidalguía de Los Cepeda* (Madrid: Editorial de Espiritualidad, 1986).

6. Norman Roth, *Conversos, Inquisition, and the Expulsion of the Jews from Spain* (Madison: University of Wisconsin, 2002).

7. Elizabeth J. Adams, "The Architectonics of Desire: Pageantry, Procession, and Protagonists in Teresa of Ávila's 'Interior Castle' (1577)," in *Things of the Spirit: Women Writers Constructing Spirituality*, ed. Kristina K. Groover (Notre Dame, Ind.: University of Notre Dame Press, 2004), 18.

8. Lawrence F. Hundersmarck, "A Study of Spiritual Themes in the Prayers and Passion Narration of Ludolphus de Saxonia's 'Vita Jesu Christi'" (PhD diss., Fordham University, 1983). See also Ludolph of Saxony, *The Life of Jesus Christ*, Part One, Vol. 1, Chapters 1–40, trans. Milton T. Walsh (Collegeville, Minn: Liturgical Press, 2018). Further volumes to follow.

9. Tomás Alvarez and Kieran Kavanaugh, *St. Teresa of Ávila: 100 Themes on Her Life and Work* (Washington, D.C.: ICS Publications, 2011), 195–98. Teresa also mentions "the Carthusian" in L 38.9.

10. See "General Introduction" in Ignatius and George E. Ganss, *Ignatius of Loyola: The Spiritual Exercises and Selected Works*, Classics of Western Spirituality (New York: Paulist Press, 1991), 19–26.

11. Elena Carrera, *Teresa of Ávila's Autobiography: Authority, Power, and the Self in Mid-Sixteenth-Century Spain* (London: Legenda, 2005).

12. The online *Encyclopaedia Britannica* defines this term thus: "In Spanish literature, the recasting of a secular work as a religious work, or, more generally, a treatment of a secular theme in religious terms. . . . Adaptations *a lo divino* were popular during the Golden Age of Spanish literature during the 16th and 17th centuries." *Encyclopaedia Britannica Online*, s.v. "A lo divino," accessed December 27, 2017, *https://www.britannica.com/art/a-lo-divino*.

13. For discussion of the disparaging meaning of the terms *mujercita* and *mujercilla* ("little woman") in sixteenth-century Spain, see Gillian T. W. Ahlgren, *Teresa of Ávila and the Politics of Sanctity* (Ithaca, N.Y.: Cornell University Press, 1996), chap. 1. Teresa sometimes explicitly described herself with these terms; see, for example, L 11, 14 and F 2.4.

14. Edward Howells, *John of the Cross and Teresa of Ávila: Mystical Knowing and Selfhood* (New York: Crossroad, 2002), chaps. 5 and 6.

15. Mary Margaret Anderson, "Thy Word in Me: On the Prayer of Union in St. Theresa of Ávila's Interior Castle," *Harvard Theological Review* 99, no. 3 (July 1, 2006): 329–54.

16. On Carmelite traditions of bridal mysticism, see Tessa Bielecki, "Bridal Mysticism (Carmelite)," in *Speaking of Silence: Christians and Buddhists on the Contemplative Way* (New York: Paulist, 1987), 38–47; Keith J. Egan, "The Éros of the 'Dark Night,'" in *Seeing the Seeker* (Leuven, Belgium: Peeters, 2008), 301–14.

17. Kevin G. Culligan, "Martha and Mary Working Together: Teresa of Ávila's Meditations on the Song of Songs," in *Seeing the Seeker: Explorations in the Discipline of Spirituality: A Festschrift for Kees Waaijman on the Occasion of His 65th Birthday* (Leuven, Belgium: Peeters, 2008), 315–29; Bernard McGinn, "'One Word Will Contain within Itself a Thousand Mysteries': Teresa of Ávila, the First Woman Commentator on the Song of Songs," *Spiritus* 16, no. 1 (2016): 21–40.

18. For a contemporary theological articulation of a similar perspective, see Karl Rahner, "On the Significance in Redemptive History of the Individual Member of the Church," in *Mission and Grace*, vol. 1 (London: Sheed and Ward, 1963), 114–70.

19. Alison Weber, *Teresa of Ávila and the Rhetoric of Femininity* (Princeton, N.J.: Princeton University Press, 1990).

20. Ibid., 15.

21. Ahlgren, *Teresa of Ávila*, chap. 5.

22. Ibid., 145–46.

23. For review and discussion of these traditions, see Barbara Newman, *From Virile Woman to WomanChrist: Studies in Medieval Religion and Literature*, Middle Ages (Philadelphia: University of Pennsylvania Press, 1995).

24. Antonio Pérez-Romero, *Subversion and Liberation in the Writings of St. Teresa of Ávila*, Portada Hispánica 2 (Amsterdam: Rodopi, 1996), 195.

# Seeking Wisdom in Common Vocal Prayers:

## Teresa of Ávila's Response to the Banning of Vernacular Books on Prayer

TARA K. SOUGHERS

FOR TERESA OF ÁVILA, the reading of Francisco de Osuna's book *Tercer abecedario spiritual* (*The Third Spiritual Alphabet*) was a life-changing event. Although she says that she had been in the habit of reading good books, after reading that book she desired no others. The path of prayer that was described there was one that she "resolved to follow . . . with all [her] strength," and for the next twenty years it was this book that she considered to be her master.[1] The type of prayer that was advocated by Osuna, mental prayer, was central to Teresa and her spirituality.[2] She began to consider how she might reform Carmelite monasteries to make them supportive of this type of prayer and the way of life it engendered, as "she felt that the way she was living was incompatible with the divine intimacy she sought in prayer."[3]

Unfortunately, by the time Teresa began to found her reformed monasteries, Osuna's book as well as many other vernacular books on prayer had been banned. The wisdom that Teresa had discovered in the *Tercer abecedario*, wisdom that she was determined to pass on to the nuns under her care, would need to be discovered in unimpeachable sources. So it was that Teresa began her search for a way to instruct her nuns in mental prayer when the wisdom of those books that had formed her was not available. She needed to find texts that could ground the practice of mental prayer in the way that these vernacular books on prayer had grounded her own practice of prayer.

In order to accomplish these objectives, Teresa would turn to the common prayers of their liturgical life. The focus of the life of a nun in sixteenth-century Spain, as well as much of her training, revolved around the Divine Office,[4] so that was an obvious place for Teresa to look for texts that could be used to support and ground the practice of mental prayer. Although she argued that other texts—any vocal prayer that they recited—could also be used,[5] she focused upon the two most common vocal prayers as examples: the Our Father and the Hail Mary. In her efforts to circumvent the restrictions of the times, Teresa would demonstrate not only her creativity but also her wisdom as a teacher, and in so doing she put into place foundational pieces of the spiritual life that would support her reform.

## The Challenge Teresa Faced

In Teresa of Ávila's first years in the monastery, there was little to mark her as someone who would start a movement of reformation. Supported by family resources, Teresa had a comfortable apartment, and she enjoyed the social life of a well-to-do woman. In her *Life*, she admits to her need to be liked. All of that changed after her uncle, Pedro Sánchez de Cepeda, gave her the *Tercer abecedario*. Unable to find a confessor who understood her way of prayer, she would find this book an important guide.[6] Because of her encounter with this text and others like it, Teresa sought to structure the rule of her reformed monasteries in such a way as to provide an environment conducive to mental prayer. She found in the primitive Carmelite Rule the structure that she needed.

The early sixteenth century in Spain, when Teresa was first encountering these books, was a time of great openness to mental prayer, and vernacular books on prayer were widely circulated. During the founding of her reformed monasteries, however, Teresa was forced to deal with a change in the religious climate that came to consider mental prayer not only unnecessary but also dangerous.[7] This climate led to the banning of books on mental prayer in the vernacular. Because of connections between the practice of mental prayer and the heretical *Alumbrado* (Illuminist) movement, mental prayer, which had been openly taught earlier in the sixteenth century, came to be seen as suspicious, a sign of heretical leanings.[8] Mental prayer was believed to be particularly dangerous for unlearned people, especially women—who were considered to be more easily deceived by the devil.[9] This left Teresa in a very difficult position. This practice she intended to promote was associated with both heresy and demonic activity, and the texts that had promoted and supported its use were banned. Her insistence upon the practice of mental prayer was potentially dangerous, both for her and for her nuns, unless she could find some recognized authority that supported it.

In order to be able to found monasteries based on the practice of mental prayer under these circumstances, Teresa needed to do two things. First, she needed to defend mental prayer as a practice that was not only consistent with church teaching but also a necessary part of the life of prayer. Second, she needed to find other sacred texts, texts that had not been banned, that could serve not only to ground the practice of mental prayer but actually justify the practice. These are the tasks that Teresa takes on in her work *The Way of Perfection*.

Vocal prayer was an expected part of monastic life in sixteenth-century Spain. Mental prayer, however, was not a traditional part of monastic discipline at this time. "Contrary to what anyone might expect today, she [Teresa] seems to have received no instruction in her novitiate about mental prayer."[10] The life of monasteries in sixteenth-century Spain, with its focus on the Divine Office, upholding of social class, and open visitation policies, was not conducive to the type of prayer that Teresa sought to foster. A different way of communal life was necessary for those pursuing the way of mental prayer that Teresa was advocating.

## The Centrality of Mental Prayer

Although vocal and liturgical prayers were important in Teresa's reformed rule, it was mental prayer that grounded the monastic life in the reformed monasteries. "Our primitive rule states that we must pray without ceasing. If we do this with all the care possible—for unceasing prayer is the most important aspect of the rule—the fasts, the disciplines, and the silence the order commands will not be wanting. For you already know that if prayer is to be genuine, it must be helped by these other things; prayer and comfortable living are incompatible."[11]

The seclusion of the nuns and the austerity of their lives were intended to allow them to focus on that which was essential; in Teresa's eyes, prayer, particularly mental prayer. Anything that could distract from that aim was to be eliminated from their lives. Much of their day was to be spent in solitude and silence in order to foster an environment conducive to mental prayer. Teresa believed that such simplification was not a burden to be assumed but a gift to be received. However, these changes in the rule toward austerity were often seen as a critique of the more traditional monastic life found in monasteries like the Incarnation (Teresa's original community), and the suspicion that mental prayer often led either to demonic influence or to heresy made Teresa's task of reformation more difficult.

In order to accomplish the aims of her reform, Teresa's nuns first needed to be taught the practice of mental prayer. Teresa could not, however, simply refer her nuns to books on mental prayer. In 1559 the inquisitor general of Spain, Fernando Valdés, had published an index of forbidden books. In this list, he placed most of the books on prayer that had been available in the vernacular, including the books that had been instrumental in Teresa's own development of the practice of prayer.[12] For Teresa, who was founding her monasteries with a rule that emphasized the importance of mental prayer, the banning of these books was a great loss. If her reform was to be continued, there was a need for works about prayer.

In order to fill the gap left by the banning of vernacular books on prayer, it would be necessary for Teresa to write her own books on prayer. Such an undertaking was risky in sixteenth-century Spain—particularly for a woman, since the Alumbrado heresy was associated in the minds of the inquisitors with women and her work, like theirs, would advocate the practice of mental prayer.[13] In this milieu, an "unlearned" woman such as Teresa could not directly claim authority. The only route left to her was to offer reflections based on personal experience and the wisdom that she had gained through her practice of mental prayer, and hope for the best.

Teresa's first attempt to write about prayer was in her *Life*, which she had composed at the urging of García de Toledo. Although she had intended the work to be useful in teaching her nuns the practice of mental prayer, her confessor at that time, Domingo Báñez, did not believe that her *Life* was suitable reading for nuns because it focused too heavily on Teresa's own spiritual experiences, giving the impression—which he regarded as inappropriate in a woman—that Teresa was a wise person or even an exemplar. In fact, Báñez was so opposed to the idea of the manuscript being distributed that he even threatened to throw it in the fire rather than allow it to be read.[14] Teresa would have to find another way to provide the instruction and wisdom her nuns needed, one that presented her in a more traditional female role. Thus, "in a time when spiritual books were removed from circulation, Teresa wrote new books out of her own living experience for those who sought guidance from her."[15]

To justify her teaching role, Teresa needed to be ordered to write by her confessor.[16] Avoiding any claims of authority, Teresa said that it was only because her nuns would understand it better coming from an unlearned person like themselves that she dared to write a book such as *The Way of Perfection*. In her prologue to the book, Teresa says, "I am aware that the great love they have for me will make what I say, so imperfectly and with such poor style, more acceptable than what is in some books that are very well written by those who know what they are writing about."[17] In response to Báñez's permission "to write some things about prayer,"[18] Teresa wrote an entire book. In *The Way of Perfection*, she developed both a defense and a method for mental prayer.

The loss of the vernacular books on prayer posed two other problems for Teresa. Not only had they served as instruction booklets for Teresa when she was learning to pray, but also they were texts that had become sacred to her because they had grounded her life of prayer. Without these revered texts, Teresa could not teach her nuns the way of mental prayer as she had experienced it, for the reading of these vernacular texts had been the starting point for her own practice.[19] Although Teresa acknowledged that there were other ways to contemplation, she claims that she had no talent for discursive thought or imagination; those ways were closed to her. In *The Way of Perfection*, she says that she "spent fourteen years never being able to practice meditation without reading."[20] Reading, therefore, was an important first step in mental prayer for Teresa, so she needed to find other sacred texts for her nuns to use in their practice.

First, however, she needed to offer a defense of the practice of mental prayer. Teresa's arguments about the importance of mental prayer would be needed to help her nuns to fend off some of the inevitable criticism they would face for focusing on mental prayer instead of being satisfied with vocal prayer and the Mass. Instead of emphasizing what was distinctive about mental prayer, Teresa made the claim that the distinctions between vocal and mental prayer were actually unimportant, saying, "Mental prayer isn't determined by whether or not the mouth is closed."[21] In her defense of mental prayer, Teresa broadened the definition of mental prayer, so that it became an essential part of the ordinary life of prayer. In fact, mental prayer became an essential element for any other form of prayer.

In order to legitimate the practice of mental prayer, Teresa argued that vocal prayer and mental prayer, rather than being distinct forms of prayer, are actually closely and integrally related. Vocal prayer done well is mental prayer. She claimed that "if while speaking I thoroughly understand and know that I am speaking with God and I have greater awareness of this than I do of the words I'm saying, mental and vocal prayer are joined."[22] For Teresa, mental prayer became less a defined method of prayer than an awareness that one is in God's presence while praying. Mental prayer, for Teresa, meant paying attention to the One to whom the prayers are addressed, something that needed to be done if one really intended to honor God with one's prayers, even when such prayers were spoken aloud.[23]

Aware that her nuns would face hostile questioning from those opposed to the practice of mental prayer, Teresa coached them in how to argue that mental prayer was indeed an essential part of vocal prayer. "If they tell you that the prayer should be vocal, ask, for the sake of more precision, if in vocal prayer the mind and heart must be attentive to what you say. If they answer 'yes'—for they cannot answer otherwise—you will see how they admit that you are forced to practice mental prayer and even experience contemplation if God should give it to you by such a means."[24] If one is really addressing God, as prayer is meant to do, then one ought to do it in full awareness of the One to whom one is speaking. If even words to an earthly king or noble need to be spoken with care, in full awareness of the one to whom we speak, then words spoken to God deserve an even greater care.[25] Although she argued that God is good and forgives our lack of manners, she is adamant that that is no excuse to be rude![26]

Teresa acknowledged that this understanding of mental prayer blurred the distinction between vocal prayer and mental prayer, but that was her intention. "You are right in saying that this vocal prayer is now in fact mental prayer. But I tell you that surely I don't know how mental prayer can be separated from vocal prayer if the vocal prayer is to be recited well with an understanding of whom we are speaking to."[27] Such a blurring of the two forms of prayer is key to her defense of the practice of mental prayer. The awareness of the One who is being addressed is the essential element of mental prayer even when spoken aloud as in vocal prayer. To speak prayers without this awareness is, in Teresa's words, to produce "poor music."[28]

In addition, Teresa argues that there is little difference in either the practice or the results when one prays well. The goal of mental prayer—contemplation—may be achieved equally well through the practice of vocal prayer. For those who believed that vocal prayer would protect them from the dangers associated with mental prayer, Teresa had a warning: even while reciting vocal prayers God may raise you to perfect contemplation, for God listens to those who speak to him.[29] What is important is paying attention to God, not words or even the lack of words. Having argued for not only the legitimacy of mental prayer but also its necessity, even for those more attracted to vocal prayer, Teresa moved to her second problem: the lack of texts in the vernacular that could support the practice of mental prayer.

The joining of vocal and mental prayer also gave Teresa a solution to her second problem. If vocal prayer could be a route to contemplation, then vocal prayers could serve as texts to ground the practice of mental prayer. Instead of the books such as the *Tercer abecedario* that had grounded her own life of prayer, Teresa urged her nuns to use familiar texts from their daily vocal prayers as the basis for their mental prayer. These prayer texts had a definite advantage over those that had been important in Teresa's growth in mental prayer. Not only could they be considered safe to use, but they were also the very prayers that those who were opposed to the practice of mental prayer insisted were necessary for the laity. In using these prayers, Teresa demonstrated that she and her nuns, unlike the Alumbrados, both followed and respected the practices of the church. In response to those who argued that all the prayers that the nuns needed were found in the Our Father and the Hail Mary, Teresa agreed.[30] "No one will be able to take from you these books . . . and if you are eager to learn you won't need anything else, provided you are humble."[31] These prayers would become the texts that Teresa's nuns would use to ground their own life of mental prayer. Not only could they serve as the texts from which to begin the practice of mental prayer, but also a close look at the Our Father showed how that prayer justified the practice of mental prayer.

## Vocal Prayer as *Lectio Divina*

Much of *The Way of Perfection* consists of Teresa's meditation on the Our Father. She refuses to call her work a commentary, realizing that as a woman such an assertion would be dangerous due to her lack of formal learning. Instead, she offers it as an aid to devotion. "I don't say that I'm going to write a commentary on these divine prayers, for I wouldn't dare. Many commentaries have been written; and even if they hadn't been, it would be absurd for me to write one. But I will mention some thoughts on the words of the Our Father. For sometimes, with regard to many books, it seems we lose devotion in the very exercise in which it is so important for us to have devotion."[32] In doing this meditation upon the words of the prayer, Teresa demonstrates her understanding of how even vocal prayer should be done. Vocal prayers are meant to be prayed in a way that opens up the meaning of the words. Once again, vocal prayer requires awareness, not simply recitation of the words.

From the opening "Our Father" of this prayer, Teresa sees in it a call to the practice of mental prayer. In meditating on this opening, one cannot avoid being aware of the One being addressed. "Does it seem right to you now that even though we recite these first words vocally we should fail to let our intellects understand and our hearts break in pieces at seeing such love?"[33] For Teresa, this prayer is designed in such a way as to bring one into the awareness of the One to whom it is addressed, and hence into mental prayer. For her, it is "an act of love to understand who this Father of ours is and who the Master is who taught us this prayer,"[34] and this understanding is prayer as it should be done.

For Teresa, the second phrase of the Our Father, "Who art in heaven," also points to the practice of mental prayer. "You already know that God is everywhere. It's obvious, then, that where the king is, there is his court; in sum, wherever God is, there is heaven."[35] In order to be in God's presence, all that is necessary is solitude, looking within oneself, and not turning away from the Guest who comes to visit.[36] In such centered recollection—awareness— God quickly joins the soul. For Teresa, the first two phrases of the Our Father, the most commonly used vocal prayer, emphasize the need for the practice of vocal prayer to include mental prayer. It is not the actual saying of the words that is important but how those words are said. Teresa criticizes those who "are so fond of speaking and reciting many vocal prayers very quickly, like one who wants to get a job done."[37] To rush through prayers in order to get all the words said is to lose "a great treasure and . . . you do much more by saying one word of the Our Father from time to time than by rushing through the entire prayer many times."[38] Without the awareness characteristic of mental prayer, such vocal prayer is not really prayer.

In describing vocal prayer in this way, these prayers take on the character of *lectio divina*. Anthony Morello notes that although Teresa does not describe a specific and distinctive method of prayer, Teresian prayer, like Carmelite prayer in general, is rooted in the monastic practice of *lectio divina*.[39] The "reading" of prayers is to be done slowly and consciously, and the goal of such prayer is contemplation. Instead of using *lectio* with passages of Scripture, whose Spanish translations were also banned by the Valdés Index, Teresa transfers this practice to readily available texts of commonly used vocal prayers. Although she focuses on the Our Father, Teresa claims that it is only lack of space that prevents her from demonstrating the same thing with the Hail Mary. She tells her nuns, "I have also thought of saying something to you about how to recite the Hail Mary. But I have been so lengthy that I have to let it go. It is enough for you to have understood how to recite the Our Father well in order to know how to recite all the vocal prayers you must recite."[40] In other words, this way of understanding the texts and using them to ground the practice of mental prayer is not limited to the Our Father and the Hail Mary but could actually be done with any of the prescribed vocal prayers.

Since any text from the liturgy could be used this way, her nuns need never again worry about essential texts being banned. The banning of books had seemed to be a great tragedy, but God still provided all that was necessary for the life of prayer. "And when books are taken away from us, this book cannot be taken away, for it comes from the mouth of Truth itself, who cannot err."[41] By linking the practice of mental prayer to that of vocal prayer and to the classics of vocal prayer, such as the Our Father and the Hail Mary, she would create a safe place for the development of a reformed Carmelite spirituality.

In linking mental prayer with common devotional and liturgical prayers, Teresa finds a way to safeguard an important element of her reform by rescuing the practice of mental prayer. Designating familiar prayers as sacred texts to ground and validate the practice of mental prayer, Teresa removed the distinction between mental and vocal prayer. By specifically using the prayers prescribed for the laity, Teresa worked to protect her nuns from the suspicion of heresy attached to mental prayer and the criticism they faced for not focusing on traditional forms of vocal prayer. Perhaps most importantly for the success of Teresa's vision of reform, she found other texts, prayers familiar to all Christians, to support the practice of mental prayer—ones that, unlike those that had served to train her in the practice of mental prayer, could never be taken away.

## Conclusion

It was Osuna's book that first introduced Teresa to mental prayer and started her on her life of prayer. For twenty years, Teresa relied on that wisdom to sustain and deepen her life of prayer. When vernacular books on prayer, including the *Tercer abecedario*, were banned, Teresa felt the loss keenly. In her loss, however, she was comforted by the Lord, who told her, "Don't be sad, for I shall give you a living book."[42] Teresa had no need for those books that had been so important to her, for she had absorbed that wisdom and she had grown in wisdom through her own experiences of the life of prayer. That wisdom could now be used in her search to find resources that could also teach and ground her nuns in their lives of prayer. Through the wisdom that Teresa had gained in her own of life of prayer, she was able to find ways to teach that wisdom to her nuns using the commonly used texts that were available to them. In the end the Lord taught Teresa in so many ways that she had "very little or almost no need for books."[43] This wisdom she was able to pass on, not only to her own nuns, but also to the generations of Christians who have followed her in the life of prayer.

### Notes

1. Teresa of Ávila, *The Book of Her Life*, in *The Collected Works of St. Teresa of Ávila*, trans. Kieran Kavanaugh and Otilio Rodriguez, vol. 1 (Washington, D.C.: ICS Publications, 1987), 67. Also Francisco De Osuna, *Third Spiritual Alphabet*, trans. Mary E. Giles (Mahweh, N.J.: Paulist Press, 1981).

2. Kieran Kavanaugh, "St. Teresa and the Spirituality of Sixteenth-Century Spain," in *The Spirituality of Western Christendom*, vol. 2, *The Roots of the Modern Christian Tradition*, ed. Ellen Rozanne Elder (Kalamazoo, Mich.: Cistercian Publications, 1984), 94.

3. Kieran Kavanaugh, "How to Pray: From the Life and Teachings of Saint Teresa," in *Carmel and Contemplation: Transforming Human Consciousness*, ed. Kevin Culligan and Regis Jordan (Washington, D.C.: ICS Publications, 2000), 118.

4. Ibid., 117.

5. Teresa of Ávila, *The Way of Perfection*, in *The Collected Works of St. Teresa of Ávila*, trans. Kieran Kavanaugh and Otilio Rodriguez, vol. 2 (Washington, D.C.: ICS Publications, 1980), 203.

6. Teresa of Ávila, *Book of Her Life*, 67.

7. Alison Weber, "Spiritual Administration: Gender and Discernment in the Carmelite Reform," Special Issue, *Sixteenth Century Journal* 31, no. 1 (Spring 2000): 124.

8. Kavanaugh, "St. Teresa," 95; Gillian T. W. Ahlgren, *Teresa of Ávila and the Politics of Sanctity* (Ithaca, N.Y.: Cornell University Press, 1996), 10–11.

9. Kavanaugh, "St. Teresa," 94.

10. Kavanaugh, "How to Pray," 117.

11. Teresa of Ávila, *Way of Perfection*, 53.

12. Ahlgren, *Teresa of Ávila*, 19.

13. Raquel Trillia, "The *Book of Her Life*: Teresa of Ávila's Rhetoric of Implication," *Studia Mystica* 24 (2003): 104.

14. Kieran Kavanaugh, introduction to *The Way of Perfection*, in *The Collected Works of St. Teresa of Ávila*, trans. Kieran Kavanaugh and Otilio Rodriguez, vol. 2 (Washington, D.C.: ICS Publications, 1980), 15.

15. Kieran Kavanaugh, "Spanish Sixteenth Century: Carmel and Surrounding Movements," in *Christian Spirituality: High Middle Ages and Reformation* (New York: Crossroad, 1987), 79.

16. Trillia, "*Book of Her Life*," 108.

17. Teresa of Ávila, *Way of Perfection*, 39.

18. Ibid.

19. Teresa of Ávila, *Book of Her Life*, 68.

20. Teresa of Ávila, *Way of Perfection*, 99.

21. Ibid., 121.

22. Ibid.

23. "Vocal prayer was always to be accompanied by mental prayer, and she urged the practice of recollection in vocal prayer." Kavanaugh, "How to Pray," 131.

24. Teresa of Ávila, *Way of Perfection*, 121.

25. Ibid., 123.

26. Ibid.

27. Ibid., 130.

28. Ibid., 132.

29. Ibid., 131.

30. Ibid., 118.

31. Ibid.

32. Ibid.

33. Ibid., 139.

34. Ibid., 129.

35. Ibid., 140.

36. "The point in the first is not that we are alone, but that we are alone 'with' him." Kavanaugh, "How to Pray," 126.

37. Teresa of Ávila, *Way of Perfection*, 159.

38. Ibid.

39. Anthony Morello, "*Lectio Divina* and the Practice of Teresian Prayer," *Spiritual Life* 37 (Summer 1991): 84.

40. Teresa of Ávila, *Way of Perfection*, 203.

41. Ibid., 204.

42. Teresa of Ávila, *Book of Her Life*, 226.

43. Ibid.

# The Prophetic Charism
# of the Mystical Life:
## The Model of Teresa of Jesus

GILLIAN T. W. AHLGREN

TERESA OF JESUS, ALREADY well appreciated as one of Christianity's great mystics, offers us a paradigm for the mystical life that may be even more holistic than we have previously understood; we have been slow to grasp the thoroughness and integrity of the mystical life that she models. Her function as a teacher of mystical doctrine has, of course, been recognized officially ever since her declaration in 1970 as a Doctor of the Universal Church, but even then for several decades she was seen as an expert in "spirituality." Thankfully, more recent scholarship has elucidated her theological contributions and established her rightful place as a theologian, not simply a spiritual teacher. What I would like to encourage, in this brief consideration, is further exploration of the seamlessness and integrity of the mystical life as she develops it. For Teresa offers us a paradigm for human living that evangelizes through deeds, speaks at all levels of God's compassionate concern for human dignity,[1] and calls the world to greater moral accountability and even holiness—a life, in short, in which God and we collaborate in work that manifests, cherishes, and nurtures the presence of God in our midst.

## Teresa's Mystical Witness

Teresa's description of the various stages of integration of the unitive life with God captivates us at first because the early stages are experientially recognizable. Amazingly, she is able, even four centuries after her death, to articulate spiritual truths that many readers can relate to their own lived experience. As she progresses into the deeper mystical levels, however, and the experiences are more challenging, more elusive, and harder to sustain, we appreciate the brilliance of her descriptions of subjective experience but begin to see greater distance between her experiences and our own. It is far easier for us to frame Teresa's writings as narratives of her "experiences" rather than as a way of inviting us to "taste and see" the unfolding of the divine-human relationship in our own lives. By telling us first the "story of her life,"[2] a life that Teresa saw as permeated by experiences of the loving-kindness of God, and then following up with *The Interior Castle* fifteen years later, as she acquired greater experiential wisdom into the dynamics of a lived partnership with God, Teresa models a life in which the divine-human partnership is gradually (but actually) fully realized.[3] Thus, as I suggested several years ago, at the outset of *Entering Teresa of Ávila's Interior Castle: A Reader's Companion*, "We have not yet developed a real definition of 'mystical knowing' that allows us to 'see' from our growing consciousness of the presence of God. But Teresa's careful documentation of the kinds of subjective transformation she herself experienced gives us clues to what happens as we learn to live consciously within the presence of God. . . . Recognizing a certain experiential wisdom and authenticity in her prose, we can explore the theological insights offered as she reveals, in her own naked soul-searching, her concurrent growing consciousness of the presence of God within and all around her."[4]

To become aware of our role in recognizing, nurturing, and bearing witness to the presence (or absence) of God in our world is a deeply prophetic act. It is to participate in God's ongoing incarnation in human history, walking in the footsteps of Christ and pointing, as Christ did, to the reign of God. In this essay, I would like to begin taking the logical "next step," as we seek to appropriate the "holistic way of knowing—through the senses, through the imagination, through the intellect, and through the awakened soul"[5] that the mystical life involves, considering the prophetic witness of the contemplative life. It will be the task of this essay then to outline, in brief, the characteristics of prophetic witness that Teresa's contemplative model bequeaths us and then to lift up one example of that prophetic witness in action. It is my hope that this preliminary exploration of the theory and praxis of the prophetic dimensions of the mystical life will lead to further understanding and recognition of the inherent coherence of contemplation and prophetic witness. Thus I hope that readers will conclude, as I have, that our appreciation of Teresa's mystical insights is incomplete, inaccurate, and inadequate without acknowledging the vital role of prophetic action in birthing the vision of God that emerges in and through the contemplative life. To appreciate Teresa is to recognize how a contemplative life takes form and shape in the world. Indeed, that taking form and shape is in itself a prophetic act, a unique witness to the reality that God can be incarnated in our midst as we grow into our partnership with God and bring it into the full range of our lives in the world and relationships with others.

## Teresa's Reform Faces a Pivotal Moment

Teresa's life as a reformer has already been well studied and documented, and there is little I can add here to decades of fine scholarship. Instead, I would simply like to remind readers of where the Carmelite Reform stood in the difficult years of 1575 through 1579—the very moment in which Teresa's contemplative wisdom was bearing such remarkable fruit both in her writing and in her foundations. In previous writing, I have suggested that Teresa's religious vocation had two complementary facets, reformer and writer; that her work as a writer of reflections on the mystical life was an integral part of her reform; and that her endeavors in both arenas awakened significant resistance even as they contributed substantively to the Catholic Reformation.[6] She had, by 1570, written two versions of both *The Book of Her Life* and *The Way of Perfection*, in each case responding carefully to both the spirit and the letter of censorial comments to first drafts. Despite her scrupulous consultation with spiritual experts and their approbation of her way of life, the *Life* was held by the Inquisition after Domingo Báñez's official assessment of its contents for the Valladolid tribunal.[7] Teresa did not take the sequestration of her book lying down. But even Inquisitor General Gaspar de Quiroga's apparent approval of it, as she reported to her brother Lorenzo in February 1577, did not result in its return to her or the circulation of the original manuscript during Teresa's lifetime.[8] In response, out of a space of even greater spiritual maturity, Teresa set out to write what became her mystical tour de force, *The Interior Castle*, that same year. In light of the fact that her previous work had been confiscated by the Valladolid tribunal in 1575 and that Teresa had had to defend herself against accusations of misconduct and unorthodox spiritual practices in an inquisitional investigation in Seville in 1575–1576, it is hard not to see the very writing of *The Interior Castle* as a prophetic act of resistance, despite its complex rhetoric of obedience.[9] We shall have occasion to examine prophetic elements of its mystical teachings below.

On the other front, that of monastic foundations, Teresa had also made remarkable progress through the 1560s and 1570s: San José in Ávila (1562) was soon followed by foundations in Medina del Campo, Malagón, and Valladolid, where she successfully recruited John of the Cross and arranged for the subsequent male foundation at Duruelo in 1568, male and female foundations in Pastrana (1569), and female foundations in Salamanca (1570) and Alba (1571). The remarkable (though not uncontroversial) success of the Discalced Reform required Teresa to develop new skills in administrative leadership—something she could not entirely have predicted when she founded the convent of San José but which she addressed ably and strategically.[10]

When Teresa found herself unexpectedly named prioress at her original (and subsequently unreformed) convent of the Incarnation in 1571, the intensity of foundation activity slowed. But her work as prioress of this large community was, in many ways, simply a new manifestation of her reforming work. In the temporary respite from founding new convents, Teresa was able to work on developing the contemplative vocations of women who could then join discalced convents. In other words, if she concentrated on encouraging the sisters' greater dedication and commitment to contemplative prayer, she could grow the discalced communities from within the order, transferring them from the Incarnation in Ávila to already established discalced convents throughout Castile.

Teresa was accustomed, at this point, to this kind of managerial authority over the growth of the reform movement. Writing to her brother Lorenzo in early 1570, she describes her situation as having significant administrative autonomy: "I have all possible freedom, from both the General and the Provincial, to receive postulants, to move nuns from one house to another, and to help any particular house from the funds of others" (Ltr 24.18). Having already experienced the significant challenges of having to accept sisters whom she discerned to be indisposed to the rigors of the discalced reform,[11] Teresa knew that establishing a "school" for mystical growth in which she or a trusted colleague could mentor women to greater spiritual maturity was indeed in the interests of sustaining the reform movement.

Thus, in a deliberate and strategic way, she arranged for the transfer to Ávila of John of the Cross, that "celestial and

divine man . . . without equal in all of Castile. There is
no one who inspires such fervor on the path to heaven" (Ltr
268, November 1578). Teresa was certain that John's care
and spiritual encouragement of the sisters at the Incarnation would inspire greater thirst for and commitment to
the mystical life. Although much as been written about the
intellectual and spiritual affinities of Teresa and John, we
have not yet fully understood what they were able to accomplish together as spiritual companions and collaborators in
reform.[12] At this point it is enough to suggest that their success in establishing Ávila as a dynamic space of dedication to
the mystical life triggered substantial resistance, as prophetic
acts so often do. Teresa's intuitions about John proved correct: the nuns at the Incarnation made great progress
through the first half of the 1570s.[13] For Teresa, too, these
were years of significant growth in the mystical life. Insights
that she could not yet articulate when she wrote *The Book
of Her Life* were becoming clearer and more comprehensible as her unitive life with God grew more integrated and
sustained. In these years, Teresa became more of a spiritual
director and teacher of the mystical life than ever before.

But the "Golden Age" of reform was about to encounter
wave after wave of challenge, even to the point of particular and direct personal assault on Teresa and John. Opposi-
tion to their reforms increased sharply through the 1570s,
beginning with the Carmelite general chapter meeting in
Piacenza in May 1575, in which Teresa was ordered to settle
at a convent of her choice and cease making foundations,
followed by her investigation by the inquisitional tribunal of Seville in 1575–1576, and John's apprehension and

imprisonment by his own Calced brothers in 1577–1578. Teresa and John's model of spiritual growth posed a significant challenge to the credibility and power of existing religious institutions and, by the mid-1570s, constituted its own small battlefront in the saga to determine how the mystical life would be taught, modeled, and represented. Teresa, John of the Cross, Jerome Gracián, and others were already deeply engaged in the trenches of this struggle to integrate spiritual maturity and religious authority and standards to assess the spiritual authenticity of religious life. All three of them, in holding fast to the key principles and values of mystical growth—for example, discernment, rigorous simplicity, and purity of heart, and the totality of one's dedication to partnership with God—ended up lacerated by representatives of the religious institutions they clung to so loyally. Certainly, their response to adversity from their own religious confreres shows them to be heroic in their efforts to maintain fidelity to the God they had come to know in their own prayer lives, to the church they loved, and to the community ideals they espoused. Against this backdrop, their struggles and their tenacity should give us more clarity about the demands of the mystical life, which caused them to take public stands, seek justice, and demand deeper respect, reverence, and support for the building up of authentic community life. Perhaps their historical witness can provide us today with a deeper sense of how to be a community that, in and through the life of the Spirit, "acts justly, loves tenderly, and walks humbly with our God" (Mi 6:8).

Having foregrounded the year 1577 with some sense of how the Carmelite Reform was progressing,[14] I would like now to focus attention on the catastrophic events of the end of 1577, a particular moment in which theory and praxis of prophetic wisdom and action coalesce with the shocking seizure of John of the Cross and his companion Germán de San Matías from their home next to the convent of the Incarnation where they had been serving as spiritual directors. November 1577 found Teresa finishing the manuscript of her *Interior Castle* (completed on November 29) across town at the convent of San José. If we review the careful language of the sixth dwelling places of *The Interior Castle* knowing what is around the corner for the reform and for Teresa herself, who truly suffers for and with John of the Cross (perhaps her truest spiritual companion), we see the uncanny prescience of her words at the outset of the sixth dwelling places: "O God help me, what interior and exterior trials the soul suffers before entering the seventh dwelling places! Indeed, sometimes I reflect and fear that if a soul knew beforehand, its natural weakness would find it most difficult to have the determination to suffer and pass through these trials, no matter what blessings were represented to it" (IC 6.1.1–2).

We can imagine Teresa's passionate dedication to this most demanding writing project, slogging her way through all the complex material on spiritual communication in the sixth dwelling places—locutions, visions, raptures, an intense desire for personal integrity and spiritual purity, and growth in the capacity to discern spirits and develop the equanimity necessary to live in the world in a holy way—all of which prepares the soul to enter into the seventh dwelling places, where one lives in permanent awareness of the presence of God.

The material in the second half of the sixth dwelling places of *The Interior Castle* presents some of Teresa's most critical teachings about the intricacies of the mystical life. Several elements characterize the spiritual maturity of the person who has reached this stage of the unitive life: courage, truth, tenderness, and extreme sensitivity to the presence or absence of God. A "purity of conscience" is the normal state of the soul as it grows into the unitive life. The experience of God as a companionate presence in one's daily life gives rise, as Teresa explains, to "a great purity of conscience because the presence at its side makes the soul pay attention to everything. For even though we already know that God is present in all we do, our nature is such that we neglect to think of this. Here the truth cannot be forgotten, for the Lord awakens the soul to His presence beside it" (IC 6.8.4). The soul walks in "deep concern about avoiding anything displeasing to God" (IC 6.8.3) and thus has a heightened sensitivity to sin—personal, social, or institutional.

At this point I would like to suggest that the sensitivity to God's presence is the root and heart of what we should call prophetic sensitivity or even the prophetic charism: the individual not only feels more sharply the burden of personal and social sin but also has an intuitive awareness of the roots and sources of unjust actions or practices—in self, in society, in church. Further, the sensitivity is such that the human person cannot tolerate injustice—resisting, as a matter of personal integrity and fidelity to covenantal relationship with God, any and all forms of personal participation in injustice and adopting practical ways of promoting life-giving relief, renewal, and personal/social transformation. The dissonance caused by difference between the love of God that the soul now knows so personally and deeply and the injustices of the world is increasingly intolerable at this level of growth, and insofar as the individual can serve as an instrument of the loving activity of God in the world, she or he seeks to do so.

Another element of this prophetic charism is clarity about God as "supreme Truth" before which all humans and human institutions fall short. Any falseness, anything less than a good-faith attempt at integrity cannot please the soul, who now desires to "walk in truth" and "live in conformity with our God and Spouse." An instinct toward greater ethical consistency in all areas of life, as well as a commitment toward greater "rigor" in love—deeper compassion, for example, and a dedication to the concrete embodiment of loving-kindness—characterizes the mystical life at this stage, for the soul now begins to participate in the very nature of the God who is love. It is this love of truth and the companionate presence of Christ that allows the unitive life to open up, dimensionally, within the soul as the mystical journey culminates in an entry into the reality of the Triune God. Thus Teresa teaches that the soul in the seventh dwelling places has been brought into the company of all three Persons of the Trinity and therefore not only understands the Trinitarian nature of God but also dwells in relational presence, where we are integrated, if you will, into the relational life of a dynamic and loving God.[15]

Thus the unitive life with God, as Teresa teaches and understands it, has relational obligations and commitments, many of which would reimagine traditional forms of religious practice and devotion. As we seek to bring the wisdom of God into the challenges of daily life, the mystical life requires different, more profound, more holistic, and actually more complex and demanding commitments from us than those traditionally described under the category of the "religious life" or even "spiritual life." Fidelity to God, for example, entails a mutual fidelity to the God present in the human community, to the body of Christ, particularly in its suffering forms. This kind of fidelity necessitates not only a compassionate response to human beings but also a proactive and protective stance toward the defense of human dignity and the capacity of all to flourish. Additionally, we must build into our homes and communities a supportive and nurturing context in which to sustain frequent and meaningful communication with God for ongoing strength and guidance. Our relationship with ourselves too must be reexamined to ensure that we sustain and cherish ourselves enough to provide God with a worthy dwelling place for the divine life. And as we look out into a world permeated with injustice, asceticism itself can bear fruit in the patiently deliberate dismantling of unjust structures, the disempowerment of forces of social and spiritual oppression, and even the careful, "wise as serpents, gentle as doves" engagement of conflictive individuals whose abuse of power threatens the well-being of others. The task of the unitive life, Teresa concludes, is to draw others toward God, enkindling others through the fire of love in oneself, awakening others to greater virtue, and transforming the world with the same fiery love that is the gift of God incarnate.[16]

We can imagine the great "Deo gratias!" Teresa sighed as she finished *The Interior Castle*, which as she admits in the epilogue, "has brought me much happiness, and I consider the labor, though I confess it was small, well spent" (IC Epil 1). Teresa clearly enjoyed sharing the fruits of her experience of God with others, empowering them too to "take delight in this interior castle since without permission from the prioress you can enter and take a walk through it at any time" (IC Epil 1). And again, she notes, "Once you get used to enjoying this castle, you will find rest in all things, even those involving much labor, for you will have the hope of returning to the castle, which no one can take from you" (IC Epil 2).

Many of the elements of prophetic sensitivity in the sixth dwelling places were about to be tested in action just days after Teresa victoriously signed off on the manuscript of *The Interior Castle*. On the night of December 3, 1577, Calced Carmelite Fernando Maldonado arrived at the house of John of the Cross and his companion Germán de San Matías, set up next to the community of Carmelites at the Incarnation to whom they ministered. Reports from the nuns at the Incarnation revealed that Calced brothers had forcibly pulled the men out of their house and beaten them severely, appropriating them and their personal possessions and whisking them away under cover of night. Appalled, Teresa returned immediately to her writing desk at the convent of San José and penned a clear, careful, and forceful appeal to Philip II on December 4, 1577.[17] Although the letter has been the focus of careful recent study, it should be juxtaposed with Teresa's reflections on the deeper stages of the mystical life that she had just committed to paper. Teresa's letter to Philip II and her subsequent protective actions, on behalf of both John of the Cross and the discalced movement, have more to teach us with respect to prophetic action than we have yet articulated. Her letter to the king allows us to see the prophetic potential of an authentic and integrated mystical life in action, for it combines advocacy, defense of ideals, a passion for truth, and clear courage under fire, upholding these Christian virtues as an integral part of the mystical life, particularly when we must live it in a world of injustice. Whether or not the letter was effective,[18] and whether or not Philip II actually read it,[19] are not the significant questions to ask. Rather, if we are to understand the prophetic dimensions of the mystical life—in other words, what actions and witness we are called to take in circumstances of injustice—then we should explore the steps that Teresa took to lament, denounce, bear witness to, alleviate, and remediate a situation that cried out for divine (and human) intervention.

Teresa's December 4, 1577, letter to Philip II was not her first letter to the king,[20] but it did need to summarize the chronology of events precipitated by the intentional program of reform that Teresa and John were fortifying. Although as so often occurs in Teresa's letters her language is careful and even encoded, it reveals the strategic and methodical implementation of spiritual direction and the cultivation of a deeper dedication to the mystical life that she intended for the (Calced) nuns at the Incarnation. As she explains in the letter, she had brought John to a house near the Incarnation to "remedy" a difficult situation—the subjection of the Calced nuns to the spiritual and disciplinary authority of their Calced confessors. In fact, Teresa's language leaves no question as to her denunciation of the Calced brothers' negative influence on the nuns, who needed "some means to free themselves from the friars, who are certainly a great hindrance to the recollection and observance of the nuns" (Ltr 218.2).[21] Teresa countered both the authority and negative influence of the Calced confessors with the more "edifying" moral and spiritual example of John of the Cross and his companion Germán de San Matías.

The "edification" of the nuns was not simply in the ways that John of the Cross taught and modeled spiritual devotion and progress toward a deeper, more committed relationship with God; it was also a profound "building up" of that life of continual improvement and growing moral and spiritual integrity and even goodness. In the same letter to King Philip, Teresa writes, ". . . I tried to provide a remedy and placed a discalced friar in a house next to them, along with a companion friar. He is so great a servant of our Lord that the nuns are truly edified, and this city is amazed by the remarkable amount of good he has done there" (Ltr 218.3).

It is notable that Teresa takes both full responsibility and full autonomy for the decision to bring John of the Cross to Ávila (*Puse allí*), and she uses the pregnant word *remedio* here, which echoes Kieran Kavanaugh's rendering of the letter, cited above. [22] Peers translates the phrase "*para algún remedio*" as "to improve matters a little." Both of these highlight the Spanish word *remedio*, which can mean a remedy, a help, or even the correction of a wrong or a solution to a problem. *Remedio* becomes a rhetorical theme in the letter; it is used four times as Teresa reaches her crescendo: a call to the king for his command to correct a situation that is both "irregular and unjust" (*sin orden ni justicia*) and that cries out for redress. "For the love of Our Lord I beg Your Majesty to order that they be rescued right away," Teresa writes, "and that you give the order that none of the poor discalced friars suffer so much at the hands of those of the cloth [i.e., the Calced] . . . for this is causing a scandal to the people" (Ltr 218:7) In highlighting the "public scandal" of the situation, Teresa is both appealing to Philip's public authority and is signaling that the situation is in urgent need of attention. Within ecclesiastical structures, the "scandal of the faithful" was to be avoided at all times in order to maintain proper respect for religious authority. As she winds down her appeal, Teresa assesses the situation rather crisply: "May God be blessed, but those who are supposed to be the means by which the Lord is not offended end up being the cause of so many sins, and each day it is getting worse. If Your Majesty does not order some remedy, I do not know how things will end, because we have no other help on earth" (Ltr 218.7).

## Action Fueled by Sorrow and Indignation

But it was in the detail of her letter to María de San José, prioress of the Discalced convent in Seville, that Teresa reveals not only her indignation at the injustice of the events but also her personal sorrow and distress. Writing on

December 10, by which time she might have heard more about the circumstances of John and Germán's detention, Teresa narrated specific details: John and his companion Germán de San Matías had been whipped several times and violently treated; when Germán was taken away, the nuns of the Incarnation said that he was bleeding from his mouth. (Ltr 221.7) Although the sisters had already suffered severe disruption within their religious community, including prohibition from the Eucharist and temporary excommunication, it was the treatment of their brothers in Christ that pained them the most. Teresa begged María de San José for her prayers, both for her sisters and for the two "saintly captives," and her language indicates that she is keenly aware of the suffering of her friends: she is keeping vigil and marking time from the day that they were seized. "Tomorrow it will be eight days since they were seized" (Ltr 221.8). In her next letter to María de San José, dated December 19, she writes again: "Although it's sixteen days from today that our two friars have been taken captive, we don't know if they have been released, although we trust in God that he will provide a remedy" (Ltr 222. 2). By this time, in fact, John had been transferred to the Calced monastery in Toledo where he was left first in the official monastery prison and then, later, in a small cell used as a lavatory.

For the next six months, Teresa used all means possible to advocate for the release of John of the Cross, considering who might be able to influence, compel, or punish the Calced who had imprisoned him. Her letters during this time reflect her efforts to secure intervention, from state and ecclesiastical officials, that would provide for John of the Cross's release and for the protection of the Discalced from the governance of the Calced.[23] Despite her efforts, John remained imprisoned until he himself escaped from the Calced brothers in Toledo in August 1578, nine months after being seized from his home. After learning of his treatment in more detail, Teresa expressed her shock and abhorrence of the injustice in a letter to Jerome Gracián, in which she encourages him to inform the papal nuncio of the entire situation.

> . . . I tell you that I carry within me what they have done to friar John of the Cross; I do not know how God permits such things. . . . Through all these nine months past he was in a cell in which he hardly even fit, as small as he is, and in all that time he could not even change his tunic, even though he was at the point of death. . . . Our Lord gave him an abundance of strength to endure such a martyrdom! And it is good that the details be known, so that everyone might be on their guard against such people. God forgive them (Ltr 260. 1,2).

Here we see both Teresa's righteous indignation and her prophetic conviction that bringing darkness and injustice into the light is a service both to God and to God's people.

Teresa's most immediate concern, in the aftermath of John's escape, was for his ongoing safety. Saddened though she likely was that she would not be near him and that their fruitful collaboration in Ávila had been ruptured, Teresa supported his relocation to Beas, in Andalusia, where he would be removed from the continuing threat of interventions from the Calced in Castile. Writing to the Carmelites in Beas toward the end of October 1578 Teresa notes, "I declare to you that I would be most happy to have my father Fray John of the Cross here, who truly is the father of soul and one from whom it benefited most in its conversations with him. Speak with him, my daughters, in total simplicity, for I assure you that you can do so as though you were speaking with me. This will bring you great satisfaction, for he is a very spiritual man with much experience and learning" (Ltr 277. 2).

For the final four years of her life, even as Teresa's energy declined, she continued to dedicate herself to the reform, both by founding new convents (or sending emissaries on her behalf when she could not go) and by working toward greater protection, support, even "edification" of the evangelical witness of her contemplative communities, designed to be light for the church at least as much as for the world. For Teresa was aware that although there were many who called themselves "Christian," there was also great confusion and even falsity about how to truly imitate Christ.[24] Teresa's attempt to teach and model an authentic life of integrity, spiritual maturity, and true evangelical witness, grounded in contemplative prayer, is both apostolic and prophetic.

What can we today appropriate from Teresa's witness? As we seek to pull together the elements of the prophetic charism of the mystical life, we could begin by observing Teresa's prophetic clarity that combines a deep love of truth with a passionate concern for protecting the sanctity of the emergence of godly presence in the human person and in the world. In other words, out of her own personal experience and out of her work guiding communities of dedicated contemplatives, Teresa saw clearly that the delicate work of spiritual growth, mediated through dedication to the contemplative life and careful spiritual guidance and direction, was a holy, transformative work. She understood the fragile intricacy of this work, the need for communities of total dedication to the dynamic work of the Spirit, and she saw this work taking place in a world that desperately needed a faithful, committed witness of truth and holiness. What this suggests is that we should see and appreciate the contemplative life as needing a space of sanctuary—active protection and advocacy for the emergence of the godly in ourselves and in our world.

As Teresa sketched out the stages of growth in the mystical life in her *Interior Castle*, she suggests that contemplation is the actuation of the God-human relationship in which individuals are empowered to draw strength from their partnership with God and to become, through that partnership, more direct conveyors of the presence of God in human life. Thus, as she articulates in the second half of the sixth dwelling places and beyond, the sense of the companioning presence of Christ, which gives the soul a keen awareness of its accountability to God, gradually moves into an even more compatible, collaborative relationship. Teresa's *Interior Castle* outlines the process of growth toward union with God that allows the soul to realize the indwelling presence of God incarnate in a life lived here on earth. The culminating stages of that life are precisely what was promised, by Christ, in the Johannine version of the Last Supper discourse, which framed the outset of *The Interior Castle* (Jn 14:2: "In my father's house there are many dwelling places . . . I go to prepare a place for you"). Thus, in the seventh dwelling places, the soul is capacitated to live into the collaborative and co-creative reality described by Christ to his disciples: first, the promise that the one who believes "will do the works I do and will do greater ones than these" (Jn 14:12); next, the promise that that believer's prayers will be heard and will be efficacious, to the glory of God (Jn 14:13); and finally, the promise of an advocate, the Spirit of truth, who actively works with God and Christ, as indwelling presence in the human person (Jn 14:16–17).

In the latter stages of her life, as she modeled and embodied the unitive life, advocacy, or life in the Spirit of truth, took on more concrete meaning for Teresa. Most fundamentally, Teresa advocated for, or "gave voice to," the possibility of living a life graced by God's incarnate presence. Thus, in her writing (treatises, letters, and other counsel) she became a living voice calling for greater awareness of and reverence toward God's presence in the midst of our communities and our daily lives. More broadly speaking, then, advocacy, as an element of the prophetic charism, is an advocacy on behalf of the body of Christ. For Teresa, this meant, as we have seen, advocacy for the presence of Christ as she had herself personally witnessed and experienced it in the affirming spiritual companionship of John of the Cross as well as advocacy on behalf of the emerging presence of Christ in the dedication and painstaking efforts at spiritual growth in the Discalced communities. Such efforts, as holy works intended to build up the body of Christ in the human realm,[25] needed protection and nurturance, even intervention and defense, when they were under attack. Teresa used both a gentle hand and a strong arm to ensure that those who had committed themselves to the challenges of growing into partnered relationship with God would both be fed by those who were able to feed them and be protected from assault and siege.

The contemplative communities Teresa established and she and John (and others) ministered to were schools of growth into the depths of the mystical life. As Teresa makes clear towards the end of *The Interior Castle*, the soul who has reached the unitive life is constantly wanting to share her joy in God with others,[26] and thus lives with a desire to evangelize, not only in words, but also in a way of life that is absolutely consistent with Gospel values. Both within and around cloister walls, Teresa understood that she and her sisters had an apostolic calling, common to all friends of Christ: the prophetic, evangelical vocation to bring souls to God, to call people to greater godliness. Whether we end up "concentrating on those who are in your company, and thus your deed will be greater since you are more obliged toward them" (IC 7.4.14) or speaking outside the walls to make appeals on behalf of the oppressed, as Teresa did in the years of persecution under the Calced, Teresa reminds us that our call is to awaken others to the desire of God to be born within us and our world: "Do you think such deep humility, your mortification, service of all and great charity toward them, and love of the Lord are of little benefit? This fire of love in you enkindles their souls, and with every other virtue you will be always awakening them" (IC 7.4.14). What should be clear to us, as we revisit these texts, is the steely resolve and inner strength that Teresa had and inculcated in her contemporaries to give witness and substance (*cuerpo*) to the reality of God in the world. The renewing Spirit of God was, in her lived experience, a spirit of *strength*, hungry for human commitment and thirsting for a more just, more humane world.

## Notes

1. Recall Teresa's lament, at the outset of the *Interior Castle*, that we are unaware of our own dignity, made, as we are in the image of God: "Isn't it a pity and regrettable that through our own fault we don't understand ourselves nor do we know who we are? . . . But we seldom consider the precious things that this soul contains or who is within this soul or its great value. Consequently, little effort is made to preserve its beauty" (IC 1.1.2; translation mine).

2. Actually, what we call *The Book of Her Life* [*Libro de su vida*] or the *Life*, for short, Teresa preferred to call *The Book of God's Mercies*, or the *Book*. The latter, more accurate title is suggestive of the dialogue Teresa recounts in chapter 26 of the *Life*: "When they took away so many books in the vernacular so that they would not be read, I was very grieved, because to read some of them gave me refreshment, and now I couldn't because they were in Latin. But God said to me: Do not be sad: I will give you a living book" (L 26.6; translation mine).

3. See Gillian T. W. Ahlgren, *Entering Teresa of Ávila's Interior Castle: A Reader's Companion* (Mahwah, N.J.: Paulist Press, 2005), 17: "Certainly, one of her [Teresa's] greatest gifts as a writer is her ability to express the depths of her subjective experiences of self and God, seeking, through words, both to express the reality of the immensely tender and awe-inspiring God she knew and to draw her readers into that reality. . . . Teresa's ability to speak through the centuries and present us, even today, with a brilliant sketch of the inner landscape of the human psyche, is perhaps the clearest indication of her theological talent. While the *Interior Castle* has

been much studied by those seeking to understand human spiritual development, readers have failed to appreciate fully the power and profundity of the theological insights—insights into the very nature of God and humanity—she offers, precisely because she has plumbed her own depths with such thoroughness, integrity, and emotional authenticity."

4. Ibid.

5. Ibid.

6. See discussion in Gillian T. W. Ahlgren, *Teresa of Ávila and the Politics of Sanctity* (Ithaca, N.Y.: Cornell University Press, 1996), 34–64, especially its framing on p. 37: "Yet prayer, penance, and monastic reform were not Teresa's only ways of realizing her desire to do missionary work. . . . In the end, Teresa expressed her desire to convert souls by her literary works, whose purpose was less to describe her own experiences than to teach and compel. Yet she encountered as much resistance to her literary endeavors as to her reform efforts." See also Jodi Bilnkoff, "Teresa of Ávila: Woman with a Mission," in *A Linking of Heaven and Earth: Studies in Religious and Cultural History in Honor of Carlos M. N. Eire,* ed. Emily Michelson et al. (Burlington, Vt.: Ashgate, 2013); Bárbara Mujica, *Teresa de Ávila: Lettered Woman* (Nashville: Vanderbilt University Press, 2009), esp. 44–102; and Alison Weber, "Spiritual Administration: Gender and Discernment in the Carmelite Reform," *Sixteenth Century Journal* 31, no. 1 (Spring 2000): 123–46.

7. For a summary of this proceeding and analysis of Báñez's assessment and its impact, see Ahlgren, *Teresa of Ávila,* 49–52.

8. See ibid., 51–52.

9. See discussion of the genesis of the text in Ahlgren, *Teresa of Ávila,* 61–62, and Ahlgren, *Entering Teresa of Ávila's Interior Castle,* 11–15. See also Alison Weber, *Teresa of Ávila and the Rhetoric of Femininity* (Princeton, N.J.: Princeton University Press, 1990), 98–122.

10. See, for example, her reflections in a letter to her brother Lorenzo dated January 17, 1570: "Tiring though I find the work, these houses do so much good in the towns where they are founded that

my conscience tells me to establish as many as I can. And the Lord helps me so much that it encourages me. . . . People have such a blind confidence in me—I don't know how they can do such things, but they seem to trust me so implicitly that they will give me as much as a thousand or two thousand ducats. So, although I used to detest money and business matters, it is the Lord's pleasure that I should engage in nothing else, and that is no light cross" (*Epistolario* carta 24, in Ahlgren, *Teresa of Ávila*, 10, 19 [trans. Allison Peers]). See also Weber, "Spiritual Administration."

11. See, for example, the carefully worded letter she wrote to María de Mendoza on March 7, 1572, about the inappropriateness of accepting a postulant María had proposed. Further insight into such problems is available in Alison Weber's study "Teresa's Problematic Patrons," *Journal of Medieval and Early Modern Studies* 29, no. 2 (Spring 1999): 357–79.

12. I shall leave for another occasion the task of considering and comparing the theology of spiritual direction that each develops, but I note in passing that their insights into the intricacies of nurturing the mystical life within communities of dedicated contemplatives are important enough to merit more attention as we seek wisdom for our time.

13. See Leonard Doohan's brief summary of this "Golden Age" in his *Contemporary Challenge of John of the Cross: An Introduction to His Life and Teaching* (Washington, D.C.: ICS Publications, 1995), 13: "Eventually John became, along with Teresa, one of the two principal spiritual guides of the Incarnation, and by the end of 1572 peace and renewal were coming to the convent. . . . While at the Incarnation, John's reputation as a spiritual guide grew, and others outside the convent entrusted extremely difficult discernment cases to him."

14. For more detail see, for example, Mujica, *Teresa de Ávila*, 40–77; Joachim Smet, *The Carmelites: A History of the Brothers of Our Lady of Mt. Carmel* (Darien, Ill.: Carmelite Spiritual Center, 1988); Otger Steggink, *Arraigo e innovación* (Madrid: BAC, 1976); and Weber, "Spiritual Administration."

15. See IC 7.1.7: "Each day this soul becomes more amazed, for these Persons [of the Trinity] never leave it anymore, but it clearly beholds, in the way that was mentioned, that they are within it. In the extreme interior, in some place very deep within itself, the nature of which it doesn't know how to explain, because of a lack of learning, it perceives this divine company." And "the soul finds itself in this company every time it takes notice" (7.1.9). See discussion of the seventh dwelling places in Ahlgren, *Entering Teresa of Ávila's Interior Castle*, 113–20.

16. See IC 7.4.12–15, especially the following: "This fire of love in you enkindles their souls, and with every other virtue you will always be awakening them. Such service will not be small but very great and very pleasing to the Lord." And "the Lord doesn't look so much at the greatness of our works but at the love with which they are done. And if we do what we can, His Majesty will enable us each day to do more and more, provided that we do not quickly tire."

17. A new translation of this letter is provided in Mujica, *Teresa de Ávila*, 231–33. See also her commentary, pp. 90–93.

18. In fact, it had no discernible effect: John remained imprisoned at the hands of his Calced brothers in Toledo until he escaped on his own on August 14, 1578, more than eight months later.

19. It is almost certain that he did not, although the contents of the letter may have reached him in a filtered review by his secretary or another agent. See discussion in Carole Slade, "The Relationship between Teresa of Ávila and Philip II: A Reading of the Extant Textual Evidence," *Archive for Reformation History* 94 (2003): 223–42; and Mujica, *Teresa de Ávila*, 90–93.

20. See Slade, "Relationship"; and Mujica, *Teresa de Ávila*, 79–83, 86–87, 90–93.

21. In paragraph 2 of Ltr 218 Teresa notes that she was brought to the Incarnation at the persistent request of the nuns.

22. Ltr 218.3, *The Collected Letters of St. Teresa of Avila*, vol. 1, trans. Kieran Kavanaugh (Washington, D.C.: ICS Publications, 2001), 579.

23. See, for example, her letter to Teutonio de Braganza of January 16, 1578, which mentions a formal complaint to the council (Ltr 226), and also her correspondence with Roque de Huerta in Madrid dated March 9, 1578 (Ltr 232), and her letter to Jerome Gracián dated March 10–11, 1578. (Ltr 233)

24. See, for example, her lament at the outset of W 1.3: "What is it now with these Christians? Does it always have to be that those who owe You the most are the ones who weigh You down?"

25. See IC 5.2.5: "See here, daughters, what we can do with the help of God! And how in this prayer of union, with our cooperation, His Majesty Himself might become our abode! It seems that I am suggesting that we can take away from or add something to God, since I say that he is the dwelling place which we may make for ourselves, and into which we can introduce ourselves. And what if we can?"

26. IC 6.6.9: "Certainly the experience takes place in this way, for the joy is so excessive the soul wouldn't want to enjoy it alone but wants to tell everyone about it so that they might help this soul praise our Lord. All its activity is directed to this praise." In the next paragraph Teresa relates the examples of Francis of Assisi and Peter of Alcántara and their evangelical zeal.

# About the Contributors

**Gillian T. W. Ahlgren** is professor of theology at Xavier University in Cincinnati. Her PhD is from the Divinity School of the University of Chicago, where she specialized in the Christian mystical tradition with Bernard McGinn. The author of six books, including *Teresa of Ávila and the Politics of Sanctity* (Cornell University, 1996); *Entering Teresa of Ávila's Interior Castle: A Reader's Companion* (Paulist, 2005); and *Enkindling Love: The Legacy of Teresa of Ávila and John of the Cross* (Fortress, 2016). Her most recent book is *The Tenderness of God: Reclaiming Our Humanity* (Fortress, 2017), in which she explores how to nurture our God-given capacity to live meaningfully and joyfully in communion with others. Ahlgren lectures widely and facilitates retreats to diverse populations.

**Daniel Chowning, O.C.D.**, is a friar and priest of the Washington Province of Discalced Carmelite Friars. He currently is based in Rome where he serves the order as a member of general council. Father Daniel studied at the International Center for Teresian/Sanjuanist Studies in Ávila, Spain, and obtained a licentiate in theology at the University of Salamanca, Spain. He has served his Province of the Immaculate Heart of Mary as novice director and in various other ministries. Before his election to the general council, he preached retreats, lectured, and published on themes of Carmelite spirituality. He has been an instructor in the Carmelite Institute's Distance Education Certificate Program and was a presenter in the Carmelite Seminar held annually at Saint Mary's College in South Bend, Indiana. With Mary Jo Meadow and Kevin Culligan, O.C.D., he coauthored *Christian Insight Meditation: Following in the Footsteps of John of the Cross*, published by Wisdom Publications, 2007.

**Kevin Culligan, O.C.D.**, is a Discalced Carmelite friar and priest. He received a master's degree in clinical psychology from Marquette University in 1970 and a doctorate in psychology of religion from Boston University in 1979. His articles and reviews have appeared in the *Journal of Transpersonal Psychology*, the *Journal of Pastoral Care*, *America*, *National Catholic Reporter*, *Spiritual Life*, *The Way*, *Carmelite Digest*, and *Mount Carmel*. Beginning in 1989, together with Mary Jo Meadow and Daniel Chowning, O.C.D., Father Kevin has developed the practice of Christian Insight Meditation through writings and intensive retreats, incorporating the wisdom of Buddhist *vipassana* meditation into Christian spirituality as taught by St. John of the Cross. He edited with Regis Jordan, O.C.D., *Carmel and Contemplation: Transforming Human Consciousness* and *A Better Wine*, an anthology of Carmelite essays, both published by ICS Publications. Now largely retired from active ministry, he is a member of the Carmelite community at Holy Hill, Wisconsin.

**Keith J. Egan, T.O.Carm.**, is a guest professor at the University of Notre Dame where he was an adjunct professor from 1983 to 2016. He is also the Aquinas Chair in Catholic Theology Emeritus, Saint Mary's College, where he founded the college's Center for Spirituality. From its inception, Keith has been a member of the North American Carmelite Forum and served a five-year term as president of the Carmelite Institute. Keith has written extensively on Carmelite spirituality. He edited *Carmelite Prayer: A Tradition for the 21st Century* (Paulist, 2004) and with Lawrence Cunningham published *Christian Spirituality: Themes from the Tradition* (Paulist, 1996). Keith has published five sets of audio programs on the Carmelite Doctors of the Church: Teresa, John, and Thérèse. He has lectured on Carmelite themes in North America, England, Ireland, and Italy.

**Constance FitzGerald, O.C.D.**, is a nun of the Carmelite Monastery in Baltimore, Maryland, where she has served terms as prioress and as formation director. Her 1984 article "Impasse and Dark Night" has become one of the most referenced essays in Carmelite spirituality. This and other groundbreaking contributions led to her being invited to give a keynote address, "From Impasse to Prophetic Hope: Crisis of Memory," at the 2009 meeting of the Catholic Theological Society of America. Sister Constance is a founding member of the Carmelite Forum and presented lectures and workshops regularly at the forum's Summer Seminar on Carmelite Spirituality. She has written on all the great Carmelite saints while focusing her most intensive research on John of the Cross. In 2017 she was honored by the Leadership Conference of Women Religious with their Outstanding Leadership award.

**Mary Frohlich, R.S.C.J.**, is professor of spirituality at Catholic Theological Union in Chicago. She was a regular presenter at the annual seminar in Carmelite Spirituality held at St. Mary's College in Notre Dame, Indiana. Her books include *The Intersubjectivity of the Mystic: Mystical Transformation in the Interior Castle of Teresa of Ávila* (Oxford, 1993) and two edited collections, *The Lay Contemplative* (St. Anthony Messenger, 2000, with Virginia Manss) and *St. Thérèse of Lisieux: Essential Writings* (Orbis, 2000). She has also published numerous articles in such venues as *Theological Studies, Horizons, Spiritus, Studies in Spirituality, New Theology Review*, and *Spirituality*. In addition to studies of the Carmelite saints, research interests include mystical dimensions of "conversion to the Earth," methodological issues in spirituality, and Sacred Heart spirituality. Her most recent book is *Breathed into Wholeness: Catholicity and the Rhythms of the Spirit* (Orbis, 2019).

**Edward Howells** is senior lecturer in Christian spirituality at Heythrop College, University of London, and from 2018, senior lecturer at the University of Roehampton. He teaches the History of Christian Spirituality, at both master's and undergraduate levels, with courses on mysticism and on Teresa of Ávila and John of the Cross. His interests are in the areas of the knowledge of God, the process of human transformation, and the reading and exposition of classic spiritual texts. His publications include *John of* *the Cross and Teresa of Ávila: Mystical Knowing and Self-hood* (Crossroad, 2002), the book based on his doctoral dissertation at the University of Chicago; and two books edited with Peter Tyler: *Sources of Transformation: Revitalizing Christian Spirituality* (Continuum, 2010) and *Teresa of Ávila: Mystical Theology and Spirituality in the Carmelite Tradition* (Routledge, 2017).

**Sandra M. Schneiders, I.H.M.,** is professor emerita of New Testament studies and Christian spirituality at the Jesuit School of Theology at Santa Clara University. She specializes in New Testament literature, particularly Johannine literature and biblical hermeneutics, and Christian spirituality, specifically biblical spirituality, feminism, religious life, and the theory of the field of spirituality. Publications include twelve books and over one hundred peer-reviewed articles. In 2014, Sister Sandra was the recipient of the Barry University Yves Congar Award for Theological Excellence. In 2013 she received the Association of Catholic Colleges and Universities Monika K. Hellwig Award for Outstanding Contribution to Catholic Intellectual Life, and in 2012 she was honored by the Leadership Conference of Women Religious as recipient of their annual Outstanding Leadership Award.

**Vilma Seelaus, O.C.D.,** was a nun of the Carmelite monastery in Barrington, Rhode Island, where she served terms as prioress, formation director, and vocation contact. A member of the Carmelite Forum, she was much loved for her insight and wisdom as a speaker, writer, and spiritual director. Sister Vilma's particular interest was making Carmelite spirituality accessible to a contemporary audience. In this vein, she published many audio tapes and CDS on spirituality, as well as articles in *Spiritual Life, Review for Religious, Mystics Quarterly, Carmelite Digest, Living Prayer, Anima,* and *The Way.* Her books include *Distractions in Prayer: Blessing or Curse?* (Alba House, 2005) and *A Lenten Journey with Jesus Christ and Elizabeth of the Trinity* (Christus, 2011). Sister Vilma was eighty-six years old at her death in January 2012.

**Tara K. Soughers** has a PhD in practical theology, with a concentration in spirituality, from Boston University School of Theology. Her work has focused on making the riches of the Christian tradition, particularly the writings of the mystics, accessible to people today. Her dissertation "Spiritual Companionship with the Saints: A Practical Theological Reading of Teresa of Ávila as a Spiritual Companion," explores how the saints can serve as spiritual companions for people today. In this work, Teresa of Ávila has been her guide, companion, and dialogue partner. She has served for over twenty years in congregational ministry as an Episcopal priest in a variety of settings, including doing spiritual direction and leading retreats. In addition, she is author of four books: *Falling in Love with God: Passion, Prayer, and the Song of Songs* (Cowley, 2005); *Fleeing God: Fear, Call, and the Book of Jonah* (Cowley, 2007); *Treasures of Darkness: Finding God When Hope Is Hidden* (Abingdon, 2009); *and Beyond a Binary God: A Theology for Trans\* Allies* (Church Publishing, 2018).

**Kees Waaijman, O.Carm.,** is a Carmelite priest and friar of the Ancient Observance. He studied philosophy and theology at the Catholic University of Nijmegen, The Netherlands, and subsequently pursued Jewish studies at the Hebrew University of Jerusalem, becoming a specialist in biblical spirituality, especially in the spirituality of the psalms and Jewish mysticism. Since 1989 he has been professor of spirituality at Radboud University of Nijmegen (formerly the Catholic University). During the last forty years, he helped build up the Titus Brandsma Institute at this same university, and from the 1990s until 2010 he was its director. His publications include *Mystiek in de Psalmen* (Ten Have, 2004) and *The Mystical Space of Carmel: A Commentary on the Carmelite Rule* (Peeters, 1999). His main work is *Spirituality: Forms, Foundations, Methods* (Peeters, 2002), which has been translated into many languages. He is currently a researcher of the Titus Brandsma Institute and editor of *Speling* and *Studies in Spirituality*.

# Index

*Page numbers followed by the letter "n" indicate notes.*

inner drama of, 263–269
memory and, 58–59, 61,
    66–68
no experience of, 75–77
Serapion (monk), 109
shamanic consciousness, 9–10
silence
    in prayer of no experience,
        74–77, 90–91n44
    theology of, 169–173
    wisdom received through,
        145–148
    in work, 110, 116–118, 121
    see also emptiness
Sobrino, Jon, 29n14
The Soliloquies (Teresa of
    Ávila), 240
Solomon, as wisdom arche-
    type, 33
Sophia/Lady Wisdom, 13,
    34–40, 129
The Spiritual Canticle (John of
    the Cross)
    desire and search for union
        in, 132–133, 135–136,
        148–152, 164–166
    memory in, 87n23
    presence of God in,
        159–160, 162–163
    solitude, silence, and
        emptiness in, 90–91n44,
        91–92n49, 190–193,
        217n4
    wisdom in, 87n23, 129,
        153–154 .

spiritual experiences. see
    mystical experiences
The Spiritual Testimonies
    (Teresa of Ávila), 240
"Stanzas Applied Spiritually to
    Christ and the Soul" (John
    of the Cross), 169
Stein, Edith, 26, 80, 82
suffering, and memory, 61–65,
    72
Summa contra Gentiles (Aqui-
    nas), 46–47
Summa Theologiae (Aquinas),
    45
Swimme, Brian, 7

**T**

Taylor, Charles, 17–18, 19
Technozoic Era, 4
Teilhard de Chardin, Pierre,
    6–7, 70, 80
Teresa of Ávila
    on call to contemplation, 46
    defense of mental prayer,
        288–295
    development of inner
        drama, 263–269
    on dignity of soul, 324n1
    discernment of authentic
        mystical experiences,
        230–235
    method for mental prayer,
        295–298
    as model contemplative, 18,
        24–25

# About Us

ICS Publications, based in Washington, D.C., is the publishing house of the Institute of Carmelite Studies (ICS) and a ministry of the Discalced Carmelite Friars of the Washington Province (U.S.A.). The Institute of Carmelite Studies promotes research and publication in the field of Carmelite spirituality, especially about Carmelite saints and related topics. Its members are friars of the Washington Province.

The Discalced Carmelites are a worldwide Roman Catholic religious order comprised of friars, nuns, and laity—men and women who are heirs to the teaching and way of life of Teresa of Avila and John of the Cross, dedicated to contemplation and to ministry in the church and the world.

Information about their way of life is available through local diocesan vocation offices, or from the Discalced Carmelite Friars vocation directors at the following addresses:

Washington Province:
1525 Carmel Road, Hubertus, WI 53033

California-Arizona Province:
P.O. Box 3420, San Jose, CA 95156

Oklahoma Province:
5151 Marylake Drive, Little Rock, AR 72206

Visit our websites at:

*www.icspublications.org*    and    *http://ocdfriarsvocation.org*